T0078112

Puja | Mumbai, Dharavi

Sanjila Shahrin Eshika

55 DAYS IN DHARAVI

INTRO BY DR. CATH MILNE
NYU EDUCATION DEPARTMENT

FORWORD BY THOMAS BLOZY
FACULTY, BROOKLYN TECH HS

REFATH BARI

authorHOUSE®

AuthorHouse™
1663 Liberty Drive
Bloomington, IN 47403
www.authorhouse.com
Phone: 833-262-8899

Published by AuthorHouse 08/27/2020

ISBN: 978-1-7283-6761-3 (sc)
ISBN: 978-1-7283-6853-5 (e)

Contents

Introduction

Dr. Catherine Milne
55 Days in Dharavi

Introduction for *55 Days in Dharavi*: Dr. Catherine Milne, Chair of Education Department, NYU

A personal and public journey through poverty and peace this book challenges its readers to look deeply at the structures emplace in all countries that serve to reinforce inequities. Indeed the current global protests highlighting the role of discrimination and injustice around racial bias provide ample evidence of such discriminatory practices. Refath Bari's book, 55 Days in Dharavi, provides a personal and public journey through poverty and understanding. His exploration is nuanced, emphasizing that the nature of poverty is complex and beset by myths, some of which have some truth but many of which are completely false. Traveling across the sub-continent either in person or in the stories of his interviewees to places such as Bangladesh, Udaipur, Delhi and the Dharavi slum in Mumbai, Bari challenges us to understand what it means to be 'extremely poor' and the role that education can play both in reskilling people to expand their options for action and in contributing to the literacy levels of countries, which opens up entire populations to new ideas and practices.

At the same time, Bari notes that the challenges in terms of health care, economics, clean water, food security, and access must also be addressed if the provocation of poverty is to be understood and faced. This book is timely for its acknowledgement that the world is also struggling with a pandemic caused by a piece of matter that exists on the boundary between living and non-living, a novel coronavirus, SARS-CoV-2. Bari, reflects on its possible impact on the already challenging lives of those living in poverty. Although India is the main focus of Bari's book, he acknowledges the global reach of this pandemic which may force the world to rethink how it defines 'extremely poor'. At the same time,

I was reminded that one of Bari's heroes, the Nobel Laureate Muhammad Yunus, argues that, rather than just restarting the engine that was stopped because of coronavirus, we should consider building a new engine that will take countries and the world on a different path. However, I share Bari"s concerns that this novel coronavirus may exacerbate the challenges the very poor face, not only in Dharavi and Delhi, but elsewhere across the globe. Part of his concern is based on his deep engagement with the citizens of India who provide the human face of questions such as, "Who are the poor?", "How do the poor earn an income?" and "What is a health poverty trap?"; which Bari explores from a global perspective. His approach helps us, his readers, appreciate the global reach of the challenges that his interview collaborators tell in their stories. The stories of the people to whom Bari introduces us, like Arajun Chauhan, Mohan Singh, and Baudghiri, help us to understand that if the poor are most in need of work and travel to earn whatever they can, then it is hard to imagine how they can benefit from the closure of commerce and transportation, which was initiated by the lockdown of countries as they tried to stem the reach of this virus.

Bari also introduces us to Gram Vikas and Joe Madiath and the importance of access to clean water and sanitation. However, Madiath's main goal is not just clean water and sanitation but his desire for equity, gender-sensitivity and egality achieved through sanitation and clean water built by communities, a social justice issue that addressed the structural cultural elements of exclusion. As Bari notes, Madiath would only commit Gram Vikas to work with communities that made a 100% commitment to building and maintaining the structures necessary for clean water and sanitation. Indeed, Bari emphasizes the importance of health because it is one of the stepping stones to being able to also make use of education. His observation of the coughing he observed everywhere he went in Dharavi, was telling I thought. One can think of health, food and education as the legs of a stool that can serve to provide people with the tools for them to live a life whereby they can make use of microloans and perhaps move away from poverty. However, as Bari's interviewees also help us to understand, even in poverty other societal issues such as drugs and alcohol can contribute to the poverty that people experience.

Finally, I want to say something about learning and Bari's nuanced exploration of how humans understand learning. Joe Madiath said that learning is experiential and I think this is what some of Bari's interviewees also discussed as they railed against their perceptions of the poor quality of educational experiences some of their children experienced in all types of schooling. Even Puja's interactions with Bari as he interacted with her and the dots in the paper show us the relational nature of learning that requires interactions with both other humans and the material world in which we live and poverty cannot take that away. Bari's and Puja's interaction also shows us that we should not only think of learning as something that is only cognitive because there was joy in that interaction and that joyful interaction was only possible because both entered into the interaction in an equitable and inclusive way. For me, these are the principles of education, cognition, joy, equity and inclusion. If we miss any of these then education will not be able to make the differences that we think it should.

This is an impressive monograph from a young scholar still negotiating the demands of high school and everyone who reads this book will learn a lot about poverty and its complexities.

Dr. Catherine Milne
Chair, Education Department
NYU, New York University

Dedication

Refath Bari
55 Days in Dharavi

Dedication for *55 Days in Dharavi*: Puja, 4 years old, Dharavi

"Nature and Nature's laws lay hid in night: God said, Let Newton be! and all was light."
Alexander Pope

There is one place in the world: Dharavi. It has no sunlight; not much clean water; electricity probably hasn't reached that corner of the globe yet. And yet there is light. It comes from Puja. Puja is a girl, only four years old. And yet, she taught me more than hundreds of lectures, classes, or books on economics could ever teach me: she taught me the power of education. Puja is a living testament to the belief that education alone is the great equalizer. Hundreds of Randomized Control Trials, and for what? No matter how large the divide – by race, creed, color, or class – education can narrow it all. And I have to thank Puja for that. Thank you, Puja. I will bring this book back to you on the narrow alleyways of Dharavi, and I hope I can find my way back to the light that inspired me so much that day.

Foreward

Tom Blozy
55 Days in Dharavi

Foreward for *55 Days in Dharavi*: Dr. Thomas Blozy, Mathematics Teacher, Brooklyn Technical H.S.

> "So let us wage a global struggle against illiteracy, poverty, and terrorism, and let us pick up our books and pens. They are our most powerful weapons."
> **Malala Yousafzai**

· The power of education cannot be denied. It is the great opportunity, narrowing the deep rifts that separate individuals based on one's race, religion, nationality and/or economic status. In "55 Days in Dharavi", Refath Bari highlights multiple societal problems he encounters in travels to Bangladesh and India, specifically the slum of Dharavi. Through observations and interactions with the residents, Refath takes the reader through substantial instances where the power of education through effective teachers and leaders can have a major impact on one's life. Refath Bari is a remarkable young man who has already led a full life at the current age of 16. His insights into the stark differences that dominate the societies of the world are strikingly real and deeply perceptive. He sees first-hand the power of education for all types of people. In the end, I believe Refath also knows the power of education for himself. This is good news for myself, one of his current mathematics teachers. Refath is currently a junior at Brooklyn Technical High School in Brooklyn New York. This New York City public high school is the largest (over 6000 students) math-science specialized high schools in the country. I have the absolute pleasure of working with Refath two periods everyday as part of the school's Applied Mathematics Major. Our course combines math research, Python programming, graph theory, number theory, and combinatorics, with the main goal being for students to write original mathematics research papers. Refath has embraced all aspects of our course and is a prized leader of the major. Beyond the major, Refath is the captain of the school's math team and the MathWorks Math Modeling Challenge. Refath has high aspirations for applying his mathematics' interests through college and beyond. He understands that education will be his means to achieving his goals. I myself have seen the power that education has to open doors for those with limited resources and as a step up to further one's life. In almost 30 years of teaching, I've worked with a full gamut of students in ability level, race, religion and socio-economic status. I've taught in public schools from a village in Ghana, West Africa to a challenging New York City zoned school to a highly successful math-science-technology magnet school. In all locations, working with an incredibly diverse group of students, the underlying theme to my education observations is that education is the one equalizing opportunity. Education gives students the ability to move beyond the limitations society has confined them in. "55 Days in Dharavi" is a journey that you will enjoy taking with Refath. One is which you will experience with him the power of education in the battle over inequalities. Enjoy.

Dr. Thomas Blozy
Mathematics Teacher
Brooklyn Technical H.S.

Chapter 1

Genius of Yunus

Refath Bari

55 Days in Dharavi

The story of Muhammad Yunus is singular in the history of Economics and Poverty Alleviation. It is rare that one man alone can affect so much change on so large a scale, and yet Yunus defied all the odds, despite being born in a poor village in rural Bangladesh, he rose to become an phenomenon in the country, pioneering the idea of Microcredit that lifted over 7 million women out of Poverty.

Keywords: Muhammad Yunus, Chittagong, Famine

1 The Origin Story

There are exactly four ways I can begin this chapter. All share a common denominator: my friendship with Muhammad Yunus. In fact, the origins of this book begins with the story of this man. Muhammad Yunus is 79 years old today, but he was exactly 63 when I met him. But let's go back – way back – to the Bangladesh famine of 1974. I was born in March, but not the March of 1974. The March of 1974 was not a month of births – it was a month of death, disease, and famine. The pictures are classic – boys with no meat in their body; their rib-cages exposed, teenage girls carrying infant sons; two living body bags in motion. These are pictures I can only see by eye, by stories Muhammad Yunus lived by heart. Great life moments – great tragedies, great accidents, and great fortune – change a man. And so they changed Yunus. On October 25, 1974, Yunus set a mission: a life devoted to the poor. Few people have the ambition to set a life mission at 34. Fewer still have the audacity/capacity to follow through. Yunus was one of those men.

1976 was the miracle year. And $27 was the magic number. $27 to 42 women made all the difference. And it was a big difference. These village women, wracked by poverty, famine, and disease – for the first time in their life – had opportunity. And it was remarkable. They seized the moment and the dividends were clear: By the month's end, each villager made 50 BDT profit on Yunus' loan of $27. And on top of it, they paid back the loan. On that day, Yunus took a small step – paving the way for a giant leap for mankind. That giant leap came in the form of Grameen Bank – a bank for the poor. Yunus created Grameen Bank to fulfill his life mission – a life devoted to helping the poor, the sick and the beat. Through Grameen Bank, Yunus afforded the poor opportunity. And opportunity is priceless. 24 years, $6.5 billion, and millions of microcredits later, Grameen Bank lifted 7.4 million Bengali Women out of poverty. That number is a testament to Muhammad Yunus and his unwavering devotion to the poor, even in the face of government corruption, death threats, and bribery. This is a man who takes the stand every day for the people he pledged to uplift. And indeed, he has done exactly that. He has fulfilled his life mission and his work is a testament to the power of unwavering devotion to the people even in times of crisis. This is Muhammad Yunus, and this is a man I am proud to call a friend. Thank you, Dr. Yunus, for affording the poor an opportunity, and affording me a deep friendship.

Chapter 2

An Enduring Friendship

Refath Bari

55 Days in Dharavi

Throughout my life, I have enjoyed the enduring and rewarding friendship of Muhammad Yunus. Yunus is much greater than the Saint or the Savior many Bangladeshis call him. He is a representative of the potential of Bangladesh – to go from zero to hero as from a nation of Rags to Riches. His concept of Microcredit has uplifted millions from Poverty

Keywords: Muhammad Yunus, Dharavi Slums, Nobel Prize, Microcredit, Microfinance

1 Muhammad Yunus: Saint of Bangladesh

I devoted my previous chapter to the life mission of Muhammad Yunus. But there is the Muhammad Yunus in the public eye, and there is the Muhammad Yunus I knew. The Muhammad Yunus I knew is a very different Yunus – no more a Nobel Laureate; no more a global titan in the international fight against poverty – but a friend. A deep friend, who I saw no more than a grandpa who supported me every step of the way. We shared an easy rapport when I was young that matured into a much deeper, grateful friendship as I grew older.

Yunus was exactly 64 when I met him. 64 is a perfect square, and Yunus was the perfect friend. He threw me a small blue ball and I bounced it around in my hand and played peek-a-boo with him, while my mom and dad stood off to the side. "Never talk to strangers", my mom always taught me, and here I was – forget talking; forget playing – I was absolutely jollying around with this man I didn't even know! Next thing I knew, I had a book in my hands. "It's for you!" Yunus said, laughing. Muhammad Yunus: The Saint read the title. "By Rashidul Bari" – "That's you, dad!" I exclaimed, pointing to my dad. "Yes, it is" he replied, smiling. Inside, I found an autograph Yunus left me – "Best of wishes, young man. You carry the dreams of Bangladesh within you". Alas, as I write this book, I realize I do not simply fulfill a dream of my own, but a shared dream – a dream of the people of Bangladesh to lead a better life, to see a stronger world, and to see a healthier people. This dream I realized 15 years ago when I read Yunus' autograph and I realize it now, as I reminisce on our shared memories.

Yunus won the Nobel Peace Prize in 2006. It was a day of true joy – a man whom we long knew had devoted his life to the poor, finally being recognized on the international stage. We flew back to Bangladesh and in a few steps, I hugged Yunus and he hugged me. And we both knew what that meant. Fame, Power, and Money changes the corrupt, but it spares the Saints. And Yunus was no less than the Saint of Bangladesh. Indeed, I recognized Yunus as the old friend I had come to play and relax with so many times before, even after he won the largest prize in the world. None of us were surprised, then, when we discovered Yunus pledged all of his $1.8 million prize money to building a hospital for the blind and towards developing Grameen Bank.

March 2009 was my 6th year of life – and my 6th encounter with Yunus. My parents took me to the Y29 Festival, and I entered with no expectations. Instead, I was absolutely riddled with Joy upon entering the festival. Inside the auditorium, I found two of my greatest idols – Jeffrey Sachs and Muhammad Yunus, sitting down for a rare public interview. I was only 6 at the time, so the words flew by me, and the ideas spilled from one ear to the other, but one thing I understood – our goals. From a young age, I realized the fundamental importance of peace and poverty alleviation, and Yunus was pivotal in that understanding. And so – I devoted my full attention to my greatest role models. And yet, I did a double-take when I heard my name from the stage: "Refath Aporbo Bari, please come to the stage." What could I do? The stage compelled me forward. As I stepped up, I just couldn't stop smiling. It was instinct more than anything. Here I was a 4 foot 7 year old, in the presence of two of the greatest titans in the global fight against poverty. For a split second, I was standing on the shoulders of giants. And what I saw from those shoulders I still see today. From the slums of India to the shanties of Bangladesh, I see the people in need – people in suffering, and I believe it is our foremost duty in this world to help those less privileged than us. And so, this book is a testament to that belief. The belief that the individual must serve his fundamental duty of fighting the common enemy of man – poverty, disease, hunger, and famine. And so, I go to India to find the edge of Poverty – Poverty so distinct that the rich millionaires of Bollywood live litteral a stone's throw from the poor shanties of Dharavi. I go to Dharavi to find the lives of the poor, to hear their stories and to live their lives. And make no mistake – I go now because now is a time more important than ever.

In this moment of crisis, humanity faces its hour of maximum danger. One virus, no more than a few millimeters thick, has brought all of mankind to its knees. Mankind – who stepped on the moon, who has traveled the seas and the stars and all in between, who has ventured to explore the unknown and go where no man has gone before – is now at risk of surrender to an enemy no eye can see, no politician can arrest, and no army can kill. COVID-19 has all but shuttered humanity from its own home. The streets are empty. The people are gone. And the only sound I sleep to is the sound of the siren; the sound of ambulances 3AM through the night. And now I ask the fatal question: What if the terror of Coronavirus attacked Dharavi? This is a question I fear to ask; and one I regret to answer. Social Distance does not exist in the most densely populated area on the planet: Dharavi. Dharavi is a slum home to one million people, and it's not uncommon to see five or six living in a closet-sized apartment. Dharavi is dense by design: the spaces are so narrow that people and cars walk on the same street. The drinking water is unfiltered, and often carries dust or fecal particles in it and garbage is often thrown into a river that in turn pollutes the entire area. So if Coronavirus ravages America, it will bring civilization in a third world slum to its knees. Those with weak immune systems are especially vulnerable to COVID19. Again, the dwellers of Dharavi fit the bill crisp – years of pollution, unsanitary water, and unregulated industry has all but scarred the immune system of millions. Stay home! Socially distance yourselves, you say. But realize that staying home is a privilege that these people cannot afford. A river separates them from those who can – million-dollar bollywood executives who can't stand the sight nor smell of the slum dwellers. Under Modi's stay-at-home order, these people will die starving before the virus ever touches them. And so is the fate of millions of other slum dwellers at this moment – they risk suicide going to work, and risk starvation staying home. It is only a matter of time before the virus arrives: a question of when, not if. When that time arrives, the infected will start small. They will seem harmless. But in the days upcoming, it will spread like wildfire – a fire that no money or politician can stop. We must stop that fire before it consumes us all. To do so, I embark on a quest – a quest to prove the fundamental axiom of life.

I seek to prove the power of hope. To do so, I take you on a journey to Dharavi, India 7776 miles away from New York. 7776 miles away is the land of the poor and home of the hopeful. To prove this universal fact, I begin with five stories among thousands; these five stories I listened to in my 55 days in Dharavi. In those 55 days, I saw darkness: the politics, the misery, and worst of all – the death. But on the 44th day, I saw beyond the dark – I saw a hope in the people; hope for a career, hope for a family, and hope for a better life for the children. I saw light transcend the dark and I saw hope transcend the hardship. Indeed, I had no plans to write a story, much less a book, but on my 55th and final day, I realized I cannot be selfish – I realized that these stories are far more than my own – they are powerful stories meant to motivate, inspire, and propel the world forward. And so, as the humble chronicler of this narrative, I see it as my duty to share these stories of hope and hardship; addiction and recovery; life and death; Of the thousands of stories I have heard – many heartbreaking, some tragic, and a few downright unreal – these are the few that demonstrate the universal power of hope. Let us commence.

Chapter 3

The Problem: Culture of Poverty

Refath Bari

55 Days in Dharavi

I begin with a Case Study: Babu Jai in Udaipur, India. I look at Babu's life holistically and isolate the main aspects of his life. I then generalize these aspects of Babu's life to the lives of all poor people. I look at these generalizations qualitatively and statistically.

Keywords: Defining Poor, Living Arrangements, Expenditure of the Poor, Health of the Poor, the Poor Man's Asset

1 Case Study: Babu Jai

It took me a hundred kilos and a buck to get to Udaipur, India. The driver dropped me off a yard from the slum. But still took me an hour to find it. It was late and I was hungry. 5 PM's not an easy time to be in India. I was already pissed after an hour of traffic and the blazing sun gave me a headache. The solution came in the form of Mr. Babu Jai: his little tin grill clinked with the sound of metal and butter every five minutes. I dropped a buck in his pan, and he shook his mini-kerosene stove. Babu dropped a cup of batter on the cast-iron griddle and swirled it with a small metal spoon. The oil drizzled around the edges, and my mouth watered and I drooled at the sight. If you're hungry, I won't torture you with the details. Better to just close my eyes. Instead, I heard the sizzling butter pop the metal griddle as the *Dosa* (the Indian pancake) became pock-marked and slid off the griddle, clean as a sliver. Babu doused the *Dosa* in his tin can of garlic green sauce, and folded the *Dosa* into a banana leaf and dropped some beans on top. All that for a buck. Or 15 Rupees. Your call. I sat on the ground for some time and stared at the wall. My forehead dripped with sweat and I studied Babu. He sat, his gaze switching from the watch to the wall, anxiously awaiting the next customer. When I came back an hour later, Babu was gone, and so was his little

Dosa stand. An hour and two alleys later, I found myself in Babu's house. Did he retire early? Apparently not: "I have to go to the field now". Babu only made *Dosas* in the day. In the night, he worked the fields, and on the way home, sold recycled trash his kids found picking the trash. "How much do you make a day?" "$1.09" he curtly responded. What a shame. A diverse man with many jobs, and yet a buck a day is all he makes. I looked around his little hut. Outside was a tin roof that looked like a sine wave. Inside were seven people crowded in the small room. The hut was basically empty, save a little cot in the corner. 7 people and 1 bed? How? Babu caught my gaze and nodded his head. "Oh yeah. They share the house with us so we pay less." Diverse *and* Savvy. There are men who work hard, and men who work smart. Here's one who did both. The three boys chased each other around the room, and the two women on the floor stared at me. It smelled quick. Not mud or dirt. It was ... fire? I glanced at the roof. Did the Sun set it ablaze? A quick check told me no. No! It was much better – the smoke was from the cigarette bobbing in the man's mouth. He stared at me. "Namaste." I greeted. "Mhmm," he struggled to take the ciggarette from his mouth "Nafaste. Tum kaun ho?" he looked puzzled. "Anik doesn't talk English. He thought you are going to share the house with us" Babu said, waving his hands around the room. I leaned on the wall, studying the room. No one was over 40, but the man in the corner looked frail. I enjoyed the silence for a while, but it was broken by a sound I'd grown all too used to: the hacking, killing cough. He cough his spit into the corner. I saw a little plastic bag by the door. This man's trash was literally my treasure. A man's trash can say a lot about him. Poking out from the garbage was a few bottles of *Desi Daru*, the Indian analogue of Alcohol, made from grass-spitting molasses, and some fine sugar canes. It was weird, I'll admit. There was no TV or Radio in Babu's hut. If not for the coughs every second and the childrens' banter, it would be silence all the way. "All work and no play makes Babu a dull boy;" I said, looking at Babu, the emotionless workaholic. Babu stared at me – "You say dull? I am working day and night brother. I am not dull, I am stressed all the time. Look at them," he pointed at the three boys, who were playing some hand game. "I picked them up from school last week. *Mal*, all over them. Pants. Gone. Shirt. Gone. I brought those clothes for 50 Rupees. 50 Rupees! But this stupid public school gave them something nasty and they got diaraheaa. I don't trust them anymore," Babu said. His blank face broke – into anger, and he started shaking. "I don't trust them anymore. They been playing with me for a long time now. Messing with me. Two years, its been, and they're the same as before school. I'm tired of that garbage 'public school' nonsense. That's why I pulled them out." No wonder the boys looked so jolly. "I'll put them in a good

Private soon, maybe Kishor Primary, but I'm still saving up. And then there's this guy", Babu gestured at Anik. "Anytime, this guy's gonna fall apart. And then what do I do? If he falls flat, I get half the money. So I work double as hard. You don't get it man," his voice broke. "You don't see it, but I am stressed. I am stressed for my life. All the time. Can't even sleep sometimes." Babu said. His pupils bore deep in his eye sockets and the bags under his eyes came clear in the harsh light. "Take some rest, brother. Do you have any holidays?" I asked. "My brother's wedding is coming up." His voice picked up a bit "The weddings are always good. Sometimes I pocket lot of the food for later. When Durga Puja comes, I go to the temples and gurdwaras (Sikh places of worship) and they give me rice with dal and green sauce and some fried chicken. But that's a long way off," he said, staring into the distance. "That yours?" I pointed to the small crop of land next to the hut. "Useless." Babu said. "Nonarable. It's dry the whole year.", he explained. I stared at Babu and he made eye-contact for the first time. We looked at each other for a few minutes before Anik's killing cough broke our gaze. "Thank you, Brother. Good luck – with everything." I turned back. "Before I leave, ... here": In my handshake, I slipped my card and a few Rupees. It was the least I could do for Babu, the man who gave me all his stories. (Chomsky 1957).

Update 1.1: Udaipur, India

Where's Udaipur now, in light of COVID19? Udaipur is in Ratjashthan, a state in Northern India, and one of India's 29 states. Udaipur has the largest COVID19 case count in the state, as of May 7, 2020, with 23 cases. Obviously, this data changes quickly, and even now, case counts are most likely an underestimate (New York Times 2020). Prime Minister Narendra Modi has relaxed lockdowns in areas largely untouched by the virus. But in a alarming sign of how quick the data can change – on May 8 (one day later), the # cases jumped to 103 in Udaipur, from a previous count of 20. Udaipur is now officially a containment zone. All offices, businesses, and establishments have been shut down and no one can leave the area without a pass. All relaxations have been suspended and curfews are being enforced in 10 police stations around the city. All movement of people have been stopped. As the designated hospital for COVID19 patients, the city's RNT mediacl college is over-capacity, new patients are transported to other medical colleges.

Refath Bari

2 Babu's List

This chapter seeks to describe the problem of Poverty. In doing so, I wish to hit 7 key points, which I will refer to as "Babu's List", in memory of my friend:

Table 1: **Babu's List**

1. Who are the poor?

2. What are the living arrangements of the poor?

3. How do the poor spend their money?

4. Do the poor have choice?

5. Are the poor in danger?

6. Can the poor help themselves?

7. How do the poor see themselves?

Upon addressing these seven key questions, I hope to establish the demarcation between the fact and fiction of poverty, after which I will compile a list of the differences between the expectations and realities one finds upon living the lives of the poor.

3 Who are the poor?

Before we supply a formal definition of the poor, we must first define Purchasing Power Parity, an important term that will come into play as we discuss the computation of poverty lines:

Definition 3.1: Purchasing Power Parity

The idea of the Purchasing Power Parity (PPP) can be translated simply as follows: the idea that "once converted to a common currency, national price levels should be equal" (Ken Rogoff). In other words, $4 in United States money should buy me a Big Mac. It should cost me no more and no less to purchase a big mac anywhere else in the world. That is the idea of PPP: Monetary Consistency. But PPPs leave a lot to be desired – they have been widely criticized by economists for their inadequacy and unadoptability to the lives of the poor (Deaton, 2004, 2006). There exist many minute nuances not incorporated into the Theory of PPPs, such as (1) Prices are usually higher in urban cities than rural regions (2) The poor typically pay a different price than everyone else, even for the same type of goods, (3) Obstacles such as tariffs, transportation costs, and non-tariff barriers make PPPs an inconsistent and infrequently updated metric.

As many of the poor gather in slums, we must formally define **Slum** before we proceed.

Definition 3.2: Slum

Slums are the housing of the poor: collections of tightly-packed decrepit huts plagued by unsanitary conditions. The growth of slums accompanied increasing urbanization during the late 20th century. However, from 1999 to 2010, the number of people living in slums dropped, despite the global urban population having increased. This is statistical proof that poverty is far from immortal – in fact, from 1990 to 2015, the number of people in extreme poverty dropped by 25%, from 1.9 billion people to 700 million. COVID-19, however, has all but erased the last decade of improvement (World Bank 2020). The World Bank estimates that 60 million people could fall into poverty, raising poverty rates for the first time in two decades.

And finally, we can now define the poor as the following:

Refath Bari

Definition 3.3: Poor

The World Bank redefined the Extremely Poor in 2015 to be those who live on $1.90 or less a day. COVID-19 will no doubt change that. The World Bank first defined the international poverty line to be $1 a day in the 1990 *World Development Report*. To create a standard for comparing poverty, we identify two reliable indicators of well-being: Consumption and Income. Consumption meaning the services we consume and Income meaning the money we make. The breaking even comes when the level of income and consumption become insufficient to support a good quality of life. This is the poverty line. Every country has its own poverty line. The poverty line of the poorest countries are averaged to find the international poverty line. That is the essence. In reality, poverty lines are largely defined by Purchasing Power Parity Exchange Rates, which are used to compute the 'uniform' poverty line. The extreme poverty line is defined by the minimum food consumption that can sustain life. These poverty lines enable economists to measure growth and progress in the first Millenium Development Goal: Eridicate extreme poverty and hunger.

---

4 What are the living arrangements of the poor?

It is well known that poor families are big. But by nature or nurture? The answer could be both. We begin with the basic facts:

Table 2: **Family Structure of Poor**

1. The Poor have large families

2. Poor families consist mostly of many children and young people

4.1 The Poor have large families

Let's quantify that. In a 2006 study conducted on 13 poor countries by MIT Nobel-Prize Winning Economists Abihijit Banerjee and Esther Duflo, the # family members in the average poor family typically ranged from 6 to 12 people, with the median being 7 to 8 people. This is in comparison to 2.5 in the United States. Banerjee and Duflo's sample size were the following 13 countries:

| | | | | Households (HHs) living on less than | | | |
| | | | | $1.08 per person per day | | $2.16 per person per day | |
Country	Source	Year	Avg. monthly consumption per capita (In PPP$)	Number surveyed	Percent of total surveyed HHs	Number surveyed	Percent of total surveyed HHs
Cote d'Ivoire	LSMS	1988	664.13	375	14%	1,411	49%
Guatemala	GFHS	1995	301.92	469	18%	910	34%
India-Hyderabad	Banerjee-Duflo-Glennerster	2005	71.61	106	7%	1,030	56%
India-Udaipur	Banerjee-Deaton-Duflo	2004	43.12	482	47%	883	86%
Indonesia	IFLS	2000	142.84	320	4%	2,106	26%
Mexico	MxFLS	2002	167.97	959	15%	2,898	39%
Nicaragua	LSMS	2001	117.34	333	6%	1,322	28%
Pakistan	LSMS	1991	48.01	1,573	46%	3,632	83%
Panama	LSMS	1997	359.73	123	2%	439	6%
Papua New Guinea	LSMS	1996	133.38	185	15%	485	38%
Peru	LSMS	1994	151.88	297	7%	821	20%
South Africa	LSMS	1993	291.33	413	5%	1,643	19%
Tanzania	LSMS	1993	58.85	1,184	35%	2,941	73%
Timor Leste	LSMS	2001	64.42	662	15%	2,426	51%

Figure 1: The sample size consisted of 13 countries scattered across the globe

And indeed, this finding closely matches reality, where we find the poor often crowded in rooms of seven of eight. But, the data tells a different story: the median # of adults in a poor family ranges from 2.5 to 5, with a median of 3 adults.

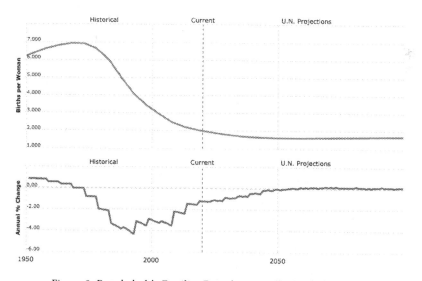

Figure 2: Bangladesh's Fertility Rate dramatically dropped in the late 20th century, following the implementation of a successful Family Planning Program

This tells us families are actually sharing the same housing with non-family members, so that the fixed cost of housing is shared amongst more people, much like Babu and his wife shared their hut in Udaipur with Anik. As we progress from extremely poor families to 'simply' poor families, the number of children in a household decreases, which holds consistent with the convention that increased socio-economic status is associated with lower fertility rates. In a direct application of this principle, we examine my home country of Bangladesh.

In what turned to be a wondrous reversal of fate for the small nation, Bangladesh went from a newly independent nation in 1971, plagued by floods, famine, war, and terrorism to a nation known for its dramatic progress in literacy and economy. Much of this dramatic success has been attributed to the decreasing fertility rate. But to understand success is just as important as to celebrate it. How did Bangladesh go from zero to hero, and how can other developing countries do the same? We start in the 1970s, when Bengali women had up to six children on average. A dangerous combination of lack of access to standard health services (i.e., contraceptives) and malnutrition meant that one in every five children died. Indeed, the child mortality rate was still 224.1 for every 1000 children. Think Middle Ages in Europe; this was Bangladesh a half a century back. This was a disaster waiting to happen. And it did – in 1974, a deadly combination of exploding population growth, and a massive monsoon flood devastated Bangladesh. It was the worst famine in decades, with over 1.5 million dead. The severe monsoon flooding ravaged the new (primarily-agrarian based) nation, destroying much of the annual rice crop, shooting up rice prices, and leading to severe unemployment. The Government was caught off guard, and their mismanaged distribution of food worsened the crisis. Despite the famine, the United States denied 2.2 million tonnes of food aid on the basis that Bangladesh was exporting Jute (a type of fiber) to Cuba. By the time Bangladesh yielded to America's demand to stop exports to Cuba, the food aid was too late. Millions died, and millions more were left destitute and bedridden. A deadly famine and diminishing resources was a wake-up call for the Government, who began considering the resources and economic prospects of Bangladesh, the new nation. In 1975, Bangladesh launched the first Family Planning Program, whose sole goal was to reduce the fertility rate. The program was riddled with failures at the start – most families in Bangladesh were oblivious to family planning, and conventional belief held that large families were the best (a common belief in Agrarian Societies, where more family members equates to more laborers and thus more income). Women had low status in Bangladesh (and much of South Asia at the time, as evident from the 'Missing Women', a phenomenon we investigate deeply in Chapter 5) and lacked access to quality health services, particularly the rural population. All of these factors proved significant barriers to the successful implementation of the Family Planning Program. But the new nation proved to be more than resilient: young married women were deployed as outreach workers to publicize the new program, provisions entitled women to various services to meet their reproductive needs, family planning clinics were established throughout the country (and especially in rural areas) to provide contraceptive and hormonal services, and the new program was publicized via mass media, education, and communal activities. The outreach workers eventually numbered in the 25,000 and other 12,000 field workers were deployed from Nongovernmental Organizations, along with 4500 male outreach workers. Each outreach worker was assigned to a corresponding village, with one worker reaching about 900 women. These outreach workers put a face on the new Family Planning Program, and humanized the country's initiative to lower fertility rates. Success came gradually, as more people became knowledgeable about Family Planning. The growth was remarkable: In the 1970s, 8% of married Bengali women used contraceptives, compared to 60% in 2004. This stunning social health development was followed by a lower fertility rate: What was once one of the world's highest fertility rates, standing at 6.9 in the 1970s, dropped to 3 in 2004. As of 2018, Bangladesh's fertility rate stands at 2.1.

Bangladesh: A Case Study in Lower Fertility Rates

Henry Kissinger dismissed Bangladesh as a basket case upon its founding in 1971. And yet, since its founding 49 years past, Bangladesh has made remarkable strides on the Millennium Development Goals. With record-setting growth rates (the Asian Development Bank projects Bangladesh GDP Growth Rate to be 8% in 2020), a stunning drop in fertility rates, and an internationally competitive economy, Bangladesh is on pace to become one of the fastest growing countries in the world (5th fastest growing country by GDP Growth Rate according to World Bank 2017). In fact, Bangladesh's Growth Rate is projected to be place it well above its Asian peers, including India and Pakistan. By all measures, Bangladesh is a rags to riches story: what started off as a nation plagued by problems of (1) High Fertility Rates: In the 1960s, one Bengali Women had an average of 6.72 children. As of 2017, that stat is now 2.06, demonstrating Bangladesh's growth as a developing country.

4.2 Poor families consist mostly of many children and young people

A young population is usually the result of high fertility, either recently or in the past. From another perspective, there are actually very few old people. The ratio of old people (>51 years old) to prime-aged people (21-50 years old) varies from 0.2-0.3 in the Urban areas (Banerjee, Duflo 2006). For reference, the comparative stat in the US is 0.6. This owes to the high mortality rates among older people, especially men (who typically suffer from respiratory illnesses as they get older). The ratio of young to old people in both rural and urban areas of the poor falls around 6 (Banerjee, Duflo 2006). The comparative stat in the US is 1. That's a very young population!

5 How do the poor spend their money?

Clearly, event cent counts. Knowing this full well, how do the dollar a day families live? This is the fundamental question we hope to address in this section. As such, it helps to simplify the answers into five key points.

Table 3: **Expenditure of the Poor**

1 The poor spend a lot on food

2 Tobacco and Alcohol are top expenses of the poor

3 Festivals are a major expense

4 Some poor invest in entertainment; Others don't

5 The poor look for a Goldilocks's in quantity and quality of food

5.1 The poor spend a lot on food

Here is the poor man's dilemma: Work as hard as he can, only to make enough to cover his basic needs the least expensive way. And indeed, the poor man can only work so hard – he barely eats enough food to keep on living. The poor man has no Martin Luther King: "If a man is called to be a street sweeper, he should sweep streets even as a Michelangelo painted, or Beethoven composed music or Shakespeare wrote poetry. He should sweep streets so well that all the hosts of heaven and earth will pause to say, 'Here lived a great street sweeper who did his job well." No one gave Babu a glance as he sweat 14 hours a day job to job. The heavens did not pause for Ashok as he toiled through the nights. No one pauses for the poor man, but the poor man pauses for all.

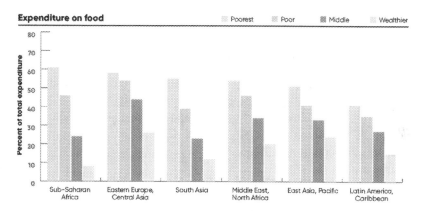

Figure 3: The poor spend more on food than the rest, making them especially vulnerable to price spikes and inflation

We have defined 'Extremely Poor' above, on the basis of Purchasing Power Parity, a insufficient income to meet needs, and most importantly – the budget required to buy the minimum food required to survive. In essence, the poor were defined as those without enough to eat. In this way, there is no life for the poor – only survival. Across 13 countries, food expenditure varied around 56% to 78% in both Rural and Urban areas (Banerjee, Duflo 2006). Even worse, the poor actually pay more for food (Chung, Myers 1999)

In 1973, Economists Chanjin Chung and Samuel L. Myers asked the exact same question: "Do the poor pay more?". Upon conducting a survey on 526 grocery/chain-stores across inner-city and suburban areas in Twin Cities (a region in the US State of Minnesota), Myers found a surprising answer: the poor pay more for grocery because the cheapest stores are not in their neighborhoods (Chung, Meyers, 1973). The moral of the story was that people who buy from non-chain stores pay more. And indeed, Myers' study found that the poor shop more often in non-chain stores. Why? If chain stores (i.e., BJs, Wal-Marts) are so cheap, why don't the poor buy from them? The key is time: time is money. Chung justifies that the wealthy value their time more, and have the transport (i.e.,private automobile) necessary to buy in volumes, and thus visit the store less frequently. Thus, with chain stores often offering large, bundled discounts,

Refath Bari

the rich often flock to them. In contrast, the poor value their time much less, and cannot afford transportation (the people who must walk to stores), which is why they can only buy a limited amount before the load gets too heavy. As such, the poor often make many trips to their local convenience store, which charges more for items than chain stores. But the poor can't afford to go to chain stores because (a) Chain stores aren't located in poor neighborhoods, often due to crime and security costs and (b) Even if they could, they can't afford to take those volume discounts home, due to lack of transport. The rabbit hole of reasons goes down much deeper, of course, to State Taxes, Discriminatory Pricing Policies, and other factors equally contributing to this crisis. But even so, not every cent goes to food. In Mexico, for instance, only half of a family's budget goes to groceries (Banerjee, Duflo 2006). Where goes the other half?

5.2 Tobacco and Alcohol are top expenses of the poor

Here's a shocker: A major expense for the poor are tobacco and alcohol. Rural or Urban, India or Mexico, the poor share one thing in common: a love for intoxicants. The amount of the poor man's budget on these 'Specialized Adult Goods', as they are often referred to, range from 4.1% in Papau New Guinea; 5% in Udaipur, India; 6% in Indonesia and 8.1% in Mexico (Banerjee, Duflo 2006).

5.3 Festivals are a major expense

Even more surprising, Festivals are a major expense for the poor – religious, ceremonial, weddings, and funerals alike, all cost the poor. The poor households of Udaipur, India spend over 10% of their yearly budget on such festivals (Banerjee, Duflo 2006). Even more striking is how many: over 99% of households in Udupair, India spend on festivals; the pattern holds in many other countries, as well: 90% of South African households living under a dollar a day spent money on festivals, and in Pakistan, Indonesia and Cote d'Ivoire, over 50% of households did the same.

5.4 Some poor invest in entertainment; Others don't

Movie, and Theatre haven't found popularity among the poor. Of the 13 countries in Banerjee and Duflo's sample, none of them spent more than 1% on any of the above forms of entertainment. The comparative stat in the US is 5%. This difference could owe to a number of factors: festivals and other social gathering may simply have outdated or overcrowded the use of Movies and Theatres as entertainment.

On the other hand, radio and TV ownership (among those living under a dollar a day) varies across the 13 countries sampled: we have radio ownership at 11% for Udaipur, and above 60% in Nicaragua and Guatemala and above 70% in South Africa and Peru. The same parity plays in television ownership: No one has a TV in Udupair, but 25% of Guatemalan households do, and over 50% of Nicaraguan households do (Banerjee, Duflo 2006).

Is this parity related? As in, does a high investment in festivals correspond to a low investment in TV/Radio (and vice versa)? That seems to be the case. In Udupair, India, where the % household budget spent on festivals is the greatest and basically everyone engages in ceremonies, the TV/Radio ownership rates are the lowest. Conversely, in Nicaragua, where barely any households invest in festivals, the TV/Radio ownership rates skyrocket to over 57% (for rural poor). One caveat is that the urban poor tend to have much higher rates of TV/Radio ownership than the rural. This may be signs of an lack of supply to meet adequate demand: perhaps the rural poor simply don't have reception.

5.5 The poor look for a Goldilocks's in quantity and quality of food

The poor seek to strike a harmony between the quantity and quality of food they consume. Here's what's counter-intuitive: if the poor of Udupair spent as much on food as they do on festivals, tobacco, and alcohol – *they could spend up to 30% more on food!* And yet they don't. These are signs of limitation: the poor don't have much choice – in a way, they are economically disenfrachised to the extent that they must significantly endanger they own health (i.e., by not buying enough food, by not going to hospital during emergencies) to have any consumer freedom. This is the poor man's dilemma – an in not buying enough food, he cannot even work hard enough before he falls ill or exhausted. And this is no hypothesis: the % budget spent by the poor and extremely poor on food is the same, reflecting that the poor feel no need to buy any more food than the extremely poor.

In short, the poor man's budget's got some slack. We look at this characteristic from another perspective: What food do the poor buy? First and foremost, we establish the efficiency of a grain by the amount it costs per the # calories it provides. By that measure, the best bang for the buck are the millet grains (Deaton, Subramanian 1996). So do the poor buy millets? Only two-thirds of the time! Of the average poor man's expenditure on grains, only 66% is on millets. Where's the rest? 20% goes to rice (costs twice as much per calorie), another 10%

Refath Bari

on wheat (70% more expensive than millets as a way to get calories). On top of this, the poor spend 7% of their total budget on Sugar, which is not only more expensive to get calories (than grains), but also devoid of any other nutritional benefits. The same sugar craze shows in Udupair: the poor spend almost 10% of their food buget on sugar. At the end of the day, for every 1% increase in the poor's total spending, that corresponds to a $\frac{2}{3}$% increase in food spending; of that increase in food spending, half goes to buying calories, and the other half goes to getting more expensive (and tastier) calories.

And here's the future: the poor are spending less and less on food. Take India: food spending dropped from 70% in 1983 to 62% in 2000. As a result, the poor are also consuming less less calories (Meenakshi and Vishwanathan, 2003), although this could be due to greater automation (Jha, 2004).

	Food	As a Share of Total Consumption Alcohol/ Tobacco	Education	Health
Living on less than $1 a day				
Rural				
Cote d'Ivoire	64.4%	2.7%	5.8%	2.2%
Guatemala	65.9%	0.4%	0.1%	0.3%
India - Udaipur	56.0%	5.0%	1.6%	5.1%
Indonesia	66.1%	6.0%	6.3%	1.3%
Mexico	49.6%	8.1%	6.9%	0.0%
Nicaragua	57.3%	0.1%	2.3%	4.1%
Pakistan	67.3%	3.1%	3.4%	3.4%
Panama	67.8%		2.5%	4.0%
Papua New Guinea	78.2%	4.1%	1.8%	0.3%
Peru	71.8%	1.0%	1.9%	0.4%
South Africa	71.5%	2.5%	0.8%	0.0%
Timor Leste	76.5%	0.0%	0.8%	0.9%

Figure 4: A summation: (1) Poor spend moderately on Food, little on Education, and sometimes invest in entertainment

6 Do the poor have choice?

Do the poor have choice in the services they consume? Or are they confined to a limited market in which they are forced to buy from a limited selection of goods? The answers may be unexpected – and sometimes counter-intuitive.

Table 4: **Fate of the Poor**

1 The poor buy goods, but they're often unproductive or undurable

2 Some poor own land, but it's not very useful

6.1 The poor buy goods, but they're often unproductive or undurable

TV and Radio ownership greatly fluctuate between countries. One factor is lack of signal, but then there's also the literal cost of buying a TV. It is a buy that removes lots of the poor man's savings. As such, it is expected that the poor own more TVs than the extremly poor: TV ownership among the poor drops from 45% to 14% when we go to $2/day poor to $1/day poor in Cote d'Ivoire; 17% to 7% in South Africa; and 21% to 10% in Peru.

	Radio	Television	Bicycle	Land
		Percent of Households with:		
Living on less than $1 a day				
Rural				
Cote d'Ivoire	43.3%	14.3%	34.4%	62.7%
Guatemala	58.5%	20.3%	23.1%	36.7%
India - Udaipur	11.4%	0.0%	13.5%	98.9%
Indonesia		26.5%		49.6%
Mexico			41.3%	4.0%
Nicaragua	59.3%	8.3%	11.1%	50.4%
Pakistan	23.1%		27.0%	30.4%
Panama	43.6%	3.3%	0.0%	85.1%
Papua New Guinea	18.0%	0.0%	5.3%	
Peru	73.3%	9.8%	9.8%	65.5%
South Africa	72.2%	7.2%	20.0%	1.4%
Tanzania		0.0%		92.3%
Timor Leste	14.3%	0.6%	0.9%	95.2%

Figure 5: The poor man has not much chocie; if he seeks to buy a durable good, he must pay for it as an expensive, lump sum, if you will.

What do the poor have by way of productive assets? Not much, actually. Obviously, transport via private automobile isn't an option, so the next best thing comes in the form of a bycicle: Of the poor, 34% own a bike in Coit d'Ivoire, but the same stat falls to less than 14% in Udaipur, Nicaragua, Panama, Papua New Guinea, Peru, and East Timor. Much like Babu's room, the poor don't come by many productive assets: in Udaipur, most households living a dollar a day have a bed, but only 10% have a chair and 5% have a table. Basic things that we take for granted are things the poor don't have. Half have some kind of watch or clock, and having an electric fan, a sewing machine, a cart, or any motorized vehicle puts you in the top 1%. And no one has a phone.

6.2 Some poor own land, but it's not very useful

And then there's land. The all-important land. Land was do-or-die in the middle ages, where much of society was agrarian-based. But today, in our increasingly industrialized and globalized society, where automation has become the new norm, land has become an almost obvious asset. Still, not all poor own land. Of those who live under a dollar a day, only 4% own land in Mexico, 1.4% in South Africa, 30% in Pakistan, 37% in Guatemala, 50% in Nicaragua and Indonesia, 63% in Cote d'Ivoire, 65% in Peru, and 85% in Panama. In Udaipur, over 99% of a dollar a day households own land. But, there's a caveat: Much of the land is non-arable dry scrubland, which can't be cultivated much of the year. Even worse, the land is too small for any productive use: the median the median amount of land owned by the poor is a hectare or less in Udaipur, Indonesia, Guatemala, and Timor-Leste, between 1 and 2 hectares in Peru, Tanzania, Pakistan, and between 2 and 3 hectares in Nicaragua, Cote d'Ivoire, and Panama (Banerjee, Duflo 2006).

7 Are the poor in danger?

The short answer: Yes! The impoverished have been demonstrated to be less willing to report or take action during medical emergencies concerning their lives or their loved ones. As such, it is of upmost importance to understand the mortal dangers the poor face.

Table 5: **Luck of the Poor**

1 Many indicators show the poor failing health standards

2 COVID-19 is endangering the lives of many slum-dwellers

7.1 Many indicators show the poor failing health standards

The poor are naturally more resistant to reporting illnesses or going to the hospital for emergencies than the rich. They are much less reactive to medical emergencies because it costs them labor productivity and the hospital bills can add up fast. And so, when the poor earnestly report of their health in Surveys, it becomes especially telling of their condition as a people.

We begin by the Indian Government's recommendation that a man with medium physical activity or a woman with heavy physical activity ought to have 2800 calories a day. By Deaton and Subramanian's (1996) measure, the poorest consume half of that in a day. By this simple estimate, we already see the cause for concern for the poor's health. But we need not resort to government estimates for warning signs: they are inherent in the people. Body Mass Index (BMI) is the first indicator. It is a measurement of an individual's body fat and is often used to guage obesity and overweightness. Udaipur's poor have a BMI of 17.8; On a broader scale, 65% of adult men and 40% of adult women have a BMI less than 18.5, the cutoff for being underweight. Even worse, among the dollar a day poor of Udaipur, only 57% report that the members of their household had enough food this year (Banerjee, Duflo 2006). There are other sporadic health problems, as well. 55% of the poor Udaipur adults have anemia (lack of red blood cells), which can be caused by a host of other disease such as sickle cell anemia or iron deficiency anemia. The poor also get sick often – in Udapir, 72% of the poor had at least one symptom and 46% had an illness that left them in the bed or in the hospital. In data, this translates to the following: of the dollar a day households, 11% to 15% report a member of the household being sick for at least a day in Peru, South Africa, East Timor, Panama, and Tanzania; 21% to 28% in Pakistan, Indonesia, and Cote d'Ivoire, and between 35% and 46% in Nicaragua, Udaipur, and Mexico. These illnesses need not be sporadic; many of them are chronic, as well: 45% of adults and 34% adults under 50 have difficulty conducting a normal activities (i.e., field work, walking, milking, etc.) Other problems, such as Diarrhea and Blind Spots riddle poor communities frequently – over 15% of the poor have vision problems, which may due to malnutrition, disease, or a dangerous combination of both.

8 Can the poor help themselves?

Aid need not be the only means of helping the poor. In fact, there are many means through which the poor can help themselves and their communities as a whole.

Table 6: **Advice for the Poor**

1 The poor can save up more money, thus accommodating for emergencies (Success Story: China)

2 Move their children from failing public schools and invest in good private schools

8.1 The poor can save up more money, thus accommodating for emergencies (Success Story: China)

The poor can save up more money, thus ensuring they won't be completely caught-off-guard by medical emergencies, crop failures, or any other disaster. Savings are the key. Take the COVID-19 pandemic – who knew the markets would shake and the shelves would empty and the prices would inflate? By the very nature of the pandemic, millions of families had to bank on their hard-earned savings to buy enough food to survive the pandemic. And those who had no savings barely survived the economic outburst of the pandemic, if they hadn't been absolutely crushed by its weight. It seems a simple way to reduce their stress, if any.

8.2 Move their children from failing public schools and invest in good private schools

The poor are far ahead of the game in this respect. Despite the World Bank's response that the poor "should be patient" (World Bank 2003: 1), and wait for Public Education to be reformed of its corruption and inefficacy before it can meet the needs of the poor, the poor have resorted to their ingenuity. 'Do well by doing good' is a common phrase in these poor communities, where poor entrepenuers, scarred by a bad education, hope to provide a better one for their own communities. These entrepenuers establish 'budget' private schools affordable to the poorest of the poor, on the poverty line or below. In Hyderabad, India, that means monthly fees as low as $1.74 in the fourth grade – this comes to about 4.2% of a minimum wage worker's monthly salary in India (Government of India, 2005, assuming 24 working days per month). Private schools are not niche – Rural and Urban, alike, they're meeting the needs of the poor effectively. In turn, many poor parents are beginning to invest more in education as they fail to see their children reaping its benefits from public education. As such, they resort to better, private institutions that place more differentiated, and individualized instruction to meet their child's needs. Indeed, the phenomenon of Private Schools is initiating a revolution in the developing countries that offer an alternate means of achieving the Second Millennium Development Goal: Achieve Universal Primary Education. But some experts worry, claiming that private schools offer 'low-quality services' that will 'restrict children's future opportunities' (Watkins, 2000: 230). Thus far, all such claims have been totally unproven. Sure, not all private schools are created equal. But they are miles better than existing public schools for the poor – in literally every aspect of comparison, the quality of private schools dominated public ones (i.e., teacher absenteeism was lower, teacher commitment was higher, and private schools had much more resources than government ones, from water to toilets to electric fans and tape recorders). But perhaps most important – research has demonstrated private schools are outperforming government ones on every key curriculum subject, from Mathematics to Reading Literacy to Science. Therein lies the power of Private Education.

Table 1	Number and proportion of schools, by school type and pupil enrolment											
	Hyderabad, India			Ga, Ghana			Lagos State, Nigeria			Mahbubnagar, India		
	Number of schools	Per cent of schools	Per cent of pupils	Number of schools	Per cent of schools	Per cent of pupils	Number of schools	Per cent of schools	Per cent of pupils	Number of schools	Per cent of schools	Per cent of pupils
Government	320	34.9	24.0	197	25.3	35.6	185	34.3	26.0	384	62.4	47.8
Private aided	49	5.3	11.4	0	0	0	0	0	0	13	2.1	4.3
Private (unaided) unrecognised/unregistered	335	36.5	23.1	177	22.7	15.3	233	43.1	33.0	77	12.5	6.6
Private (unaided) recognised/registered	214	23.3	41.5	405	52.0	49.1	122	22.6	42.0	141	22.9	41.2
Total	918	100	100	779	100	100	540	100	100	615	100	100

Source: Survey of Schools data, 2003–4 (Tooley and Dixon, 2006b)

Figure 6: Private Schools are growing increasingly popular a viable – if not better – alternative to failing government ones.

On this note, I should mention the role of education in the lives of the poor. Chapter 6 will greatly expand on this, but we examine an overview now. The extremely poor – the dollar-a-day people – invest very little in education, mostly because they send their children to public or government schools. In the countries where parents do invest more, it is often due to the government charging fees for schools, or parents moving children from flailing public schools to better private schools. The poor genereally spend around 2% of their total budget on education. The facts are these: The poor of Pakistan spend 3%, on average;

Refath Bari

Indonesia has 6%, Cote d'Ivoire has 6%, but Guatemala has 0.1% and South Africa has only 0.8%. By no means does this mean the poor are missing out on education – far from it. In 12 of the 13 countries in Banerjee and Duflo's sample (exception of Cote d'Iviore), over 50% of both boys and girls 7-12 years old in dollar-a-day households are enrolled in school. In just half the counries, over 75% girls are enrolled and 80% of boys are enrolled.

9 How do the poor see themselves?

Are the poor self-aware of their ranks on the social ladder? Do they know the forces at work against them – by nature and by man? And most importantly – do the poor *feel* poor? These are some of the heavy questions we tackle in this section.

Table 7: The Poor's Perception of the Poor

1 The poor are aware of their social rank

2 They suffer from psychological and financial stress

9.1 The poor are aware of their social rank

And yet – despite knowing and *feeling* that they are poor – the poor aren't particularly sad or depressed (Banerjee, Duflo, and Deaton, 2004).

9.2 They suffer from psychological and financial stress

Much like Babu, a lot of the poor suffer from a great deal of financial and pscyholcial stress. A lot of this comes from health concerns (cited by 29% of respondents) and lack of food and inevitable death (cited by 13% each). In Udaipur, for instance, 12% say there's been a period of a month or more over the year that their stress has interfered with regular activities like sleep, and work. This stress isn't unfounded: over the year, in almost half of the dollar-a-day households of Uiapur, adults have had to cut their meal. Over 37% of these dollar-a-day people haven't eaten a meal for an entire day over the year. Good meals are have strong correlation to hapiness.

10 Moral of the Story

By reading the Part I of the problem, I hope you've had some of the epiphanies
I've had, in realizing that the lives of the poor are much more nuanced than the
dualistic thinking we often project upon them. The poors face truly unimagine-
able choices both economically and socially. Here is a brief review, if you will,
that establishes the line between fact and fiction of the world of Poverty.

Table 8: Breaking the Falsehoods of Poverty

Fiction	Fact
The poor spend everything on food	There are two problems with this: (1) They can't, (2) They don't. (1) The poor have other, auxiliarly costs just as crucial to their survival – this could vary from housing to transportation to small fees (2) As we've seen, the poor have significant slack in their expenditure, and they often spend money on nonessential things such as tobacco, alchohol, and festivals.

This intermission is a fine time to speak on a topic of deep interest to me:
The United States' denial of 2.2 million tonnes of food aid to Bangladesh in the
fatal year of 1974. The United States Ambassador to Bangladesh who was the
harbinger of this bad news was Davis Eugene Boster, an American Diplomat.
Boster, whose name was often mistaken for "Booster", took a great liking to
Bangladesh's founder, Sheikh Mujiber Rahman, finding him charistmatic and
humble as the leader of a new nation, analagous to what George Washington
was for the United States. In an interview by Charles Stuart Kennedy, Boster
described Sheikh Mujb as "the George Washington ... who led them to independence, but did not have the managerial talent to administer the affairs of
State ... Mujib was a political success and a managerial failure." Soon after the
famine, Mujib was assassinated during a coup, but the new government didn't
last very long. At the same time, tensions with India were growing, to which
Boster remarked "...the tension between the Indians and the Bengalis grew. The
Indians had played a special role in helping Bangladesh achieve independence.
One might have thought therefore that the relationship would have been ex-

tremely friendly for a long time. In fact that did not happen. They had border disputes which were pretty lively and not easily solved. The relations between the two governments became almost tense." Regardless, the US government played along, their foreign policy interests in Bangladesh solely 'humanitarian'. While the United States' actions at the time seem ruthless in retrospect, as Catherine Bertini, Former Executive Director of the World Food Program, said herself, "Food is power. We use it to change behavior. Some may call that bribery. We do not apologize".

Table 9: Breaking the Falsehoods of Poverty

Fiction	Fact
Poverty is immortal; the eternal given. As long as humanity lives, some of us will be the poorest.	Poverty is by no means immortal. Let me point you to the many, many indicators that demonstrate humanity's growth since the early 1990s. Lower fertility rates, higher primary enrollment, lower child mortality, greater life expectancy, and hundreds of millions less in poverty. Poverty is subject to change, and while COVID19 may provide to be a setback, we must nevertheless persevere.

Table 10: Breaking the Falsehoods of Poverty

Fiction	Fact
The poor man doesn't understand the value of education, which is why they don't invest in it.	Right result, but wrong method. Due to social outreach programs, poor families are beginning to understand the importance of education, and the fruits of government labors are paying off. Primary School Enrollment has grown from 71.68% in 1970 to 89.41% in 2018. Instead, families are really debating whether to place their children in public or private schools. Each one requires a sacrifice: the former, intellectual and the latter, monetary.

Table 11: Breaking the Falsehoods of Poverty

Fiction	Fact
Poor people pay more for food because stores exploit them for higher profits	Once again, right hypothesis, but wrong conclusion. The problem with poor people paying more for groceries is that they're simply situated in the wrong neighborhoods – neighborhoods where cheaper chain stores aren't located. Even if these chain stores are pressured to move to poor neighborhoods to help the poor, chain stores would have to increase their prices – not due to discriminatory pricing policies (may play a role), but due to other factors such as security and surveillance costs that are especially prevalent in a small neighborhood.

Chapter 4

The Problem: A Rationale

Refath Bari

55 Days in Dharavi

> Once again, I begin with a Case Study: Mohan Singh in New Delhi, India. I examine
> Mohan's life during my stay in his house in New Delhi and isolate the main aspects
> of his life. But this time, the key is to offer a Rationale for the Poor Man's behavior.
> That is – in essence – the bread and butter of this chapter. I then generalize these
> aspects of Mohan's life to the lives of all poor people. I look at these generalizations
> qualitatively and statistically.
>
> **Keywords:** Migration, Poor Entrepenuers, the Poor Man's Finance, Network

1 Case Study: Mohan Singh

Look, I'm no addict. I can shake a wager of 6 bucks and still bet a mile. I wake at
6, conduct my daily jumping jacks, and drink no more than 6 oz. of milk a day. In
short, I'm a healthy guy's healthy guy. And yet, my lungs looked like a smoker's.

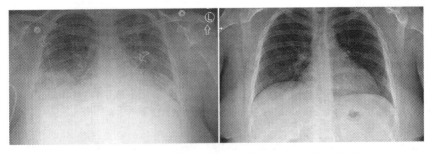

Figure 1: My left and right lung scans during my study in India

This is a common story in India, where the Air Pollution threatens billions
of lungs every day. Dr. Arvind Kumar, one of the lung surgeons I met in North

Refath Bari

Delhi, told me over half of his lung cancer patients are non-smokers. I digress. That's not the point of this story – the point is Mohan Singh, or as he put it, "Call me Mo, bro.", shaking my hand vigorously. "I'm a cool dude in loose mood, baby. I just say let it go. Just go with the flow, baby, you know. Groovy, wooh!". Not exactly the type of dollar-a-day guy I expected, but this was it. This really was Mo Singh. Mo was selling some bananas next to the South Delhi Municipal Corporation.

Figure 2: Mo and his Banana cart next to S.D.M.C.

Well, some would be an understatement. "I got 500 bananas, from Namkeen & Sweets for a bulk discount. You want?" I couldn't let the Mo down, and as a healthy young man myself, I was happy to oblige. "5, *krpya*", I said, clasping some rupees in Mohan's hand. These were no normal hands for a man of Mo's age –

his palm was pock-marked with rough scratches and I felt like I grazed against leather. His thick biceps looked foreign to a teenager's body and hours of standing in the blazing Delhi Sun did nothing to this young man's posture. You carry all this?, I asked, peeling the banana. Mo nodded. My father and I buy in bulk the night before from Namkeen and we carry it next to the parking lot in the morning. "Hey how's the banana?" he asked. "Very high quality. Just how I like it." "I told you, brother. Only the good stuff for you." How's business? Mo shook his head. "You're my first." he sighed. "It's like this everyday, for god's sake." He reminded me of Babu, as he looked over my shoulder, anxiously awaiting the next customer, drumming away his fingers on the solid wood cart. I welcomed the interim silence, though Delhi is never really silent. I stroked my non-existent beard in search for a solution to Mo's problem. Why don't you do other jobs? I exclaimed. It was, after all, what Babu and thousands of other poor slum-dwellers did. "That's what the buckets are for" he wagged his fingers at a few heavy jugs of water. Mmmm, how could I miss those? I go door to door, giving them water as needed, Mo explained. "After all, Mo jobs, Mo money, am I right?" Mo said, giggling like a girl jumping on a trampoline. I changed the subject: Where's your parents?, I said, noting the distinct lack of a parental presence, despite Mo's young age. Mo hesistated, "My father is doing his own work, sometimes slapping up the cow dung and drying it to sell as fuel, and from evening to night, he's recyclcing, picking, and selling trash." he looked at his foot, "He leaves me the softer work." And your mom?, I asked "Ahh, yes. My mom." he looked into the distance. "She's gone off a few miles to Karol Bagh for work" his voice broke mid-sentence. Hey, at least she's still in Delhi, I reassured. "Yeah." I grasped my imaginary beard, but my palms clasped empty air. "Hey! Here's one" I leaned forward. "Go to the Central Bank, and get a loan. Boom! Your mom doesn't need to migrate for work, and instead, she can get a small business loan" Mo shook his head before I even finished. "Too much. The central bank could give a damn about us poor workers. They bail out the bollywood stars and the billion-dollar businesses that need no help, but when it comes to the small people, it's like we don't exist to them." Mo's nose flinched as his demeanor shifted. Sorry. Don't you have any friends you can loan from?, I asked. "There's Johan, but I'm scared of the guy." Mo said, dragging his feet across the pavement. "Mess uf one fayment and I'll make your interest go through the daamn roof!", Mo mocked Johan's thick English accent. I don't know, brother, you miss 100% of the shots you don't take. Mo smacked his lips, apparently in search for deep thought. "It's too much hassle, but I'll give it a shot", he promised. Worst comes to worst, you can even join one of those savings clubs, and they can keep you in check so you don't end up with a loan default, I advised. How's school?, I piped. "Non-existent. I dropped out after the fifth grade. After all, primary's all that matters, eh?" he chipped. Can't argue with that, I lied. "Plus, we're running low on cash, so this is our back-up". Mo popped a pill in his mouth. "Take a chill pill" he laughed, slapping my shoulder with his thick leather hands, when he saw my mouth agape. I have a natural adversity to pills. "You sure that's good for you?" I interrogated. "Nope. But doc says it's all good. And hey, at the end of the day, you can't control anything so don't even try." he said nonchalantly, smirking behind the cart. "Alright brother, I guess I better start heading out." I saw Mo's evergreen eyes, and he saw mine. We struck on a level far deeper than age. "Come here," Mo said quick. It was just the sort of hug you'd expect from a guy like Mo. "Hey Mo, one last thing: what's your middle name?" "Four actually: Mohit Mohammed Mohammedy Mohammadan", he said. We chuckled. Mohan Mohit Mohammed Mohammedy Mohammadan Singh, 18-year old fruit seller. Yep, sounds about right. As I did for Babu, I clasped all the rupees I had in Mo's hand. Among the crisp bills was a ten digit number inscribed on a paper. It was all I could do for the boy who gave me all his stories. Maybe someday, I could give him some of mine. (Chomsky 1957).

Update 1.1: New Delhi, India

Where's Delhi now, in light of COVID19? As of May 16, 2020, there's 9,333 confirmed cases in the state, an uptick of 433 from the day before. It's worst in Central Delhi, where 184 of the 9333 confirmed cases reside. But testing still leaves much to be desired. Of New Delhi's population of 21.75 million, only 143,637 have been tested thus far. In other stats, 471 out of every 1 million people in Delhi have tested positive for the virus. We can inspect this from the perspective of the SIR disease model, with S = Susceptible, I = Infected, and R = Recovery: for every 100 confirmed cases, 57% remain infected, and 42% have recovered. That doesn't quite add up: the remaining is the mortality rate of 1.38%. This past week from May 10 to May 16 , the average growth rate of infections has been 5%.

---

2 Mo's List

Now we come to a greater question: How do the extremely poor really live on a dollar a day? This what the first few questions hope to address. In doing so, I wish to hit six key points, which I will refer to as "Mohan Mohit Mohammed Mohammedy Mohammadan Singh's List", abbreviated as "Mo's List'.

Upon addressing these six key questions, I will offer a rationale for the poor man's behavior through questions seven through twelve. Afterwards, as I did the previous chapter, I hope to establish the demarcation between the fact and fiction of poverty, after which I will compile a list of the differences between the expectations and realities one finds upon living with the poor.

Table 1: Mo's List

1. How do the poor earn money?

2. What's wrong with more jobs?

3. Why don't the poor get rich quick via small businesses?

4. Why don't banks lend to the poor?

5. Do the poor really own their land?

6. What's wrong with poor infrastructure for poor people?

7. Why don't the poor specialize?

8. Why so many entrepreneurs?

9. Why don't the poor eat more?

10. Why don't the poor invest in education?

11. Why don't the poor save more?

12. Why not migrate longer if you can earn more?

3 How do the poor earn money?

Where does the dollar in dollar-a-day families come from? How do the poor actually earn money? Governmental programs? International aid? Jobs?

Table 2: **Poor Man's Money**

1 The poor are entrepreneurs

2 They have diverse job portfolios

3 They migrate for short periods for jobs

3.1 The poor are entrepreneurs

In every sense of the word, the poor satisfy the definition of an entrepreneur: raising the capital, executing the investment, and being the full residual claimants of their original investment.

3.2 They have diverse job portfolios

And they are diverse entrepreneurs at that! I obviously met Mo, who bought bananas in bulk from his local grocer, Namkeen & Sweets, and then sold his goods at a marked up price. But there's so much diversity in the poor man's jobs that stuns any middle-class family: there's people like Babu, making *Dosas*, and recycling trash and there's water deliverers like Mo. There's also women like Latika, who buy *saris* (Indian women's clothing) from a local dealer and stitch small gems and jewels on the cloth, in the hopes that women will buy them during festival season. The true scope of the poor man's job is captured by the data of Abijhit Banerjee and Esther Dueflo in their 2006 field study on the lives of the poor in 13 countries, as shown.

	Percent of Households that own land	Median Area Of Land Owned	Percent of Households in which At Least One Member: Is Self Employed in Agriculture	Is Self Employed in Other	Works for a Wage or Salary in Agriculture	Works for a Wage or Salary in Other	Percent of HHs That Receive Income From Multiple Sectors
Living on less than $1 a day							
Rural							
Cote d'Ivoire	62.7%	300	57.2%	23.9%	52.4%	78.3%	72.1%
Guatemala	36.7%	29	64.4%	22.0%	31.4%	86.4%	83.6%
India - Udaipur	98.9%	69	98.4%	5.9%	8.3%	90.7%	94.0%
India - UP/Bihar		40	72.1%	40.2%	2.0%	18.9%	41.9%
Indonesia	40.6%	50	40.8%	36.6%	11.1%	34.3%	56.4%
Mexico	4.1%		4.9%	20.4%	2.8%	72.6%	13.2%
Nicaragua	50.4%	280	54.7%	11.0%	9.3%	42.8%	12.4%
Pakistan	30.4%	162	72.1%	35.5%	32.0%	50.9%	66.8%
Panama	83.1%	360	59.1%	17.7%	9.0%	6.0%	19.2%
Peru	65.5%	130	71.7%	25.2%			34.8%
South Africa	1.4%		8.0%	9.1%	27.9%	26.6%	8.4%
Tanzania	92.3%	182					
Timor Leste	95.2%	100	78.5%	12.0%			10.4%
Urban							
Cote d'Ivoire	57.3%	300	35.0%	6.0%	92.3%	26.3%	47.4%
Guatemala							
India - Hyderabad	17.6%	29	0.0%	12.0%	0.8%	89.8%	11.5%
Indonesia	10.7%	1	9.6%	50.8%	15.6%	77.9%	56.9%
Mexico	37.1%		27.3%	20.7%	24.3%	36.3%	24.2%
Nicaragua	13.9%	350	24.9%	37.7%	9.0%	31.8%	2.5%
Pakistan	1.3%	121	17.6%	51.2%	4.2%	67.7%	[illegible]
Peru	8.8%	100	5.2%	57.6%			21.9%
South Africa	0.0%		0.0%	5.6%	4.0%	46.4%	0.0%
Tanzania	71.9%	162					
Timor Leste	89.8%	100	80.6%	7.0%			2.1%

Figure 3: Occupations of the poor

The poor's time is split between agircultural and non-agricultural activities. In Peru, a South American country, 69% households living under $2 a day in urban areas had a non-agricultural business. This is no fluke: Indonesia and Nicargua's comparative stats range from 47% to 52%. Much of the rural poor also operate farms, with responses ranging from 25% to 98% of dollar-a-day households reporting being self-employed in agriculture. In addition, the rural poor also own non-agricultural businesses, ranging from 7% in Udaipur, India to 36% in Panama, Central America.

The data tells us much more in regards to the variety of the poor man's jobs. It seems to be a common trend that the poor have resorted to a diverse range of jobs, whether the country be India, Mexico, or Africa – we see the poor engaging in many industries. In Hyderabad, India 21% of $2-a-day households have multiple busnesses, with 13% owning a business and having a labor job. This is an international trend: In Cote d'Ivoire, the African country, and Indonesia, over 47% of urban households receive their income from multiple sources; 36% in Pakistan, 20.5% in Peru, and 24% in Mexico.

The trend of multiple jobs becomes especially prevalent in rural areas. Take Udaipur, India, for instance. Everyone's got land, but only 19% say working the fields is their main source of income. Instead, over 98%of $1-a-day Udaipur households claim daily laboring is their main source of income.

Agriculture used to be do-or-die in the Southeast countries, especially India. But increasing automization, industrialization, and machinery has disrupted the convention. In 2006, Abjijit Banerjee, the Nobel-Prize winning economist, randomly sampled 27 vlllages from West Bengal. The survey revealed that even households that owned land spent only 40% of their time tending to it. Gender doesn't do much to change the data: men and women alike tend to the farm through such activities as animal rearing, teaching, household work, gathering fuel, growing fruits and vegetables, and embroidery. The survey revealed that the median family has three working members and up to seven different jobs. This is in direct agreement with Banerjee and Duflo's original assessment that the median number of adults in an extremely poor household is 3. As such, it makes sense that poor families are taking maximum advantage of all their available labor.

Rural households, as mentioned previously, also have a tendency to diversify their job portfolio. In Guatemala, the Central American country, 65% of the $1-a-day poor receive some income from agricultural self-employment, 24% are self-employed in non-agricultural jobs, and 86% work as laborers in non-agricultural jobs. In Pakistan, 35% of the $1-a-day rural poor make earnings from

Refath Bari

non-agricultural businesses, whereas 51% make earnings as laborers in non-agricultural activities.

3.3 They migrate for short periods for jobs

The worst kind of livelihood is often for the poor living in rural areas, those lacking even basic services to meet their needs. And yet, they manage a way, despite their inherenet geographic disavantage: often-times, these are the people an hour or two away from the closest road. So how do they find all these non-agricultural jobs? Here comes the Occam's Razor answer: Migration!

Migration for jobs is demanding in that a laborer must leave all social and fam-lial activities behind for a new job. And yet, it is a standard practice among the poor. In Udaipur, for instance, 60% of the $1-a-day households said a family mem-ber lived outside for apart of the year for work activities. Much like Mo's mother herself had migrated a few mlies off from New Delhi to find work, thousands of poor laborers migrate for parts of the year in the search for better, newer, or more profitable jobs. These migrations are neither long, nor far: the usual migration span a month, and only 10% of migrations exceed three months; 28% of migrants stay in tthe same district (Udaipur), and 42% leave Rajasthan, the state.

This makes permanent migrtion all the more rare. Indeed, if we examine ur-ban areas for migrants who were born elsewhere and came for work reasons is negligble: only 4% in Pakistan, 6% in Cote d'Ivoire, 6% in Niaragua, and 10% in Peru. According to the 1991 Census of India, only 14.7% of males live somewhere they weren't born.

4 What's wrong with more jobs?

After all, to quote Mo, "Mo' jobs, mo' money". Unfortunately, Mo could never be more wrong. Moral of the story: don't spread yourself too thin and risk losing more money for less risk. Let me explain.

Table 3: **Death of a Poorman**

1 The poor don't specialize

4.1 The poor don't specialize

And therein lies their downfall: they have many occupations, sure, but none of these occupations require much skill, and thus are not associated with higher earnings. They have land, and they do conduct some agricultural activities – but they don't go all the way: they don't take full advantage of it by renting, sharecropping, or buying more land. What's more, they don't invest in irrigation technology that enable land to be usable for a greater part of the year, stagnating potentially higher earnings. Even when they migrate, they do so in short bursts (median of 18 weeks for Udaipur), instead of moving for longer periods, earning a potential fraction of what they could otherwise. Much of the poor's income is derived from outside jobs, so they're missing out on a lot of potential earnings. What's worse, these short bursts of outside work mean the poor don't learn their job extensively, and thus miss out on promotions, or advancements. What's worse, of the many occupations shared by the poor, most require no skill: In Hyderabad, India, most businesses are general stores, tailors, auto owners, telephone booths, fruit vendors and milk sellers. Save for a tailor, many of these jobs require no skill.

5 Why don't the poor get rich quick via small businesses?

The story of rags to riches is foreign for the poor, who are often too stuck in poverty traps to increase their Socioeconomic status. Why don't their small businesses help? The answer is in the name itself: *small* businesses.

Table 4: **Extremely Small Businesses**

1 The poor run unprofitable businesses

5.1 The poor run unprofitable businesses

And really, it has nothing to do with the quality of their products or their demand. Instead, the answer is in the name itself, *small* businesses. We begin with Agricultural Businesses: the average landowning poor man has very little land at all. Even worse, they don't have the capital to irrigate it the dry scrub lands, so it's unusable for much of the year. In addition, the poor don't rent or buy more land, making the problem even worse. In short, these agricultural businesses have a very limited capacity for growth or profit, a problem exacerbated by limited resources, and capital.

Non-agricultural businesses share the same burden: few assets and limited staff limit the potential growth and efficiency of a business. Take Hyderabad, for instance, where most businesses have tables, and scales, but only 20% have a separate operating room (most are run from home). In Pakistan, 40% of businesses under $2-a-day have vehicles, but only 4% of those vehicles are motorized and none have machinery (i.e., sewing). And what about staff? These non-agricultural businesses consist mostly of family members, who are usually never paid (read: existential internship). An average of 1.4 (Peru) to 2.6 (Cote d'Ivoire) people operate businesses. The people operating these businesses live under $2-a-day.

6 Why don't banks lend to the poor?

I lied to myself many times that I knew the answer: the bank lenders were mean. Occam's Razor says it best: sometimes the simplest explanation is the best. Unfortunately, here's an important exception to the rule.

Table 5: **A Poor Man's Economy**

1 The poor get informal loans

2 They don't have reliable savings accounts

3 Formal insurance is rare for the poor

4 Informal insurance has many cons

6.1 The poor get informal loans

Your best friend really is your worst enemy when it comes to loans, due to a combination of high interest rates, high defaults, and lack of government guarantees. But before we investigate this specific scenario, let's examine the state of the poor man's financial situation.

We begin with debt: the poor man's outstanding debt varies widely between 11% in Timor, an Asian country, to 93% in Pakistan. To exacerbate the problem, very few of the poor get loans from formal sources such as Banks. Loans are very common for the poor, who typically require small financial nudges to start a business, or weather an emergency – whether it be health or financial. In Udaipur, India, for instance, 67% of the poor had a loan during the study. The breakdown is unsettling: only 5% of loans are from actual commercial banks.

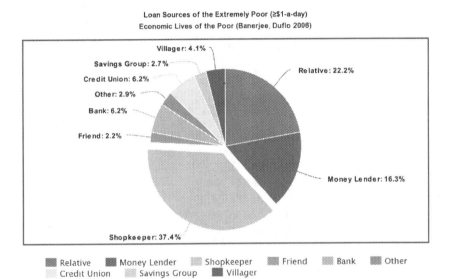

Loan Sources of the Extremely Poor (≥$1-a-day)
Economic Lives of the Poor (Banerjee, Duflo 2006)

Figure 4: Much of the Poor Man's Loans originate from Shopkeepers and Relatives

This isn't isolated to Udaipur. It is a general trend that the poor tend to loan from informal sources, with one exception: Indonesia, where the Bank Rakyat Indonesia (BRI) has made micro-finance a reality to over 30 million retail clients and had a revenue of 111.6 trillion IDR, as of 2018. Bank Rakyat Indonesia has enabled over a third of the rural poor to borrow loans from a formal bank or microcredit institution.

Loans from informal sources are expensive: they have high credit and interest rates. We turn to the data: In Udaipur, the $1-a-day poor pay 3.8% monthly for credit from informal sources. This drops to 3.13% for those who live on $1 to $2-a-day. This reflects poor are less dependent on informal sources than the extremely poor, and thus benefit more from formal sources that require less credit. Income definitely gives in advantage in that aspect. Land is even better: for every additional hectare of land owned, the poor man's interest rate drops by .4% (if from an informal source). Take Hyderabad, the Indian City of 7 million; the interest

Refath Bari

rates are even worse – 3.94% monthly for the $2-a-day poor. That means most of these poor have no land to use as collateral.

Why so high? These expensive interest rates are only partially explained by defaults. While defered payments are the standard in poor countries, default isn't: Economist Dasgupta finds that default accounts for only 23% of interest charged across informal credit markets in India. Moreover, Pakistani Economist Abdul Aleem, finds that the median rate of default in Pakistan is only 2%. High interest rates yet low defaults? What explains this paradoxical nature of informal credit markets?

It comes down to human nature. The very act of borrowing a loan is a social contract, one that must be closely monitored by the lender and adhered to by the borrower. Lending money is very much a question of security, and as courts are reluctant to punish poor borrowers, it's up to lenders to ensure their money is rightfully paid back. This is the burden of contract enforcement. In an attempt to enforce the loan contract, banks spend a lot of money on security and maintenance, expenses which may not be covered by negligible profits from interest paid back on small loans by poor borrowers. This is worth repeating: most banks do not lend to the poor because the security expenses of monitoring the poor will not be covered by interest on the poor man's small loans. Therein lies the primary reason for banks' reluctance to lend to poor borrowers: lack of credit makes their trustworthy questionable, lack of collateral – especially for the landless poor (after all, if you have no assets, what can a bank seize?) makes them especially vulnerable in the case of a missed payment, and lack of large loans means security/monitoring expenses will not be compensated by interest from small loans. The exact shortcomings of the bank are the very reason most of the poor man's loans comes from informal sources such as friends, relatives, or shopkeepers. These people are in much closer vicinity to the poor, both in terms of socioeconomic status and actual physical proximity. As such, they need not waste as much money (if at all) on security or monitoring expenses. So if they have much smaller expenses, why do they mark up interest rates so much? The problem is in that these people pay much higher for deposits than commercial banks would – these higher costs are passed onto the borrowers (they do not have the either the capital or government guarantees of a commercial bank), who in turn are plagued by high interest rates. The gap in deposit payments by commercial banks versus informal sources is tremendous: Aleem finds that money-lenders pay 32.5% for the cost of capital, whereas banks pay only 10% for their deposits

6.2 They don't have reliable savings accounts

Where do the poor save their money? Stashing it at home isn't the best way to protect your money from getting devalued from inflation. And the poor man is only human: he has the same temptations to resist spending his savings that we do (Ashraf, Karlan, Yin 2005).

How to save is one question, but how *many* save is another entirely: Of the $1-a-day families, less than 1% have savings accounts in Panama and Peru. The stat varies between countries (with the exception of Coit d'Iviore), but the trend is the same: most of the poor don't have savings accounts.

Thankfully, the poor man has his ways: through a ingenious combination of Savings Clubs (the savings analogue of Alcoholics Anonymous, where every member ensures others are saving), Self-Help Groups (much like a savings club, extended to provide members loans from accumulated savings; these groups sometimes partner with banks to form partnerships and increase savings), and Rotating Savings and Credit Associations (these enable borrowers to lend to each other through a rotating scheme, effectively teaching borrowers what it's like to be a lender), the poor have effectively taken control of their financial life. The poor have come up with a multitude of means of ensuring their savings are kept in order: some pay deposit collectors to collect their money and deposit it to the bank; others store their savings at a post office or with a money-lender. Yet others resort to the recently popular option of Microcredit (coined by Nobel Laureate Muhammad Yunus), which resounds with the poor exactly because it efficiently affords them the opportunity to both a) access goods and services they couldn't otherwise and b) have the experience of paying down a loan, and thus saving your money. But for all the buzz, you'd think the poor would rally around their semi-formal savings institutions. Unfortunately, the reality is that the poor don't actively participate in these institutions: only 10% of the poor in Hyderabad and Udaipur engage in Rotating Savings and Credit Associations, Self-Help Groups, or even Microfinance Institutions.

6.3 Formal insurance is rare for the poor

The poor man is financially disenfranchised: banks won't lend to him, governments won't incentivize his assets, and insurers won't insure him. Data says less than 6% of the extremely poor have health insurance, with the exception of Mexico, where 50% of the dollar-a-day have health insurance. The numbers don't fare much better in India: Of the dollar-a-day poor, only 4% in Udaipur have health insurance, and only 10% in Hyderabad have it. Weather Insurance is equally absent

Refath Bari

(Murdoch 2005), despite the evident fact that one wrong monsoon can devastate an entire nation (look no further than Bangladesh's 1974 famine – the monsoon was the catalyst in a quickly crumbling nation; fortunately, it was a wake-up call for the government, who proceeded to implement the first family planning program).

Rotating Savings and Credit Associations and Savings Clubs are just formalized versions of what already exists in the wild: informal networks of poor borrowers and money-lenders exchanging loans to and fro. These dense networks are comprised almost solely of friends, relatives, and neighbors of borrowers and lenders. The loan term, interest rate, and amount repaid are all dependent on both the lender and borrower's financial situation. India, in particular, has an interesting case of these informal loan exchange networks, where money changes hands between different lines, castes, and religions alike.

Given that the poor experience distressing emergencies on a daily basis, these informal networks are hardly enough to cushion them against financial disasters such as health emergencies or crop failures that can devastate a family and severely reduce their expenditure on commodities and entertainment such as festivals or weddings. Indeed, this is a common case in poor populations around the world, where the declining health of the breadwinner or head of the family leads to declining expenditure on such goods as alcohol, tobacco, or other entertainment-value goods. To give a sense of just how large these expenses can be, they are 1) often covered by borrowing loans or spending savings and 2) experienced by over 24% of poor households in Hyderabad during the study (Banerjee, Duflo 2006)

They don't have insurance; they don't have formal loans; they don't have credit; what do they have? How do the poor survive a crisis? Much like Mo dropped out of fifth grade from the private Adarsh School to save his parents some money, many poor families take their children out from school in times of emergency. A more disturbing outcome comes in the form of health: we see girls suffer a much higher mortality rate during drought years (periods of economic stress, when land stays unarable due to lack of rain, and when poor families lose essentially all their hard work in the year). When children suffer medical emergencies, mix in a bit of gender discrimination and financial burden, and what you have is a dangerous combination of factors that result in parents not taking their daughters to the hospital, in fear of high medical bills. This is not just for daughters – parents too, avoid going to the hospital to save money; in Udaipur, of the poor who were sick, more than 50% did not seek treatment, of which 34% cited lack of money as the sole reason. In this way, lack of insurance damages the poor during periods of economic stress, but also during the regular season: farmers, for instance, don't invest in irrigation technology or new grain seeds, fearing to lose their investment, ultimately overlooking potential profits.

We are examining the four players in this game of finance: the bank, the informal loan exchange networks, the lender and the borrower, and finally – we've arrived at the last piece of the puzzle: the government. Most countries guarantee free health care for all their constituents. And yet health care is rarely, if ever, free. Look no further than the richest economy in the world. Rich or poor, first-world or fourth-world alike, universal health care remains an enigma. Instead, in most poor countries, government-partnered public health-care providers charge for services. These services are so second-rate that the poor often resort to private health care providers for quality health services. Some governments also sponsor "Food for Work" programs that provide the poor food on the basis that they provide labor. Unfortunately, these programs often discriminate against the poor, and do little to alleviate the insurance crises faced by the poor.

6.4 Informal insurance has many cons

Informal insurance doesn't protect the poor against risk, as shown above. It does little to cushion the poor against health and agricultural emergencies. It should come as no surprise that informal insurance is dependent on the ideal of altruism: that the more fortunate are willing to help those with lower socioeconomic status. As expected, this altruistic behavior has its limits, and the fortunate are only willing to give so much. In addition, these informal loan networks aren't diversified and thus spread much risk over a few households with similar socioeconomic statuses, occupations, and incomes.

7 Do the poor really own their land?

Usually not. Titling issues, idiosyncratic governmental policies, and discriminatory schemes make the poor *agents*, rather than true *owners* of their own land.

Table 6: **Finders Keepers: Land Edition**

1 Many poor don't have titles to their land

2 Poor don't take full advantage of land

Refath Bari

7.1 Many poor don't have titles to their land

Land is the crux of the poor man's assets. What does he have other than land? Nothing. It is land that is the sole potentially income-generating asset that he has – he can rent it, sharecrop it, buy more of it, title it, irrigate it, grow it. But does he? No. Far from it – he does no more than cultivate the land he already owns for a fraction of the year. No more; no less. Here comes the kicker: most of the poor don't have titles to their land. In developing countries, where land records are incomplete and land disputes happen often, land titles become especially important. A land title proves ownership; it supersedes any and all informal forms of proof of land ownership, such as rent receipts or handwritten notes. This may be the root of all other problems: if you don't title your land, that makes it harder to sell, rent, or mortgage it – all problems that the poor face with their own land. The issue becomes even worse for the poor, who usually live on recently cleared or lived-on land. They could lose the right to their land at any time, and as such, some poor (i.e., in Peru), rightfully spend much of their time protecting their claims to their land (although these claims have negligible significance in the legal arena). Peruvian Economist Hernando deSoto spent much of his life pioneering and advising foreign nations to act on his idea of "dead capital" – capital locked up in land that belonged to the poor, but which they didn't legally own due to lack of land titles. When titles are imperfectly enforced, it is the poor who suffer. In Ghana, for instance, the cultivators – the poor – only have the right to use land; the land itself is owned by the village or some past lineages. The poor man now faces a dilemma: does he fallow the land, thus making it more productive and earn more money, yet simulatenously risk the village taking his land? Or does he not fallow his land, risk making his land *less* productive, and make less earnings? In this way, we have effectively trapped the poor man – he cannot take full advantage of his land, otherwise the village would seize it; whereas if he doesn't take advantage of his land, he makes less money. Why then does land exist in the first place?

7.2 Poor don't take full advantage of land

There has been a historical lack of incentives for the poor to take full advantage of their land, demoting them to agents of their land rather than true owners of it. An effective policy reformed incentives such that landlords were forced to provide sharecroppers more of the agricultural output, thus increasing the sharecroppers' incentives, and simultaneously granting them secure rights to the land. This reform policy alone increased productivity by 50%.

8 What's wrong with poor infrastructure for poor people?

It's fair. It's equitable. For southeast countries like Bangladesh, India, and Pakistan, the poor are truly the heart and soul of the national economy. As such, better infrastructure for the poor would equate to a better economy.

Table 7: **State of Infrastructure**

1   The poor have varying access to basic infrastructure

2   Lots of absenteeism in both healthcare and education

8.1 The poor have varying access to basic infrastructure

We begin by defining basic infrastructure as the basic physical commodities we take for granted everyday – ranging from power lines, roads, health facilities, school infrastructure, public health infrastructure (i.e., water fountains, public toilets, sanitation, etc.). It is stunning who widely basic infrastructure can vary between poor countries. We begin with basic physical infrastructure such as tap water, electricity, and latrines (basic communal toilets).

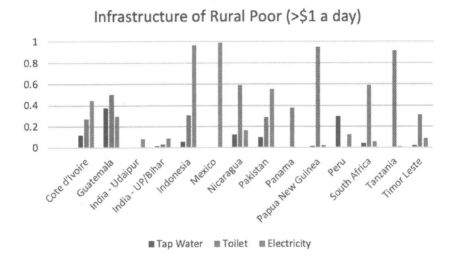

Figure 5: The paradoxical nature of the poor man's infrastructure

Refath Bari

What's so strange about the poor man's infrastructure is it's variety: take Indonesia, for instance, where over 97% of the dollar-a-day households have access to electricity, but only 6% have access to tap water. That means you can watch the news, but you can't drink the water. How does that make sense? I give credit where credit is due: Some governments, most notably Guatemala, provides poor rural households with both water and electricity; as a result, over 38% of the rural dollar-a-day households have tap water and 30% have access to electricity. And then there's governments that take an effectively hands-off, laissez-faire approach to infrastructure, especially as it applies to the poor: Across Udaipur, South Africa, Papua New Guinea and East Timor alike, the number of dollar-a-day rural households with access to tap water or electricity is less than 5%. Two small trends in the data: the urban poor have greater access to water and electricity than do the rural poor (which may be better, since it is the urban poor who must deal with dense living conditions ripe for disease and infection). And as expected, the poor ($1-$2 a day) have greater access to both commodities than the extremely poor ($1 a day).

8.2 Lots of absenteeism in both healthcare and education

At the turn of the century, there was hope: many developing countries were making an effort to ensure rural and urban poor alike had access to basic health services and primary education. Indeed, school enrollments shot through the roof and the government began taking infrastructure of the poor seriously. But establishing infrastructure much different than maintaining it. There is no question that infrastructure has been established; the Indian government did not leave that to doubt: the fact that any Delhi household (rich and poor alike) now lives in the vicinity (15-minute walk) of up to 70 health care providers is in itself an accomplishment. In addition, most Indian villages now live within a kilometer of a school, and there is one health service center for every 10,000 people. Then again, the government isn't keeping the closest eye on matters on the ground: absenteeism is plaguing both the healthcare and education industry, both pivotal industries for the poor. Among teachers and health workers in developing countries such as Bangladesh, India, Uganda, Peru, and Indonesia, health workers are absent 35% of the time and teachers are absent 19% of the time, on average (Chauduary et. al. 2005). Even when they're not absent, it's not clear whether these individuals are a) actually doing their jobs, b) performing to the best of their ability. Health worker and Teacher absenteeism rates fare better in richer areas than poorer ones, perhaps due to a lack of governmental incentive.

Absenteeism is one concern, but the actual quality of these workers is another question entirely. Every Delhi resident lives 15 minutes walking distance of up to 70 healthcare facilities. But these service centers vary widely in quality: most of the centers are operated by health providers without an MD, while a handful of private doctors do operate with an MD (or an MBBS in India). This difference in quality carries stark warnings for whatever patient chooses to seek a health service provider without an MD: a fatal combination of misdiagnosis and over/under-prescription of drugs may in fact cause more harm than good to patients. Therein lies the 'competence gap' between doctors operating in the poorest and richest districts. And although the study was conducted only in India, this gap in quality health services between the rich and the poor offer lessons to all countries around the world.

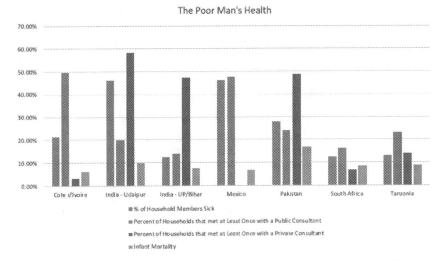

Figure 6: While India's Health Infrastructure has been established, it hasn't neccesarily been mantained

Moral of the story: Quality Infrastrucutre can save lives. Countries that spend more on health have lower mortalities. That's just a fact. And we must acknowledge that fact if we hope to uplift the poor from poverty. The worst poverty trap is the health one: the trap in which a family resorts to spending their savings due to health emergencies and thus cannot escape their socioeconomic status as a result of reduced income. That is the health poverty trap, but we can possibly eliminate it by not just building more quality infrastructure, but mantaining them – ensuring the absenteeism rates are not through the roof; ensuring health-care

Refath Bari

workers are actually performing their jobs adequtely and have the qualifications to perform their jobs in the first place; ensuring that facilities do not lack the resources they need to adequately address the needs of their patients. This is the very definition of good infrastrucutre. Believe it or not, good infrastructure can save lives – it can reduce mortality. Take infant mortality (calculated by dividing deaths before one year old by # live births) – it is 2020, and yet infant mortality rates are unacceptably high among the dollar-a-day poor in countries like Pakistan (16.7%), Udaipur (10%), and South Africa (8.7%). And these aren't even the true mortality rates – they're underestimates, since many developing countries don't even have complete records of premature infant deaths. In measuring malnutrition and child mortality rates in various countries, World Bank economist Adam Wagstaff found in 2003 that the mortality rate in a country is directly correlated with the health spending per capita in said countries.

Here's a paradox: how do you end up with 99% student enrollment and 0% student achievement? Although the question is slightly exageratted, this is exactly the case in India, where 93.4% of children ages 6-14 are enrolled in school (75% in public or governmental schools) It's no surprise that low quality public schools result in lower student achievement outcomes. , and yet 35% of children age 7-14 can't read a simple second-grade paragraph. It gets worse: 41.1% can't subtract and 65% can't divide. Even worse: of children in grades 6-8, 22% can't read a second-grade text (Pratham 2005). And this was 2005. Like Babu, some parents have decided it's enough. Where public schools are failing, the privates are taking their place. In fact, many of these private schools are improvised by once-frustrated poor parents who sought to create a differentaited educational environment for their own children. We look at the data: where public school abseentism is highest, so is the % of children attending a private school. Private schools do have their downsides, however: despite lower teacher absenteeism, private school teachers are signficantly less qualifid than their government peers, as they usually lack a formal teaching degree.

The trend follows in the health-care industry, as well: private health service providers take the role of public ones, with less absenteeism but less qualifications, as well (Das and Hammer 2004). But there is a striking difference: in public education, most parents keep their kids in public schools despite their second-rate quality; we do not see the same picture in the health-care industry. The public flock to private health care providers when they deem their public counterparts unfit. Take India: in regions where public health care providers are absent up to 40% of the time, 58% of the dollar-a-day households have resorted to a private health service provider. Peru turns the tables: where health care providers are rarely absent (25% absenteeism rate), only % of the dollar-a-day households have gone to a private health service provider in the month of the study.

9 Why don't the poor specialize?

The old moral still holds true: don't spread yourself too thin, like butter on fried toast. While lack of specialization does have its pros, among them a diversified job portfolio and thus inherently lower risk, its disadvantages may be far greater: unprofitability.

Table 8: He who chases two rabbits will catch neither

1 Poor specialize to spread risk

2 Productively use wasted time

3 Can't raise the capital to specialize

9.1 Poor specialize to spread risk

OK. I will begin with land: land is great. Land is the poor man's key to climbing up the socioeconomic ladder. But, there is a caveat. And for the poor man, the caveats don't stop coming: first and foremost, is the issue of titling. Because of idiosyncratic governmental policies, poor people throughout much of the world, have been unable to title their land. This makes it extremely difficult to rent or buy more land, due to various agency problems. Given the size of poor families and relatively small amount of land they own, it makes sense that they should be consumers of more land – once again, caveat stands in the way: lack of access to proper credit for the poor makes it nearly impossible for them to cultivate more land than they began with. And then there's weather insurance against crop failures or monsoons, or other natural disasters – insurance that the poor don't have access to. All of these reasons compile to make one case clear: a second job is all but essential to secure one against the risk of the inherent risks of agricultural work.

First and foremost is risk. The poor diversify their job portfolios to spread their risk amongst various jobs. In doing so, they tend to avoid specializing in any one job. The poor man sees it as such: keep a foot in agriculture to resist

Refath Bari

over-dependence on non-agricultural jobs; and keep a foot in non-agricultural jobs to avoid succumbing to traditional agricultural caveats such as crop failures, monsoons, etc.

9.2 Productively use wasted time

It's not the first thing to come to mind, but productively using one's time is an important ideal for the poor man. For the poor man, every second counts. After all, poverty trap or not, he will likely remain in the same socioeconomic status for much his life. As such, it is absolutely crucial for the poor man to devote every single second of his waking hour to generating profit. Take Agriculture – due to lack of credit, the poor man cannot afford to irrigate his dry scrub land, making it usable for only a fraction of the year; as such, the poor man resorts to finding other jobs when his land remains unarable. In doing so, he productively spends the time he would be wasting otherwise. But this picture leaves a lot to be desired: instead of making *Dosas*, or delivering Water Jugs, why doesn't the poor man pick a job to specialize in for the remainder of the year? In answering this question, it is best we follow Occam's Razor.

9.3 Can't raise the capital to specialize

That's exactly it: the poor man doesn't have the capital necessary to buy the assets required to specialize in any one job. We've already seen that the poor man's business operates with minimal capital, staff, and assets. As such, the poor man doesn't have the capital required for specialization.

10 Why so many entrepreneurs?

Maybe the Nobel Prize Leaureate says it best: "We are all entrepreneurs. Human beings are not born to work for anybody else. For millions of years that we were on the planet, we never worked for anybody. We are go-getters. We are farmers. We are hunters. We lived in caves and we found our own food, we didn't send job applications. So this is our tradition.", Mohammed Yunus told the Guardian.

Table 9: **Poor Entrepreneurs**

1　No Skill + Small Capital = Entrepreneur!

10.1 No Skill + Small Capital = Entrepreneur!

There it is! Therein lies the equation that expresses the poor man's most famous tendency: entrepenuership. Given the poor man's affinity for multiple occupations and his limited access to the credit markets, it becomes clear why he
chooses to be an entrepenuer – what other choice does he have? Becoming an en-
treprenuer is in many ways more accessible than a job; whereas jobs may select
laborers discriminatively, sometimes selecting against the poor – entrepenuership is an absolute democracy! Poor and rich; urban and rural alike can engage
in entrepenuership. Indeed, this is exactly what the poor man does: he collects
cow dung and dries it to sell as fuel; he picks up trash and recycles it to sell it
anew. Therein lies the poor man's ingenuity.

   Let us not romanticize this behavior, however. Their lack of capital, collateral, and reliability makes borrowing extrmely risky for the poor, and no moneylender would be sane to give money to them. The poor man's venture is extremly
small, and contribute negligibly to a country's economic status. These small,
short bursts of entrepenuership need not be recognized or hailed as heroic deeds,
but as desperate means of survival – a means that does not create more jobs at
that, since the large families of the poor can afford a lot of labor from in-house.
This tendency of restricted jobs makes it harder for any poor man to find a job
in the first place, and thus the cycle begins anew.

11 Why don't the poor eat more?

This is a particularly vexing question, and one of the many paradoxes we re-
counted in the previous chapter's demarcation of the line between the facts and
fictions of poverty. And yet, as we transcend the economics and examine the
families, the rationale becomes clear: the poor have their own way.

Table 10: A Vexing Paradox

1 Food offers no resistance against disease

2 Entertainment > Food

Refath Bari

11.1 Food offers no resistance against disease

That's number one. And disease will inevitably come: nutrition or not, disease will ravage not only a poor family's overall health (as all members are in close vicinity), but also leave their financial status in ruins. We thus conjecture that eating more will not necessarily postpone disease. This does, in part, explain the poor's resistance to eating more, despite their low Body Mass Index (half of what's suggested by the government, as it pertains to India). And more food can make the poor man work only so much harder, no? As a matter of fact, increased nutrition has in fact been correlated to greater labor productivity (Thomas et. al. 2004). In addition, eating is a big factor in the poor man's happiness, or lack thereof.

11.2 Entertainment > Food

Self-control doesn't answer it either. From what we see, the poor value saving up for significant entertainment in the future in exchange for loss of additional food on the plate in present. That doesn't exactly fit the picture of lack of self-control (i.e., the poor spend so much on nonessential goods like alcohol and tobacco that they don't have enough for food), especially because much of the poor man's entertainment is derived from televisions, festivals, and weddings, expenditures that require long-term savings.

Even the poor feel peer pressure. Indeed, that may be the very reason they value entertainment over additional food – they simply want to keep up with their neighbors. Indeed, in a 2005 survey conducted in Nepal by World Bank and Stanford Economists Forhad Shilpi and Marcel Fafchamps, they find that the poor's expenditure was strongly negatively related to their responses of whether their consumption of food, clothing, health-care, and other commodities was adequate.

12 Why don't the poor invest in education?

Education is at the crux of poverty – no doubt, primary education has been hailed as a significant contributor to increased socioeconomic status for poor families, and even higher education has its own economic returns. So why aren't the poor invested in education?

Table 11: **Schools for the Poor**

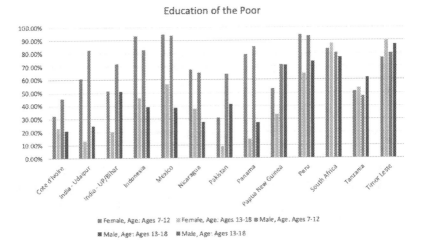 Parents don't recognize if kids are learning

12.1 Parents don't recognize if kids are learning

No, really. How can you recognize if your kids are learning how to read if you can't read yourself? Indeed, this is the dilemma faced by many poor parents, who struggle to cope with these questions. In every sense of the word, poor parents are being nonreactive to public schools in that once they drop their children in, they have no means of measuring progress or achievement! A survey taken in the east of Indian state Uttar Pradesh finds that parents have limited success in predicting whether their children can read (Banerjee et al., 2005). Indeed, we ask why poor parents are so nonreactive, given that it is their children's future at stake – why don't they lobby against the schools? Why don't they send their kids to private schools – and then we realize the caveats. First and foremost, how can you send you children to private schools and expect better if half the teachers in the private school aren't even qualified to be a teacher? And by simple arithmetic, the poor can by no means afford or have the know-how to lobby or pressure the government.

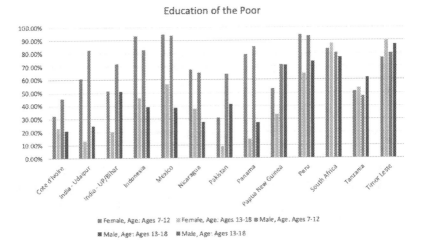

Figure 7: Be warned: Enrollment by no means reflects the mathematical or literary competencies of children in any country

13 Why don't the poor save more?

We touched much on the poor man's market, but this alone doesn't explain why the poor don't save more. Is at a lack of self-control? Or perhaps factors the poor can't control? Savings are the key to a secure life for the poor, as they endure crises and emergencies ranging from health issues to crop failures on a daily basis. As such, answering this question has become all-important.

Table 12: The Poor Man's Finance

| 1 | Self-saving is hard |

13.1 Self-saving is hard

I best begin by giving the poor man the benefit of the doubt: why doesn't he save up more money? Well, first and foremost, he has no bank to store his money in, that could otherwise pay him some interest on his principal. That right there is one reason. Second, we mustn't ignore the human tendency of the poor man to simply spend his savings, much like the rest of us – although, if they can save up for televisions or festivals, it doesn't seem implausible to save up for an emergency, health or otherwise. We then look at the poor man's physical environment: his home is ripe for a stealing. If he's the average poor man, he'll store his savings somewhere under the pillow – a place accessible to his teenage son, and his wife, not to mention that devalues his savings under inflation. Therein lies the key reasons why the poor man does not save: it's a hassle. I mean – consider this: how many caveats, nooks, and crannies must the poor man navigate to do what the rest of us do in the flip of a click? By all measures, the poor man must truly go out of his way to save money.

But now, let me play the role of the devil's advocate: the poor man has every reason to save. I mean, sure, it is by all means a hassle – but a hassle worth the price. First and most importantly, savings cushions the poor man against emergencies, so that he doesn't have to resort to 'improvised insurance' such as not going to the hospital or feeding himself or his children. That right there is the biggest selling point for savings, and boy is it a selling point, considering the uncertainty the poor man faces on a daily basis. What else is there besides emergencies, trip-ups, and false starts for the poor man? Given the scale of the poor's debt and their high interest rates, it benefits the poor significantly to pay down these debts – indeed, paying down debt is really another means of savings. What's more, how much can getting ahold of a stock or two hurt the old man? The most it can do is lose a small, negligible investment – but at its best, investing is the path to climbing the socioeconomic ladder, and this is a key practice the poor man must adopt.

Now comes the element of self-awareness: is the poor man aware of his own temptations to splurge his savings on alcohol, tobacco, festivals, and such? As a matter of fact, he is! In a survey given to the people of Hyderabad, an Indian state, 28% of the poor said they'd reduce their expenditures. Of those that wished to do so, over 44% sought to cut down on alcohol and tobacco spending, 9% sought to cut sugar, tea, and snacks spending, and 7% each sough to cut down on festivals, and entertainment, respectively. Unfortunately, self-awareness may kill the cat here. Not knowing your own temptations may actually enable you to buy your asset faster than if you knew you had temptations and that resisting them would most likely lead to future unhappiness. Ignorance truly is a bliss (I myself know that fact quite well).

Here comes a curious excercise in self-control: Fertilizer to Kenyan Farmers. Fertilizer is a popular farm chemical, and most farmers who use it one season return to it the following season. But not these people. When researchers went farm to farm, hoping to teach the farmers how to use the fertilizers effectively, they found that only 10% of the farmers agreed to use fertilizer next season. What did these poor farmers have against the pesticide? It came down to money – the farmers told researchers that bottles of pesticide cost too much and would eat much of their savings. But this was by no means a complete story: fertilizer can be purchased in relatively modest amounts that even the poorest farmer can afford, especially after a fine harvest. The researchers proceeded to concoct an ingenious plan to test the farmers' true affinity for pesticide: they provided the farmers vouchers right after the harvest (when they had the most money) to buy fertilizer in the future. Instead, most of the poor farmers brought the fertilizers after researchers brought it to their farms, and stored the fertilizers for use later. The program was effective: 39% of the poor farmers who were offered a voucher brought the fertilizer – the voucher enabled the poor to truly commit to saving for and buying the fertilizer. So what just happened? What's the moral of this story? The moral is that the farmers had the ability to buy the fertilizers themselves, but chose not to until researchers went out of their way to bring the fertilizers to them. In essence, the poor man has a natural inertia, a natural tendency to resist saving up lots of money to buy assets; this may simply be a reflection of their perception of themselves – perhaps they do not want to face the fact that they

Refath Bari

must save up for months in order to buy assets we can afford in the span of a few days. Perhaps this natural inertia towards savings is simply the poor man's psychological defense against his natural condition.

14 Why not migrate longer if you can earn more?

This is perhaps the most human question of all. Of course, money triumphs all, but the poor man may indeed sacrifice profit for family. There come human moments where the idiosyncratic tendencies of man defy logic – this may be one of them.

Table 13: Social Network

1	The poor man values his social network

14.1 The poor man values his social network

That sums it up: the poor man's reluctance to stray from his home for long periods of time reflects the value of staying close to one's social network. The value of the poor man's social network is in its potential as an informal loan exchange network. By leaving the rest of their family behind, the breadwinner ensures that they at least some of their social links are preserved by their remaining family members. Or we resort to the Occam's Razor approach: the poor is reluctant to work in conditions with bad livelihood. We can also analyze the idea from the perspective of opportunity cost: it may just be that the income earned from outside jobs is simply not worth the cost of leaving one's family, one's social network, and one's informal loan exchange network.

15 Moral of the Story II

The entire point of Chapter 4 has been (1) to describe the trials and tribulations faced by the poor man on a daily basis, but also to go further: (2) to offer a rationale, an epic finale, if you will, that sumrises all the decisions made by the poor man. I hope this chapter has helped you to understand the magnitude, if not the weight of the decisions made by the poor man. Now I want to take the time to establish the line of demarcation between the facts and fictions of poverty.

Table 14: Breaking the Falsehoods of Poverty

Fiction	Fact
The Banks don't loan to the poor because of discriminatory policies and stereotypes	This is a perfectly common misconception to carry – indeed, I used to believe this very notion myself. But this is a very dangerous misconception to hold. Commercial Banks, co-operatives, and other formal sources don't lend to the poor because of three major reasons: (1) Lack of collateral – without collateral, there's no way to secure a loan. In the event of a default, what will the bank seize? Thin air? Sounds about right. (2) Security Expenses not recouped by interest repaid: the poor will take out small loans; banks can't monitor the poor in a hope to enforce loan contracts – it's simply a waste of security expense (3) Lack of reliability: With no credit score/collateral, lending to the poor is a gamble: How does the lender know he'll get his money back?
The poor man doesn't use his land because he doesn't have the know-how	Land is a curious concern for the poor man: there's so much he can do, and yet so little. He can rent it, buy more, sharecrop it, mortgage it, irrigate it – the possibilities are endless. But so are the barriers: lack of credit ensures that selling or mortgaging land is all but impossible. It also means the poor are risk-averse, and don't invest in technologies such as new seeds or irrigation, which carry potentially high profits. Lack of weather insurance also means land is left uninsured against natural disasters like monsoons, and droughts.

Refath Bari

Table 15: Breaking the Falsehoods of Poverty

Fiction	Fact
The poor man doesn't have savings because he has no self-control	This is a hard myth to break, because it may very well be that the poor don't have much self-control. Then again, it is our human tendency to spend our savings on the next trend. So what is it that makes the poor different? Well for one thing, the poor certainly have enough self-control to save up for expensive assets such as TVs or Radios. As such, it may very well be that they choose not to save money in an effort to consume the goods they seek effortlessly.
The poor have a tendency to become entrepreneurs because they have special business models and receive government grants for their small businesses	This is most certainly *not* the case in many poor countries. Becoming an entrepreneur is much like a right of passage, or 'natural selection' for the poor. In essence, they do not choose to become entrepreneurs, but their lack of skill and capital make entrepreneurship a necessity, since it's much easier than finding a job. These small businesses are operated on with nearly no assets, and no paid staff; most employees are family members. And yet, we should not romanticize these ventures: in creating these temporary bursts of extremely small businesses, the poor close their own businesses off from others in their community. Thus, when the next poor man goes hunting for a job, only to find them populated by family members, he will seek to create his own business. And then he will become an entrepreneur. And so the cycle continues.

Table 16: Breaking the Falsehoods of Poverty

Fiction	Fact
The poor man with electricity has all other standard commodities, such as tap water and toilets guaranteed	This is truly unsettling, but the reality is that there exists some people in the world who have the news, but not the water. Indeed, this is the very issue we examined in the infrastructure section of the chapter, in which over 8.3% of extremely poor rural households have electricity, but no-one has toilets or tap water, as of 2006. The COVID19 pandemic will only exacerbate the crises faced by these poor people.
The larger the family the better! Likewise, the more jobs, all the better!	I now quote none other than Mo Sigh himself, who exclaimed on the streets of Delhi, "Mo' Jobs, Mo' money!". As the famous English proverb replies, "He who chases two rabbits will catch neither". Indeed, that is the dilemma faced by the poor man: understandably, his first concern is to reduce risk, since he faces so much uncertainty and emergency every day. Through a purely risk reductionist perspective, the concept of multiple occupations seems almost obvious. But then we come to see that a sacrifice must be made: hopping job to job means one doesn't learn, or become specialized at any of one's jobs. It's behavior typically associate with millennials, but the poor do this often. As such, one avoids catching a job specialized towards one's talents and thus associated with higher earnings. But the poor man does not see this pitfall; instead, he sacrifices future financial success for present risk aversion.

Refath Bari

Table 17: Breaking the Falsehoods of Poverty

Fiction	Fact
Rotating Savings and Credit Associations and Self-Help Groups have collectively enabled many poor people to open savings accounts and save money	Not really. In India, a country where Self-Help Groups have high visiblity, due to the presence of Non-governmental Organizations, and their partnerships with Banks, Self-Help Groups have helped only a limited number of individuals. Your typical Self-Help group is comprised of a group of eight to ten women from 20-40 years of age; sometimes, all of the women collectively save and deposit the money in the Self-Help Groups in the case that a future villager in need, or the village itself. These Self-Help Groups' funds are often linked to commercial banks and microfinance institutions for the express purpose of delivering mico-credit to the extremely poor.
The best money-lender is your friend, because he keeps your best interests in mind when giving you a loan	I don't blame you for this one. I had it myself. And indeed, what's not to like about your friend, relative, or shop-keeper giving you your loans? The problem is three-fold: (1) These informal sources must be much higher costs for deposits, an expense that gets passed onto poor borrowers (2) These sources often have high interest rates, in excess of 3% monthly, so keep that in mind, and lastly (3) These informal sources lack the government guarantees and the capital necessary to effectively lend money, making it unprofitable to loan from an informal source, due to a combination of high interest rates, and expenses.

Chapter 5

Health

Refath Bari

55 Days in Dharavi

For decades, the Southeast Asian countries have been the laughing stock of Western Nations. Secretary of State Henry Kissinger dismissed Bangladesh as a "Basket
Case". President George Bush promised he'd "bomb Pakistan back to the Stone
Age". Lyndon B. Johnson, the "Machiavelli with a Heart", gave India limited food
aid on a month-by-month basis depending on whether the nation adopted market mechanisms and US directives, even during the 1965-66 worsening food crisis
in India. Now the tables have turned: in the face of a spiraling global pandemic,
the poor southeast nations have fared surprisingly well compared to the economic
superpowers that have suffered major losses. This is a simple excercise in health.
Now I come to Health: the crux of all life. I wish to investigate nine key aspects
of health, beggining with a case study of Arjun Chauhan, a 18 year old Water Deliverer in Kerala, a Southern Indian State. Through Arjun's story, I establish the
idea of a poverty trap. I then adress nine key points throughout the chapter, all in
regards to health: (1) Child Mortality in Developing Countries and its causes, (2)
Low-Cost, Low-Used Treatments (3) Innovative NGOs (i.e., Gram Vikas, Population Service International, Together Against Malaria, Seva Mandir) and their field
work on Health (4) Innovative Leaders and Public Health Contributions (5) The
poor man's health dilemma (6) Incompetent Public Health Workers and their Private Counterparts (7) The Poor Man prefers Expensive Cure to Cheap Prevention
(8) The Role of Faith in the Poor Man's decisions on Health (9) One small nudge for
the poor is one giant leap of mankind. I explore each of these themes through ten
key questions. We conclude with a demarcation of the fact and fiction of the poor
man's health.

Keywords: Child Mortality, Belief, Vaccines, Governmental Interference, Public
Health, Cost-Effective Treatments, NGOs, Health Poverty Trap, Water, Sanitation,
Malaria, Nudges

Refath Bari

1 Case Study: Arjun Chauhan

He packs it all up under his legs and behind his shirt: five huge plastic cases of water. He got beat up real bad by the Palakkad police a couple of times for over-speeding, but he doesn't mind. Everyone does it here in Kerala, he says. Arjun's only 18, but he's already got five sons, or so he says. Arjun is in a bad state of affairs – he dropped out of school early to work for his family and married young, as per the advice of his mother. Now he's a water deliverer by day and a trash recycler by night. I met him at a red light (believe it or not, they do exist in some parts of India). He gave me a curious look when I insisted I was just a journalist. "I've never been interviewed. Thank you." he said, shaking with sweat and burn. "You know I can't stand", he reassured. I nodded. All those precariously stacked bottles of water were gonna spill in a bohemian mess.

Figure 1: The One Man Band: Arjun and his five precariously stacked cases of water, 10 gallons each, he promises

I nodded. "It's alright; where you going?" Arjun struggled to pull a smudged paper out of his pocket. *Mercy College, Pallippuram, Palakkad, Kerala.* Hmmph. "Somewhere important?" I guessed. "Look, it's water. Poor or rich, we all need it, Bhai. You want?" he offered me. Wow – guy was a real oppurtunist. Not sure how I was gonna carry a ten gallon case of water home, but I brought it. "That's 50 rupees" said the curt man. I gave him 60. "Keep the tip" I insisted. "So, what do you want? I gotta go soon. People need their water, bhai" "Alright: I'll buy another case if you answer a bunch of questions" I was practically shouting over the traffic "You pay, I talk. No water, no interview" Arjun said, shaking his head. Five minutes and the kerala Sun forced us to make a deal: he would talk 20 minutes, I'd buy his water, and he'd on his merry way. "How long you've been doing this?" He looked at his watch for some reason "5:40 PM". "No, how, long, are you giving water" I said slowly. "Oh, two weeks". "Before then?" "My wife's got eye problems, so now I have to work more to make the same money" Arjun pointed to his squinched left eye. "She got hurt bad in this one" "So pay for her meds, take her to the doctor," I insisted. "I did. That's the problem," he said through gritted teeth. Guy wasn't even looking at me anymore. "She can't work anymore, and now I – one man – has to feed 6 people. How? How?" he threw his hands up in anger. "What, you gonna help me? He's gonna help me? You say go to the doctor, give her meds – you think the doctors care about her? Huh, you must be new to this town" he said, squinting his eyes at me, holding back either tears or anger, I don't know. "Come on," I insisted, and he followed: "Half the time, the doc's not in the house. And then what do I do? I walk half a mile with my sick wife to a doctor that doesn't even care. What, I go to another one? Then I lose work for the whole day. So I don't get the doctor or the money – what do I get? Misery" he blinked back tears. "You tried private?" I whispered. "What?" Kerala was roaring over us. "I said – did you try a private doctor?" "That public crap tortured me long enough. That's what they do – say everything is free, but then make it so garbage that you waste time, money, energy, everything!" he shot his arms up in desperation. "No, but did you try a private one?" "Thank god I did, but it wasn't easy. I took a loan from Rahul, that swine-smelling basta-" he cursed under his breath. "Interest?" "10% on 2000 Rupee loan" Goddamn. That's one big loan – "500 Rupees for the medicine and 1500 Rupees for food for all when she was recovering" "How much interest you paid back?" He darted his eyes, checking behind me. "Show me your ID", he said real quick. "What?" "Show me the ID, the ID" he trailed. I did. "Good?" He calmed down. "Good. I thought you are Rahul's agent – that swine-smelling basta-" he swore a curse under his breath. "OK, OK, come on. I said 20 minutes, right? We almost done." he said, tapping on his little plastic watch. First he harasses me, now he hurries me up. What a guy. "OK. OK. So again: the loan is done, or not?" "Far from over, brother: I'm in debt now. Big debt. I missed three payments," he said, showing his pock-marked fingers. "Now he's threatening me" "Tell the police!" "I can't. He has all the right; I signed the loan contract and now he says he'll take everything" "Who?" "Rahul – that swine-smelling basta-" "OK, OK" I cut him off. "OK, let's see: you're wife's done, she's got the meds. Your kids are fed. So why don't you just pay off the loan?" "OK, OK" Arjun closed his eyes, muttering something quick – probably a swear to Rahul. "I can't. Every month, whatever I pay off, it goes up by more", his eyes shone in tears. "And it's worse now!" he pounded his fists on the motorbike's handle. One of the water cases dropped behind his back. I picked it up. "One of my sons has measles, and you know, it goes round fast" he said, his chest heaving. "I can't get any meds for him, and the private doctor costs money. I can't do anything for him." I was stuck in words; this time it was me cursing under my breath, "Sorry". Arjun went on, "Now he can't even go to school every day. No doctor, no meds, no school." he said counting off his tire smeared fingers. He glanced at his watch and I guessed my time was up. Arjun screwed one of the case caps and doused his face with water. Arjun was not Mo. But I hugged him the same way. Because at the end of the day, we were all drowning in our own problems, and equally deserving of a good life. I slipped a few Rupees in Arjun's hand before wishing him farewell. Mo and Arjun were the same age, but far different characters. He sped off real quick after our talk – must have been up to something; Poor guy – just a few seconds later and he got pulled over by the Palakkad police. Thankfully, it was just a warning.

Figure 2: Arjun showed this to me proudly; Other names blurred for privacy

2 Arjun's List

Health is a big idea. Maybe the biggest lesson from this chapter is that the health of the poor isn't much different from our own. One factor separates the poor man's interaction with health from our own: nudges. This factor will be the basis for our understanding of the whole chapter, and our overall understanding of the health of the poor.

This chapter will examine eleven key themes – each of these themes are associated with their own key questions. After examining each of the key themes and their questions, we will explore health in the developing world in the larger context of COVID-19. We end by considering the demarcation of the facts and fictions of the poor man's health, of which there are many. I hope this chapter will teach you the importance of health in your own life, and the many small 'nudges' that support your life from birth to old age – nudges that do not become apparent until we come to the poor man's home.

(I) Health Poverty Traps

(II) The Child Mortality Problem in South Asia and Subsaharan Africa

(III) Low-Cost, Low-Used Effective Treatments

Refath Bari

(IV) A Poor Man's Logic: Expensive Cures over Cheap Prevention

(V) Poor Man's Burden: Unreliable Public System; Incompetent Private System

(VI) The Government's No-Blame Approach to Public Health

(VII) The Role of Faith in the Poor Man's Health Dilemma

(VIII) Innovative NGOs Pave the Way via Randomized Control Trials

(IX) Persistent Leaders' Significant Contributions to Public Health

(X) One Small Nudge for the Poor is One Giant Leap for Mankind

These are the ten key themes, each of which are associated with essential questions. We begin with our first major theme: Health Poverty Traps.

3 Health Poverty Traps

Any living organism comes with inherent risk: it is by nature a biological machinery that requires constant nutrition, nurture, and energy to subsist. Health, alone, is the basis for many poverty traps – think malnutrition, disease, illness, etc. – these alone can afflict an individual such that they fall into the poverty trap. As such, it is crucial we establish the Health Poverty Trap in two dimensions: conceptual and analytic.

Table 1: **The Health Trap**

1 What is a Health Poverty Trap?

2 How do we model a Poverty Trap?

3.1 What is a Health Poverty Trap?

Arjun told me best: "[My son] He's got the measles. Now, he goes to school half as much as before. Now he gets what? No meds, no doctor, no school. He's gonna end up like me – his mother will tell him to marry early and forget school and then his son, and his son's son. *Yah kahaan samaapt hota hai?* (Where does it end?)". Therein lies the poverty trap: The trap that ensures that Arjun and his next generation are effectively knee-deep in a generational poverty. That's the conceptual idea of a poverty trap: a family does not make sufficient earnings to break living life on the edge.

3.2 How do we model a Poverty Trap?

Now we take a more analytic approach: an approach we'll expand on in Chapter 8, Money. What makes a poverty trap? Ask yourself that. To even begin modeling this socioeconomic phenomenon, we need to begin to understand what factors create it. And indeed, there is only one: Capital! When it comes to Poverty Traps,

Refath Bari

Capital is the name of the game. Capital makes the difference between the poor man who spirals into debt and the poor man who has begun escalating the ranks of economic development. But the difference between the former and the latter is only one word: Capital. And the poor must receive a Capital boost, whether by means of foreign aid, microcredit, or social business – the bottom line is that the poor man mmust receive a capital boost to begin ascending the ranks of secio-economic status. This is how the stoy starts: the story of the six forms of capital:

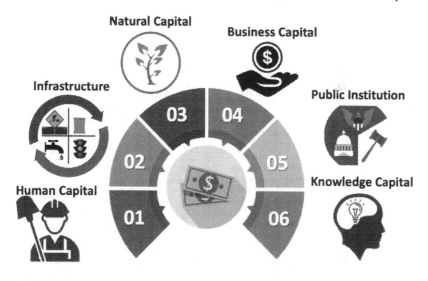

Let's expand on each of the 6 Forms of Capital – each fundamental to the poor man's ascension through the ranks of economic development.

(1) **Human Capital:** Health is at the crux of human capital – for without health, there is no labor! Indeed, this simple idea is one many poor economies fail to appreciate.

(2) **Infrastructure:** We've discussed Water, Sanitation, Toilets, Latrines, and Electricity as some of the pivotal infrastructure that the poor lack. By establishing and maintaining these infrastructures, we maintain the health of a society and it's economy

(3) **Natural Capital:** Now comes all things agricultural: from land to fertilizer to soil fertility. The key here is to ensure that there exist natural arable land that can be used to grow crops, especially in cases of natural disasters

(4) **Business Capital:** Here comes small businesses, which often use household savings as loans (with banks acting as middle-men); they require assets, transport, facilities, and machinery

(5) **Public Institution:** Here comes effective distribution and division of labor, judicial systems, executive law, and social services from the government. These are often funded by tax-payer money.

(6) **Knowledge Capital:** Perhaps the most important, Knowledge Capital means open borders so that there is absolutely no friction between a nation's economy and the talent that it seeks

Now: we've understood the importance of Capital. Here it is: without capital, the poor man cannot even begin climbing the ladder of socioeconomic development. Now – how can the poor man accrue capital? First and foremost is savings – the poor man must save! And yet, from Chapters 3 and 4, we know very well how relunctant he is to do so. Perhaps this comes from a psychological friction – an idea we will adress later in the chapter. Capital is also accumulated through government taxes on individuals' income (i.e., to build infrastructure, finance public works, etc.). That comes to postive capital accumulation. Negative capital accumulation comes in the form of losing skilled workers, by disease, by war, or simply through an older, unproductive, and unskilled population. Here we come to the bigger picture: a poverty trap occurs when the capital per person decreases from generation to generation – one sign of this is when household income decreases from one generation to the next. That ratio is of upmost importance: the ratio of capital per person. When the capital decreases, but population growth skyrockets (as it often does in poor, primarily agrarian-based economies, where the standard is that bigger families mean bigger labor potential, which may explain the high fertility rates) – the ratio of capital per person decreases. On the other hand, even if capital grows, the capital per person will still decrease if the capital cannot grow fast enough to keep up with the population expansion. OK. That is the big idea: that delicate balance of capital accumulation and population growth that can slap a vulnerable country into a poverty trap. That's the key idea of a poverty trap, which will be a recurring theme throughout this book – one we will encounter in our conversations about Food, Income, Money, and more.

Now we come to the mathematical picture. Now I introduce a different perspective: Poverty Traps are all about Income Potential. How likely is it that you'll make more today than tomorrow? This is the core of a poverty trap – when the extremely poor have limited opportunity for income growth, but the slightly less-poor have dramatically greater potential for growth. That's the idea. Where the

Refath Bari

poor have sufficient capital to invest in health, business, education, etc. and that capital levels off for higher incomes, there exists no poverty trap.

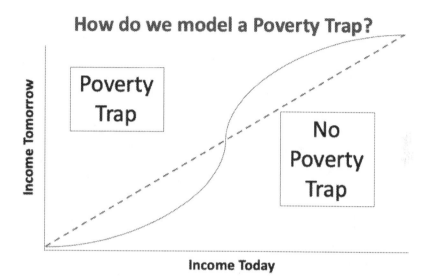

That is the might S-Shaped Poverty Curve. That curve alone holds the key to the restricted economic development of much of the developing world. Let's try to understand it: we begin by the horizontal axis, the Income Today – this is everything, all the assets, that a family has today. Of these assets, the family can either spend or save – saving will lead to positive capital accumulation, whereas spending is the all-too-traveled road that the poor typically take. On the vertical axis is the income of the future – this may come in the form of savings that were invested and are now available in the future, or income-producing assets such as land which may produce income in the future. Those are the axes. Now we find the diagonal line. Being on that dotted blue diagonal line means living on the edge – the Goldilocks's zone, if you will – on tip and you've fallen off the ledge and into the left side, the dreaded side: The Poverty Trap. This is where the income you make in the future (tomorrow, next week, next generation even) is less than the income you make today. On the other hand, should your income tomorrow be greater than it is today, we have no poverty trap.

Our graph paints a basic picture of the poverty trap: Low income means that the poor can't even cover their basic needs, such as proper nutrition and health. Malnutrition can decrease labor productivity, and so the poor man works less, thus earning less, and so the cycle repeats. Eventually his dependants will inherit their father's trap.

4 The Child Mortality Problem in South Asia and Subsaharan Africa

Child Mortality is still a 21st century problem, despite the remarkable progress we've made over the last two centuries. There's a lot left to be desired: 5.3 Million Children Under 5 died in 2018. We begin this section with a statement of the United Nation's Fourth Millennium Development Goal: Reduce Child Mortality by 66% from 1990 to 2015. By 2015, the progress made was substantial: The child mortality rate has been cut by more than half in those 25 years: from 90/1000 live births to 43/1000. We see now the Child Mortality Rates:

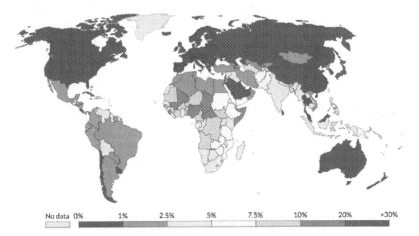

Table 2: **Child Mortality**

1 What is the state of Child Mortality in developing countries?

2 What diseases contribute to most Child Mortality?

3 What non-disease factors contribute most to Child Mortality?

Refath Bari

4.1 What is the state of Child Mortality in developing countries?

As Max Roser puts it – "The world is much better; The world is awful; The world can be much better" (Oxford Economics Research Director) We thus examine the state of child mortality in third world countries in these three stages: it was far worse, it's gotten better, and it can get a lot better.

We begin at the first stage: the world is much better. The Child Mortality rate in the poorest countries today (10%-13% in Subsaharan Africa, for instance) is far better than the richest countries of the past (30%). It's hard to imagine the remarkable strides we've made over the past few years, but the fact of the matter is that in the 1800s, given the high fertility rates (the average woman had 5-7 children) and high child mortality rates (30% in the richest countries), parents would see every second child die. It is a difficult truth, but it was a common norm.

Now we transcend to the second stage: from the mid-20th century to present day. Imagine just how divided the world was in the 20th century: we had wars of magnitude unwitnessed in previous history, all whilst going through a ravaging pandemic (Spanish Flu). And yet – in spite of all this – child mortality in the richest countries dropped to 5% – that's still 1 in every 20 children dying, but progress nonetheless. With this decline in fertility came a decline in mortality: the average woman in the richest countries in the 1950s was having 2-3 babies. For the first time, parents didn't have to lose a single child, due to remarkable strides in medicine, technology, and sanitation. But recall that this is 1950 – it remains a divided world: Children in the rest of the developing world were still suffering from unbelievable mortality rates, with most countries in Asia, Africa, and South America have 33% mortality rates. That percentage does not convey the scale of deaths that a parent would witness: at best, a parent would witness one of their three babies die before making it to five years of age. We now arrive to 2015, where the child mortality rates of the poorest countries are comparable to the richest ones in the 1950s.

But, we can – and must – do better: in 2018 alone, 5.3 million children died. Roser asks the pivotal question: "Are we born at that unlucky moment in modern history at which global progress has to come to a halt?". The answer is right before us: where the richest countries were 50 years past, the poorest are now. We must bridge that gap and ensure that the richest countries of today are the poorest of tomorrow. Iceland, for instance, has a child mortality rate of .7 per 1000 live births as of 2018, whereas Subsaharan Africa has a child mortality rate of 78 per 1000 live births – 100 times higher than Iceland and 15 times higher than children born in the average high-income country. So the truth is this: if we can boost the rest of the developing nations to the child mortality rates that the rich countries are at today, we will make definitive progress towards a world where there is no concept of child mortality.

4.2 What diseases contribute to most Child Mortality?

Every single day, about 15,000 children under 5 die. We never find this on the headlines, but it happens every single day and sums to an unacceptable number by the end of the year. What are the diseases that take their lives?

(1) **Pneumonia and Respiratory Diseases (15%)**: Almost 1 in 7 of every children who died in 2017 was due to Respiratory Diseases. The respiratory illness that took the most lives was Pnuemonia, which is caused by bacterial infection.

(2) **Preterm births and Neonatal disorders (12%)**: Preterm births are premature births (more specifically, one that occurs before the 37th week of pregnancy). The problem with premature births are birth complications, which can be the platform for numerous fatalities including birth injuries, undeveloped organs, and infectious diseases.

(3) **Diarrhea (10%)**: Diarrahea is one of the greatest regrets of Public Health, especially in developing countries: it is both a treatable and preventable disease and treatments are cost-effective to implement. Why governments don't implement them is a whole different question entirely.

(4) **Birth Defects (9%)**: These are birth complications present during a child's birth: abnormalities such as heart defects, Down syndrome, neural tube defects, and problems in the growth of the spinal cord. These may be the consequences of a neglectful parent (i.e., one that drinks alcohol)

(5) **Infectious diseases (45%)**: These are the biggest killers of children. They involve household names like Malaria and Measles, both of which are preventable and have cost-effective treatments. But the data doesn't reflect the magnitude of improvement in the area of infectious diseases: The # Measles Cases, for instance, has declined by 86% since 1990, largely due to effective national vaccination programs. The World Health Organization states that measles vaccines alone have prevented 21 million deaths in Africa since 2000-2017. Therein lies the power of public health.

Refath Bari

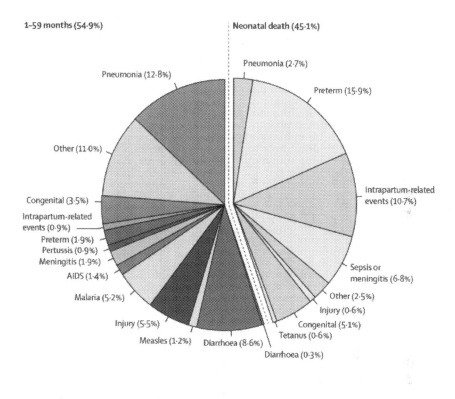

1-59 months (54·9%)　　　　　Neonatal death (45·1%)

Pneumonia (12·8%)

Pneumonia (2·7%)

Preterm (15·9%)

Other (11·0%)

Intrapartum-related events (10·7%)

Congenital (3·5%)

Intrapartum-related events (0·9%)

Preterm (1·9%)

Pertussis (0·9%)

Meningitis (1·9%)

AIDS (1·4%)

Sepsis or meningitis (6·8%)

Other (2·5%)

Injury (0·6%)

Congenital (5·1%)

Tetanus (0·6%)

Malaria (5·2%)

Injury (5·5%)

Measles (1·2%)　　Diarrhoea (8·6%)

Diarrhoea (0·3%)

4.3 What non-disease factors contribute most to Child Mortality?

Three factors: Ineffective Treatments, High Fertility, and Household Income. The first factor we will investigate in the upcoming section, but the other two we will discuss now.

We begin with High Fertility Rates. We discussed at length the importance of low fertility in the economic development of third world countries, but now it becomes especially evident: it goes in two ways. First, lower fertility rates typically results in lower child mortality – with less babies, families (especially poor ones with a low ratio of capital per person that are strained to invest resources between children) have more resources to invest in each one of them. But it also goes the other way – lower child mortality can create lower fertility rates, as there exists less demand for babies as the existing children's chances of survival from baby to adult increases. It can go other way, as well – if parents seek to have 'excess' babies in developing countries, knowing that not all of them will survive.

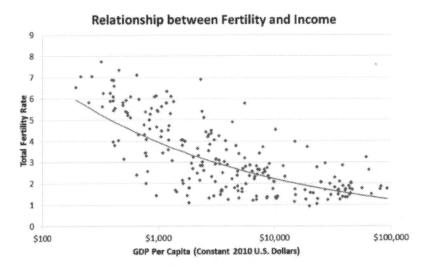

Figure 3: Every dot is a country – richer countries, those with higher GDP Per Capitas, tend to have lower fertility rates. The converse – poorer countries tend to have higher fertility rates – is also true. We thus have an inverse relationship between Fertility Rates and Income

In regards to Income and Fertility, there exists an inverse relationship between two factors. We see this clearly on the global scale, as richer countries with higher GDPs have much lower fertility than poorer countries. We observe the same phenomenon upon closer inspection: individual households also have the same tendency – richer ones opt for less babies than poorer ones. Associated with richer households is more education, and indeed, women with higher education and higher social status often have less babies.

5 Low-Cost, Low-Used Effective Treatments

It makes it especially painful that most of the under-five child mortality deaths are *preventable*. Right there: they're not only preventable, but the treatments are cost-effective to implement! So why don't governments implement them? The answer is a mix of on-the-ground nuances and bureaucratic nonsense, but I hope this chapter establishes that the solution does exist. It just needs to be implemented by those that have the power to implement them.

Refath Bari

Table 3: **Cheap Prevention**

| 1 | What cost-effective treatments can prevent disease?

5.1 What cost-effective treatments can prevent disease?

We address this question in three stages – cost-effective treatments for (1) Diarrhea, a leading factor in Child Mortality, (2) Infectious Diseases (with Malaria and Measles as Case Studies), which account for over 45% of deaths of children under 5, and (3) Miscellaneous Diseases (ranging from Respiratory Diseases to Birth Defects), which account for another 36% of diseases

We begin with Diarrhea, a leading cause of child mortality under five. Let's establish the quick facts first: Diarrheal disease is the second largest contributor to child mortality under five. Between 2005 and 2015, child deaths from Diarrhea dropped by 30%; however, while these are signs of progress, repeated bouts of diarrhea can stifle physical and cognitive development in young children. How do we prevent it? Thankfully, the solutions already exist and they are not only preventable, but also cheap. But cheap does not imply easy-to-implement, and therein lies the caveat. Here they are:

(1) **ORS+Zinc:** Fluids are the name of the game when it comes to Diarrhea. That's exactly what Oral Re-hydration Solutions provide – it's a simple, do-it-yourself, cheap homemade solution that supplies the body with extra fluids – breast milk, juices and other fluids – prevents it from drying up, which in turn stops Diarrhea.

(2) **Chlorine:** How do the poor drink water? They can't just take it off the river or the stream – both of these means have the risk of waterborne diarrhea, which can be simply avoided by Chlorine, a cheap and effective means of cleaning and purifying water.

(3) **Others:** There are a variety of alternative ways to prevent Diarrhea, all of which are accessible to the poor, including exclusively breastfeeding up to six months,

The great thing is that neither of these methods are costly. As a matter of fact, ORS is a low-tech solution that has been demonstrated to have widespread efficacy: It has saved over 70 million lives since its introduction in the late 1970s. What's more, if scaled to 100% usage amongst all the developing nations, it could drastically reduce the number of diarrhea-caused child deaths. In fact, the World Health Organization's official advisory for treating diarrheal diseases is as follows: "The WHO-recommended treatment for acute diarrheal disease is ORS and zinc supplementation and continued feeding. If scaled to 100% coverage, ORS could prevent up to 93% of diarrhea deaths, and zinc can reduce the duration of illness by 25% and prevent recurrence of disease for 2-3 months." (Diarrhea and Pneumonia Working Group 2016 report, Progress over a Decade of Zinc and ORS Scale-up). I found the efficacy of ORS to be particularly telling under the story of Dr Mathuram Santosham MD, a professor of pediatric infectious diseases at John Hopkins. Dr. Santosham's passion for fighting infectious diseases began on an expedition to a remote Nigerian village where he accompanied the World Health Organization as a consultant to conduct an ORS training program. In the doctor's clinic, ran a mother no older than 16, desperately screaming for her baby, who was afflicted with diarrhea. The doctor shook his head as he trailed the stethoscope around the young boy's belly. "Sorry", was all he could say, as his voice broke. The mother refused to believe the fact, and she grabbed the sethoscope and slapped her baby's belly with it; she frantically dragged the sethoscope's bell around the little boy's belly-button – perhaps awaiting a medical miracle. But none came. The only miracle that day was Dr. Santosham walking out of the clinic, declaring he would dedicate the rest of his life to preventing such disasters – create a treatment, promote a campaign, or start a revolution. And start a revolution he did – while Dr.Santoshon alone was not responsible for creating the ORS mixture, it is due to the contributions of doctors, physicians, and leaders like him that the world is equipped with this cheap, homemade, low-tech solution to a global crisis. All we need to do now, is use it.

We have arrived at the second stage of child morality: infectious diseases – these alone account for over 45% of child mortality rates, and range a wide spectrum of diseases, from Malaria to Measles. Now we examine Malaria as a case study in the power of cheap, disease preventative technology. Here they are:

(1) **Bed Nets**: Insecticide-Tested, Durable Bed Nets are the key to cheap malaria prevention. In 2008 alone, Malaria killed a million children, mostly African. Studies demonstrated that in regions where Malaria is common, these cheap Bed Nets alone can reduce the number of cases of Malaria by half.

(2) **Piped Chlorinated Water**: Piping Ready-made chlorinated water to the poor man's house can reduce diarrhea by up to 95% and significantly reduce other diseases including Malaria and Trachoma, all of which are diseases which can kill children or make them unproductive adults; furthermore, it ensures

that even if the poor man forgets to chlorinate his water, he nor his family will risk attaining waterborne diarrhea or malaria.

There it is: two cost-effective solutions to Malaria that have been proven to drastically reduce the incidence of Malaria Cases. We now arrive at the last and final stage of cost-effective treatments: preventative treatments for Miscellaneous Diseases ranging from Pneumonia to Birth Abnormalities. Here we begin. I associate each type of disease/illness with a cheap, preventable treatment.

(1) **Neonatal Disorders**: Measles Vaccines, Breastfeeding (which is free), regular anti-netal procedures such as a tetanus shot for prospective mothers, insecticide-treated material

(2) **Birth Defects**: DTaP Vaccine (which can prevent Diphtheria – which can lead to paralysis or death; Tetanus – which can cause painful muscle contraction that leads to symptoms like unable to open one's mouth; and Pertussis – also known as Whooping Cough, and can lead to severe coughing that prevents conducting daily activities), Folic Acid and Iodine can also reduce the possibility of defects.

(3) **Pnuemonia**: DTap, Rotavirus, Measles, and Pnuemonial Vaccines, Breastfeeding, and Zinc can all effectively prevent the possibility of Pnuemonia, which claimed 810,000 children in 2017

6   A Poor Man's Logic: Expensive Cures over Cheap Prevention

From high-up, it seems paradoxical: why would one value expensive cures over cheap prevention? Especially when one has limited capital to invest in his health? This is the poor man's rationale – one confounded on a host of theories, accumulated from myths, guesses, and beliefs alike, the poor man's misguided health decisions are in large part due to an inconsistent health system that refuses to serve them well.

Table 4: **Cheap Prevention**

1 What is the extent of the Poor Man's Resistance to Cheap Preventative Technologiess?

2 Do the poor engage in the Sunken Cost effect: Cheap = No Value?

3 What is the Role of Faith in the Poor Man's Health Dilemma?

4 Spooky Action at a Distance: Does it Haunt the Poor Man's decisions?

6.1 What is the extent of the Poor Man's Resistance to Cheap Preventative Technologies?

The poor man's resistance is complex, unpredictable, and hopeless – it is, in essence, a shot in the dark. He does not have the education necessary to differentiate ineffective technologies from effective ones; nor does he have the reassurance that we do from a never-ending supply of expert doctors. The poor man runs in the dark, making at best – hopeless guesses, and worst – dangerous ones. These guesses are the consequences of many parties to-blame: the government, the incompetent doctors, and even the education system. The root of the crisis begins with understanding the extent of the poor man's rationale in making these shots in the dark, and the extent to which he does so.

In Zambia, a East African Country, the Nongovernmental Organization Population Service International has subsidized costs of chlorine and promoted it throughout the country. Indeed, there is no reason *not* to buy Chlorine – it is cheap and widely available; at the cost of $.15, a family of 6, which is the median size of a family in a poor country, can buy enough bleach to purify their entire water supply. And yet, only 10% of families use it. This is no isolated case. As of 2014, the % of children with Diarrhea who received Oral Re-hydration Therapy is 77% in Bangladesh and 38% in Pakistan. In some places, it's actually getting worse: India dropped from 39.3% usage in 2014 to 20.5% usage in 2016 – in a matter of two years, the nation of a billion essentially regressed in Childhood Mortality Development. On average, only 44% of children with Diarrhea receive ORT as of 2019 (according to UNICEF).

Refath Bari

6.2 Do the poor engage in the Sunken Cost effect: Cheap = No Value?

Your turn: Would you be more likely to read this book (cover-to-cover) if you a) borrowed it from the public library or b) brought it physically from Barnes & Nobles. It's a common sense answer – B! And yet, this simple physiological phenomenon – termed the Sunken Cost effect – communicates that you're more likely to invest more into an endeavor if you've already invested significant resources (time, money, energy, etc.) to it. Indeed, this may be the basis for much of the poor man's decisions in regards to public health. How so? We begin with the basic facts: the poor man knows that he has limited capital, of which he can invested only so much in his Health. Now take the sunken cost effect and wind it in reverse: if you don't invest much in a product, you're not very likely to use it. So given the remarkable strides in cheap disease prevention technology, are we aiming for the wrong goal? Is making disease prevention cheaper actually making the poor resist it more? After all, you'd be more likely to use a insecticide-tested bed net for preventing malaria if you paid more for it, no? As a matter of fact, this is not the case. TAMTAM, an NGO formed by Harvard Economist Jessica Cohen and Stanford Developmental Economics Pascaline Dupas, sought to answer exactly that question: whether the poor used free or paid bed nets more. It turned out the difference was negligible. Even if the sunken cost effect contributes to the poor man's psychological decision of whether to invest in cheap preventative technologies, it does not make a statistically significant difference in his behavior in regards to public health.

6.3 What is the Role of Faith in the Poor Man's Health Dilemma?

And now, we come to faith: the all-important believer. What role does the poor man's beliefs play in the public health decisions he makes? This is a critical question to ask, and one that gets obscured in the face of the larger ideas. Faith is very important, especially for some of the poorest – some of whom rely on faith for hope, motivation, and reasoning. But faith can be very misguided at times: to understand this, we look to vaccination. First and foremost – even in the richest economy in the world, where we can afford all the doctors, nurses, and experts we want – there is a lack of public belief in the efficacy of vaccines. We need look no further than the "Vaccines Cause Autism" movement, with individuals claiming anecdotal evidence that vaccines cause various disorders and diseases, among them Autism. These claims are often based on conspiracy, superstition, or even sincere belief. One can imagine how the scenario can be much worse in a third world country like India, one that cannot afford to educate its whole public on the importance of vaccination; a country where the public health system suffers from doctor and nurse absenteeism and the private health system suffers from incompetence. Who can the poor man trust? The unqualified doctor who blindly over-prescribes him medication, or the qualified nurse who's never there for him, but assures that a vaccine will prevent pneumonia? It gets worse: vaccines such as DTaP prevent only a host of diseases, but not all. As such, when the poor man suffers symptoms from another disease because he has not received his full set of vaccinations (as most do), he becomes suspicious of the vaccine's efficacy – as he should. Even worse, if the poor man receives a vaccination and rightfully never contracts the disease, he will have no way of knowing that one shot saved his life. The poor man then resorts to superstition, visiting herbal doctors that wave magical prescriptions out of thin air and give the poor man some nonsense mixture. Due to the fluctuating nature of disease symptoms, the poor man may feel slightly better in a day, but much worse in the days to come, and he knows not what to prescribe the symptoms to – the vaccine, the herbs, or something else. There's just too many false lines to chase and too many dangerous outcomes to consider. To make matters worse, most of the poor have – at most – a primary-level education, and are unable to solicit true treatments from bogus ones. And so, the poor man is left alone, to fend with decisions of life-and-death importance on his own – decisions that are just shots in the dark.

6.4 Spooky Action at a Distance: Does it Haunt the Poor Man's decisions?

It never ends for the poor man. His strife is continual, everlasting, and unwinding. Here we come to some spooky action at a distance – does the poor man consider the implications of his actions today on his life tommorow? Indeed, this is an insensible question to ask, given that the extremely poor live hand-to-mouth; check-to-check; and day-to-day. He cannot afford to think of tomorrow if he cannot even live today. And yet this is an important question to ask nonetheless. It gives us insight into the poor man's behavior: the poor man goes to the doctor for minor, sideline problems, but not for major health issues. In fact, the poor are much less likely to go to the hospital for a life-and-death disease than for diarrhea or fevers. This is mostly because the poor can't afford to spend so much on elective surgeries, or expensive treatments, as the rich can. In fact, the poor man in Delhi spends as much on short-term problems like fevers as the rich man – but the rich man spends much more on chronic diseases, as well. For those riskier ailments – the life-and-death scenarios – the poor man resorts to herbal healers and superstitious healers. Remarkably, this phenomenon isn't in just poor

Refath Bari

countries: it's general human behavior to resort to faith when we encounter a particularly cryptic illness, such as back pains or depression, that are not as well understood. As such, we often go back-and-forth between psychics, healers, and chiropractors. Here's the big idea: we think about the present much differently than we do about the future. Small incentives in the present (i.e., a birani in front of me) may deflect me from my original goal. Think a heavy Christmas dinner (or a *Eiftar* for us) blocking out all desire to exercise. It goes the other way, as well: a small cost may deflect an individual from taking a life-saving drug, or jogging every day, even if may prevent a heart attack in the future. Think about your New Year's Resolution. Now think about the one time you kept it. Not many thoughts, right? The same "time inconsistency" comes for the poor man – a few cents is all it takes for him to avoid a life-saving bed net or Oral Re-hydration Therapy. Bottom line is that we are impulsive in the now, easily distracted by quick incentives or small costs. That's why retrospection is so powerful – these small pros and cons become minuscule in the grander scale of life. Here's our logic, poor man and rich man alike: if there's a cost today, do it tommorow. But when tommorow comes, our same instinct applies, and soon enough, the cost is accepted too late, if at all. You have two choices: a life saving bed net for your family, or a bag of chips for your desperately pleading son. It's gotta go to the latter – you know the net will save you many harsh nights, but you postpone that cost until later, because there's a better bang for the buck.

7 Poor Man's Burden: Unreliable Public System; Incompetent Private System

Health, or Education; Life or death; the poor man consistently receives the short end of the stick. This is especially frustrating when it comes to public health – a matter of actual life-and-death. We begin by examining the ravaged public health care system in the poor country, specifically India, where clinics, hospitals, and health providers alike are plagued by severe staff absenteeism. And so the poor man finds no-one in the public clinic, only to be referred to a private one where the doctor a) turns him away for money or b) is unqualified and overprescribing and misdiagnosing the patient. Therein lies the deep flaws of the both public and private health systems of poor countries: they are ravaged by absenteeism, unqualifications, and all-round subpar standard health services.

Table 5: **Poor Man Gets Short End of the Stick**

 What is the state of the Poor Man's Public & Private Health System?

2 Why does absenteeism plague the public and incompetency ravage the private health care systems?

7.1 What is the state of the Poor Man's Public & Private Health System?

We know the poor man cares about his health. It's the biggest reason for his stress and one of his biggest expenditures. But does health care about the poor man? At first glance, everything's fine: the infrastructure is there – there exists public health clinics everywhere from the most rural farms to the most urban cities. The positions are filled, ... but are the people there? Upon closer inspection, we see huge abseenteism in across the health care industry. As a result, the poor have shunned the public health system – they don't even care for it anymore. We see this from the data: adults in extremely poor households visit health care providers once every sixty days, of which less than a fourth were to a public facility. More than 50% of the visits were to private facilities, and the rest were to spiritual healers.

The poor man has chased the wrong tail: he goes to the private doctor, who is expensive, and he seeks cure over prevention, which is even worse! This would make sense if the private doctors are more qualified, but they're not. In fact, their degree of qualification makes them far from useless – it makes them dangerous. First we look to the state of their qualifications: only 50% of private doctors have a medical college degree, and 33% didn't even go to college. It gets worse: Of the people helping the doctors, 66% don't even have formal qualifications in medicine. This is not good. And then, there's the cycle. The goddamn cycle. When the most educated poor – some of whom drop out of high school – find no jobs due to lack of skill and lack of capital, they set up as "Bengali Doctors", colloquial for unqualified doctors. Of course, things wouldn't be so bad if these Bengali doctors had the humility and self-awareness to only guess-prescribe for some patients and refer the rest to a local hospital for cases they didn't know how to handle. Unfortunately, most don't, and therein lies the problem: unqualified doctors overprescribing and misdiagnosing patients all over. We understand this phenonomenon from an innovative study done by World Bank Economists Jishnu Das and Jeff Hammer, who sought to answer "How much do these doctors actually know?" To answer the question, Das and Hammer gave doctors, rural and urban, public and private alike – scenarios. These scenarios involved a patient walking in with some typical symptoms that clearly resembled a very particular disease. To clarify and confirm what said disease was, a qualified doctor would ask a specific series of questions designed to understand and correctly diagnose the patient's condition. Das and Hammer's study had striking results: the fact of the matter was that the very *best* of the doctors asked less than half of the questoins neccessary to correctly diagnose a disease, and the bottom quartile asked less than 16% of the required questions. One can imagine how off-track the diagnoses can be. Unqualified private doctors fared the worst in the rankings, and public doctors were in the middle, and qualified public doctors fared the best – but then again, there are only so many qualified private doctors to go around in the first place. The bottom line of Das and Hammer's study was that these bad doctors tended to overprescribe and misdiagnose. The data comes in scary: only 3% of doctors actually performed a test on a patient, before giving them a shot (66% of visits) or a drip (12% of visits). Instead of providing cheap solutions like Oral Rehydration Therapy, doctors excercised the most unnecsary measures to treat diarrhea, including some antibiotics or steroids. But this isn't just unnecesary – it's dangerous. As doctors prescribe these antibiotics more and more, the viruses that cause these diseases can become resistant to the anitboitics, reducing their efficacy. This is no speculation: across the develpoing natoins, antioboitc resistant viruses are increasing. Even worse, when doctors prescribe steroids, patients may it first use feel much better (because that's exactly how steroids are designed), but will never realize that in ten years time, they'll look fifty years older, and in fact, die sooner as well. Believe it or not, it gets worse: many doctors neglect to even sterilize the needles, thus increasing the risk of disease spread throughout a community. It is said that in the Indian district of Udaipur, one doctor infected the entire village because he didn't sterilize his needle. the Public System suffers from unreliability and the Private one suffers from incompetency.

7.2 Why does absenteeism plague the public and incompetency ravage the private health care systems?

It really comes down to three levels of beaurocrartic incompetence: Ideology, Ignorance, and Inertia (Banerjee, Duflo 2006). We take it to Ideology, first and foremost: the good-willing beauracrat envisons a certain future for the public health system and that founded on his ideology that the executors of his vision – pharmicists, doctors, and physicians alike will be not only be willing to execute his vision, but be motivated to do so. Therein lies the first and foremost caveat: the wrong ideology. The beauracrat's small mind is blocked by the hobgoblins of politics, and thus he fails to consider the pragmatic effects of the laws that he signs. We see this in action with the problem of Absenteeism in Udaipur, India. Seva Mandir sought to reduce the severe absenteeism problem with one method: monitoring. Every nurse with assigned a stamp, with which they would prove their presence at the clinic. If they were absent more than half of the time, their wages would be put on-hold. Independent researchers and Seva Mardin staff checked regularly to ensure nurses were actually coming to the facility and marking their presence on the time sheets. And indeed there were – for a time. Nurse attendance jumped from 30% in 2003 to 60% by August 2006. But then the tables turned: in just a year, Nurse attendance in the experimental clinics (where Seva Mardin was monitoring) had dropped *below* attendance in standard control clinics: now, Nurses were coming only 25% of the time. What's worse, Seva Mardin was receiving no complaints of the Nurses' absences. When they checked the time sheets, recorded absences were low, ... so how come they were gone 75% of the time? It was the excused absences – days when nurses claimed they had meetings and professional development sessions to go to, but actually didn't. Someone who was supervising the nurses was wilfully ignoring the 30% jump in excused absences. This willfull ignorance, combined with negligent nurses creates a serious health problem – but it all begins with beauracract.

See, the burcreat had a misguided ideology – that the nurses would be eager to execute his vision of prenatal clinics throughout the villlage. This was wrong. Far from it – the nurses didn't even understand the importance of selling sterilziatoin to the villagers. As such, when the executors of an initiative are not motivated by the same vision as its founder, the initiative won't even take off from the ground. Now comes the next problem: ignorance. The burcrat had no idea what he was subjecting these nurses to – the reality was this: the nurses were expected to wake at six, commute for two hours, sign in and stamp their time onto the log, walk to a village – sometimes three miles away and in 100 degree blazing heat – and make the rounds, advertising sterilization services to the villagers, then come back into the clinic, stamp and sign out, and commute back to home for two hours. This was the routine that the buearcrat envisioned. But now, upon actually writing it down, the pure unpragmatism of the vision becomes real – nurses can't do this every day. And yet, the beauracrat's ignorance to what truly happens on the ground blinds him from creating effective programs.

Finally, the bureaucrat's inertia – his resistance to change the pre-existing law inhibits further development of an initiative. To begin change, you must first

Refath Bari

admit what you were doing is wrong. Unfortuantely, this humility is not one many leaders possess, and that is a sad truth. To begin changing this dismal trend of absenteeism in public health programs and government initiatives alike, we must take the first step: reforming the ground-level work that health care workers need to do such that it is a) pragmatic, b) efficient, c) a vision that the workers themselves support.

8 The Government's No-Blame Approach to Public Health

What do you do when the government wants to take no-blame for deplorable standards of public health care in their country? This is the exact dilemma the poor man faces.

Table 6: **An Unfortunate Government**

1 What role does the government play in the public and private health care systems?

8.1 What role does the government play in the public and private health care systems?

Let's talk Governmental Incentive: disease prevention is a straight road to economic prosperity. To understand why, let's go back to poverty traps: these traps are founded on the idea that future generations receive less capital per person than present ones. But the trap is easily broken: set one generation loose, and the rest are home-free – future generations will have the opportunity to scale the socioeconomic ladder as they choose. We need only look to Malaria for a guideline: countries where more than half of the population has been exposed to Malaria have per-capita incomes less than a third of countries that don't. Being so poor means that these countries don't have the capital to invest in health, which in turn makes the population less healthy, making it more unproductive, and thus continuing the negative feedback cycle. But, it is for this exact reason that public health investments are so valuable in poor countries: they will benefit tremendously from the smallest capital investment in health. In other words, these poor, malaria-infested countries would typically be stuck in a poverty trap, on the left side of the income graph. But, if they were to receive the smallest capital boost, they would definitely end up on the "No Poverty Trap" side of the S-shaped curve, thus on their way to economic prosperity. The moral of the story is this: there is enormous incentive for governments to invest in disease prevention and eridication, specifically and public health, in general. To understand why, we need look no further than Latin America: malaria-free children there earn 50% more annually for the entire life than a child with malaria. It is probable, then, that the GDP growth rate of a country with a malaria-infested population is significantly higher than a country whose population does not suffer from the disease. This phenomenon is not isolated to Latin America – the same findings have been established throughout India, Sri Lanka, and Paraguay. To understand the power of a small investment, we descend from a macroscopic examination of the population to the microscopic – a single poor household:

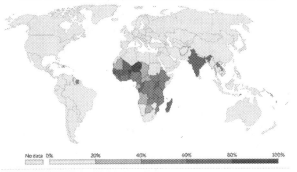

Share of children sleeping under insecticide-treated nets, 2017

Figure 4: Niger, a West African country, has the highest usage of Insecticide Treated Bed Nets, with over 95% of children under five years old sleeping under an insecticide treated net to prevent malaria infection, as of 2015

I ask you to imagine the following scenario – a family of six buys one durable (>5 years), insecticide-treated bed net, which costs $14 USD PPP in Kenya. That small cost will be more than made up in just a few years: as the family becomes more healthier, their labor productivity will increase and so will their income. Let's find the economic returns: A malaria-infected adult makes half the money in Kenya than a healthy one: $295 per year for an infected adult. But now – that adult will be making double the money – for every year of his life! And that's just for $14 investment. The returns are fantastic – the benefits, undeniable.

Just how effective can one small investment be? We look to Bed Nets – I myself being one of their primary beneficiaries, can endorse their utility: I used to be fond of them in Bangladesh, where we would prop them up around our beds whenever Summer came. The nights that we forgot to prop the nets, I would

Refath Bari

wake up a mysteriously red pock-marked skin the morning after. It's not just my anecdotal evidence: the World Health Organization recommends universal coverage of Long Lasting Insecticide Treated Nets (LLINs) such that they are distributed to and used by all people in malaria-infested regions. Since 2000, over 6.8 million lives have been saved by these nets, so there is no question about their efficacy.

9 Innovative NGOs Pave the Way via Randomized Control Trial

I will focus on the works of four major Non Governmental Organizations: Seva Mandir, Together Against Malaria, Gram Vikas, and Population Service International, and the efforts they have led in promoting vaccination campaigns, rural public health infrastructure, and immunization programs throughout developing countries. Their fundamental efforts in improving the lives of millions of children every day give us hope that poverty can indeed be eradicated – or in the words of Nobel-Prize Winning Economists Abihijit Banerjee and Esther Duflo, "it is possible to make very significant progress against the biggest problems in the world through a set of small steps, each well thought-out, carefully tested and judiciously implemented".

Table 7: **An Unfortunate Government**

1 How did Population Service International subsidize prices of Chlorine (for Water Purification) in Zambia?

2 How did Gram Vikas implement piped water and sanitation throughout rural India (for preventing Diarrhea)?

3 How did Together Against Malaria measure demand for mosquito bed-nets (for preventing Malaria)

Table 8: **An Unfortunate Government**

1 How did Seva Mandir organize monthly immunization camps in commu nities and sharply reduce staff absenteeism in health facilities?

9.1 How did Population Service International subsidize prices of Chlorine (for Water Purification) in Zambia?

Population Service International's work is exactly that – International. Their work ranges from distribution of subsidized insecticide-treated durable bed nets in Rural Kenya to subsidized chlorine for water purification. Their broad reach and subsidized prices make it convenient and affordable for the poor man to have access to the public health goods he needs. PSI aims to treat malaria, child survival, and reproductive health around the world by collaborating with both the public and private sector.

9.2 How did Gram Vikas implement piped water and sanitation throughout rural India (for preventing Diarrhea)?

I take this picture: clean water and a toilet alone can save millions of lives, children and adults alike. This is a universal truth, but not a universal reality: I have gone to great lengths to illustrate this painful fact. In 2008, according to WHO and UNICEF, 13% of the world didn't have a tap or well – what's worse, 25% didn't have any safe water to drink (I know many of the poor in Dharavi, India who have no choice but to drink water from fecal-infested rivers). Tap water varies from 1% in rural villages like rural Rajasthan and Uttar Pradesh in India to 37% in Guatemala, where the government receives support from institutions such as the Inter-American Development Bank and the World Bank. As Income and Urbanization increases, so does a families' access to water and sanitation infrastructure. Sanitation is even harder to come by: 42% of the world lives without a toilet. To give you just the magnitude – the scope – of change that a single toilet and water can bring to a people: from 1900 to 1950 – Infant Mortality declined by 75% because of better sanitatoin, and water chlorination. Piped water and sanitation can reduce diarrhea up to 95% and prevent a horde of other diseases, from Malaria to Teataphaus. So where is it? Where are the toilets and the clean water? Nonexistent – they're just too costly. At $20 a house per month, that's way above the heads of most poor countries. Implementation of rural sanitation and toilets isn't even an option. That's where Gram Vikas comes in.

Gram Vikas cut the price of implementation from $20 a house per month to $4 a house per month, an 80% reduction in price cost. Here's how: it begins with CEO Joe Madiath, an activist from an early age – who at 12, organized labor on his father's plantation. Since then, Madiath has been afflicted by the plight of the poor, and came to Orissa, India in the 1970s when a cyclone ravaged the poor. He set up shop there, persuading some 400 students from a local university to help in distributing recovery materials to the poor. After he thought his work done, he left Orissa, only to come back a few years later, explaining the allure of long-term foundational change had attracted him back to the village. There in Orissa, he sought for ways to fundamentally change the long-term lives of the poor so that they could begin climbing the ladder of economic development. He found his calling in Water and Sanitation. Gram Vikas functions on the idea that everyone in a village be connected to the same water mains – so that the rich, high-caste Indians must ultimately share water with the poor, low-caste people. This principle alone was the basis for much of the early resistance Gram Vikas faced, but Madiath held steadfast – the NGO would not begin construction of toilets, and water taps in a village until absolute consensus was reached by all the villagers. Once everyone in the village agrees, the NGO begins construction and builds for one to two years, after which they connect every house in the village to the same mains. Simulataneously, Gram Vikas checks the frequency of villagers' visits to the local health clinic due to diarrhea, malnutrition, and other preventable diseases. After turning on the water system, these visits drastically drop: incidence of severe diarrhea drops by 50& and malaria drops by 33% – and Gram Vikas celebrates its overnight victory. Maintanence and all, the monthly cost of the entire system is $4 a household. It's not short-lived either – the effects of Gram Vikas' interventions last years into the future, and diarrhea, malaria, and tetaphanus cases drop significantly and stay low in these villages. And therein lies the power of social entrepenuership.

9.3 How did Together Against Malaria measure demand for mosquito bed-nets (for preventing Malaria)?

Nets are life-savers when it comes to Malaria. That was the sole reason why Economists Pascaline Dupas and Jessica Cohen created TAMTAM (which translates to "Together Against Malaria, Tunapenda Afya na Maisha", which in Swahili means "We love health and living" in the Busia language): to distribute insecticide-treated bed nets to the poor throughout health clinics in Kenya. But at the same time, PSI, the other NGO, was also doing the same. To determine whether their organization was still neccesary, the pair began varying price levels to perform a sensitivity analysis – how much did the poor man's demand for bed nets change in relation to the price? It was a lot: demand surged when nets were free, and dropped nearly to zero when they were subsidized to the PSI price ($.75). It was strange phenomenon: we touched on the financial impacts on buying a bed net – it increases labor productivity such that an individual's annual income will increase by at least 15%, on average. And yet, people with more income don't tend to buy more nets, even though that would be the common-sense thing to do: people who are 15% richer are only 5% more likely to buy a net than others. And therein lies the problem: even if you give everyone a *free* bed net, it would increase the # children living under a net from 47% to 52%, a mere 5% increase – negligible, at best.

Now here comes the real kicker: just because you buy, doesn't mean you use. That's exactly the caveat Together Against Malaria set out to answer: Do the poor actually use the free nets? 60%-70% of women who brought the net were actually using it. And there was negligible difference in usage between those who paid for it and those who didn't. To this day, Together Against Malaria continues its crucial mission of delivering nets to the poor in Africa, and has been endorsed by Nobel-Prize Winning Economists, Developmental Experts, and Journalists throughout the world for its essential and life-saving work.

9.4 How did Seva Mandir organize monthly immunization camps in communities and sharply reduce staff absenteeism in health facilities?

Seva Mandir means "Temple of Service" in Hindi. Indeed, the NGO has deployed all sorts of services for the poor; its contributions range from village develpoment to women empowerment to informal childrens' education. To highlight the scope and magnitude of the work Seva Mandir has conducted, I look to a few highlights of its work since its founding in 1968.

The state of immunization is dismal in India. In the particular village Seva Mandir was working in, less than 5% of children were receiving up-to-date immunizations. Given their potential (1.5 million die every year due to vaccine-preventable diseases) and cheap cost (free for these villagers), it seems nonsensical that villagers refused to take these life-saving ailments. It all came down to negligent nurses – one wrong cog tripping the entire system – who were often absent from their posts; mothers would walk all day to find a clinic, only to find it was empty. The frustration left villagers in pain, as they realized it was better not to bother going to the clinics anyway. That's where Seva Mandir stepped in. In 2003, Seva Mandir started up its own clinics, offering state-of-the-art, high quality full immunization services to the people of the village. It was a no-brainer: free, healthy, convenient, and reliable: the clinics operated on a regular basis, and staff were available on-site at all times. Now one problem of the health care machine was fixed: the negligent nurses. Now came another: the poor man himself! In the Seva Mandir villages, 77% of children received at least one vaccine. And yet,

Refath Bari

despite their initative, the % full immunization rates increased from 6% to only 17% – a meager 11% change. It wasn't publicity, either: Seva Mandir staff went village to village, door to door, advertising the initiative. All that work, and for what? A population that doesn't even demand the service! We're now stuck in a loop: these NGOs are going out of their way to provide the poor man effective vaccination, but the poor man refuses. What do you do when the subject refuses the service? The poor man goes out of his way to seek unreliable, incompetent health care, and yet refuses to accept the highest quality services when they're right in front him. Therein lies the poor man's paradox.

Despite the failure of the attendance monitoring system, Seva Mandir persisted and set up their own immunization clinics for the poor, but different from their past trail. This time, to entice the villagers to complete the full immunization course, they offered two pounds of dal (a mixture of dry beans and *johl*, or spice) for every vaccine shot and a bunch of cutlery and silverware for completing the whole course. These rewards were by no means expensive – the villagers themselves could have brought two pounds of dal with half-a-day's work, but nevertheless, Seva Mandir remained committed that the positive incentives would entice more villagers to complete their full immunizations. It was no less than a miracle: where vaccination rates used to 6%, they now shot up to 38%. Even better, it reduced the cost of immunization per person, because the government nurses (who were paid in advance) were working 24/7. After the tremondous success, Seva Mandir began working with the likes of Nobel-Prize Winning Economists to implement the save immunization programs elsewhere around the world, but came upon some resistance: many politicians, and even doctors claimed that they should 'Go Big or Go Home' – citing the fact that 38% immunization rate was far from perfect; WHO guidelines state that herd immunity is only reached upon 90% immunization of a nation, and 80% immunization of each district. And yet – we don't need herd immunity for a healthier community – by vaccinating one child, we prevent those around him (classmastes, teachers, and friends alike) from contracting disease. This alone is a public health milestone, and it can be accredited to the remarkable work of Seva Mandir.

10 Persistent Leaders' Significant Contributions to Public Health

This entire section was created for one man: James P. Grant. This man alone saved 25 million people – one man saved more lives than all of Hitler, Stalin, and Mao killed. Who is this man? Why is he not enshrined upon the thrones of history?

This section is devoted to the incredible and enduring life work of James P. Grant – who as the executive director of UNICEF – championed vaccination programs, promoted social entrepreneurship, and in the process saved millions of lives.

Table 9: An Unfortunate Government

1　How did one man save more than Hitler, Stalin, and Mussolini killed?

10.1 How did one man save more than Hitler, Stalin, and Mussolini killed?

Flip to any page in Time's 100 Most Influential. Any year. Any decade. Do you see the name "James P. Grant"? You shouldn't. Because he's not there. Search his name on Youtube, and you find no results. Who is this man so cryptic, yet so influential? This man alone saved more lives than Hitler, Stalin, or Mao combined killed. And yet he is not enshrined upon the thrones of his history. I hope to instill in you some sense of hope – that despite COVID19; despite Global Warming; despite all the headwinds and the backfires that the world throws at us, we can – and we will defeat poverty, if only we have some Jims to guide us along the way. Upon becoming the executive director of UNICEF, Jim launched the "Child Survival Revolution", because of which the worldwide vaccination rate quadrupled from 20% to 80%. By 1992, 4 million deaths were being prevented every year due to the immunization and diarrhea relief programs that Jim promoted. Millions of people, children and adults alike, have been the prime beneficiaries of Jim's work: millions of people with polio, Vitamin A deficiency, iodine deficincy, and otherwise health abnomoralities have had their lives saved by this one man. He is a man who consistently produced miracles – no more, no less. He *is* the miracle man – but his outcomes were no miracle. They were the results of decades of absolute dedication. He slept at 3 AM and woke at 6, shuffling between heads of state, insisting that they deploy vaccination programs, or diarrhea relief initiatives. He got personal, asking Presidents if their children visited the doctor routinely, and transitioned the conversation to the plight of the poor. He had a major breakthrough upon persuading the President of El-Salvador to hold a cease-fire during the El Salvador Civil War in early 1985. He convinced the president to hold that day of silence so that all the children on the ground could be vaccinated. Ever since, nations worldwide have recognized "Days of Tranquility", in which they hold cease-fire so that children get vaccinated. Jim Grant was a remarkable man, of remarkable stature, and he lived in his last days in his UNICEF

Refath Bari

Office, refusing to lay rest until his time came to pass: he led UNICEF until he resigned on January 23, 1995 and passed a few days later. And now – I end with his favorite quote: "'This is the true joy in life, the being used for a purpose recognised by yourself as a mighty one. I am of the opinion that my life belongs to the whole community and as long as I live it is my privilege to do for it whatever I can. Life is no brief candle to me. It is a sort of splendid torch which I have got hold of for the moment, and I want to make it burn as brightly as possible before handing it on to future generations.'" (Jim's favorite quote, with which he concluded his last State of the World's Children Report)

11 One Small Nudge for the Poor is One Giant Leap for Mankind

This section is dedicated to an idea: that one Small Nudge for the Poor is One Giant Leap for Mankind. This is one of those big ideas: the idea that I am alive because of a million tiny, incremental mechanisms that ensure my survival everyday, implemented by the government, private organizations, and public institutions alike. To illustrate the importance of a nudge, I ask you to look no further than water: if you are a poor man, you must remember to chlorinate your water *every, time* you drink water. This is no easy task, and one mistaken cup of unchlorinated water is all it takes for the waterborne viruses to invade your body. And here's the thing: if you put one drop too many of chlorine, it can cause all sorts of problems with one's health – asthma; and lung, skin, and eye irritation. And yet, I do not have to worry about this: the government pipes chlorinated water to my home. There. That one nudge has saved me countless visits to the hospital, bouts of diarrhea, and saved us lots of money. How can you nudge a community with no chlorine to pipe filtered water? Michael Kremer suggests a solution: install a chlorine dispenser that spits just the right amount of chlorine into a cup, and then mix it with your drinking water. Then I have this: schools, private and public alike, will refused your kids if they're not up-to-date on their vaccinations. That nudge right there saves me from the worry that my children will get infected from a horde of diseases at school, and forces me to vaccinate my child so he can receive his education. Small, effective nudges like these from the government may seem paternalistic, but they are the reason we are alive today. Understanding the importance of these small nudges is the key to ending poverty.

12 Moral of the Story III

I hope you grasped the key idea of this chapter – that being that there is very little that differentiates the poor man from his rich counterpart. Indeed, without the benefits of a free market, a democratic government, a capitalist economy, and an autonomous press – it is unlikely that could manage all the aspects of our own health (as the poor are left to do). And so, the morals of this story have far-ranging implications, from the pandemic we are living in today (May 2020, as of this writing) to our common psychological tendencies, there is many similarities between the poor man and his rich counterpart – and these are some of the similarities I want to highlight in this section. And now begin – the demarcation between the facts and fiction of poverty.

Table 10: Breaking the Falsehoods of Poverty

Fiction	Fact
What differentiates the rich man and his poor counterpart is the rich man's ability to be self-sufficient in his health – he takes all responsibility for his health, for exercise to calorie intake	I cannot speak for every individual in the world, but for the vast majority of us, this fact holds true: we *cannot* be self-sufficient. There must be some aspects of our life that the government is willing to regulate, from vaccinations to water purification to many other aspects of our health that we have come to take for granted. Later, we'll see how a developing nation can use 'nudges' to effectively implement public health initiatives. As such, we are indebted to the poor for teaching us the importance of small, incremental strides in public health, and how we subsist on those strides every day.

Refath Bari

Table 11: Breaking the Falsehoods of Poverty

Fiction	Fact
The poor man does not go to the doctor for life-threatening diseases because he doesn't care about his health	The truth couldn't be more different: the poor man stresses for his health day and night – indeed, the poor man is severely afflicted by stress, the primary cause of which is his health. Health is the poor man's ticket to Economic Development; Health affords the poor man nutrition, which affords him greater labor productivity and thus a greater standard of life. The poor man understands the importance of health. But sadly, he cannot come to pay for it. As such, we understand the source of the poor man's resistance as one of money, not belief.
Implementing rural water and sanitation is just unpragmatic. Look it: $20 a household every single month comes out to $240 annually just for one house.	This couldn't be farther from the truth. Gram Vikas is proof that affordable rural infrastructure can and does exist – by the sheer will and conviction of its Founder Joe Madiath and the thousands of public health workers it employs, Gram Vikas has implemented an infrastructure that entire governments and nations have failed in doing – the affordable infrastrcture of rural toilet and water. What's more, it has done so through full cooperation of all the communities it involves. Many of the communities that have agreed to work with Gram Vikas never had the high caste sharing anything with the poor. As such, Gram Vikas is proof that despite resistance, affordable rural infrastructure can be implemented.

Table 12: Breaking the Falsehoods of Poverty

Fiction	Fact
Given the decreasing rate of COVID19 cases around the world (as of May 2020), reopening schools and businesses and the economy will be of no danger to the public health.	Reopening the economy too quickly can lead to a public health disaster (i.e., South Korea). While this is a crisis still in the making, by the time you're reading this book, you know the end of the story. Nevertheless, I conjecture this: if we open the economy too soon, given the fact that people have not been up-to-date on their vaccines for quite some time (look no further than Michigan for evidence of this), it makes the public extremely vulnerable to disease outbreaks such as Measles, which have indeed been occuring prior to the outbreak. Let's not make rash decisions and sacrifice the health of our communities.
The poor man may buys treatments such as Oral Rehydration Therapy or Infesticide-trated bed nets, but he will use them, because they've been subsidized, and as such he does not value them.	There are all too many stories of people using their bed nets for – shall we say – creative purposes. Some have repurposed them as wedding veils, bathroom shower curtains, and flower pots. But, carefully conducted research shows that this anecdotal evidence is overblown, and far from the majority. We need only look to Jessica Cohen and Pascaline Dupas' NGO TAMTAM to observe the usage rates of subsidized bed nets: the pair found that over 60% of women who brought a net was using it. In other villages, over 90% of women were using the nets despite subsidized prices, and the usage difference between subsidized and market prices were statistically insignificant.

Refath Bari

Table 13: Breaking the Falsehoods of Poverty

Fiction	Fact
It will take too long for child mortality rates to drop significantly enough in poor countries to reach the rates of today's rich countries. Just extrapolate the data: it took 50 years just for the poor countries in the 1800s to catch up to their rich counterparts of the 1850s.	This is surely "the-glass-is-half-empty" perspective: technology has a way of acting as a catalyst. We need look no further than the Industrial Revolution or Green Revolution for evidence of this – during which resources came out of practically thin air. Thankfully, Thomas Malthus' bleak world view that high fertility rates would be the death of the world did not come to fruition. Technology, as Arthur C. Clark once so elegantly put it, has a way of being "indistinguishable from magic". I am optimistic that our medical and scientific breakthroughs will lead the way towards a brighter future for the children of the world.
The beauracrat is purposefully posing initiatives that will appeal to the public politically, but then does not consider how pramatic said initiatives are in the first place.	I'm not pointing fingers here. The bureaucrat has his own set of constituients he must report to and indeed, his initiatives are founded upon their reception to his policies and programs. However, I think too few leaders are aware, or even consider the type of ground-level work that must be conducted by health workers on a daily basis to execute their vision. This must be the danger in implementing public health initiatives – the founder and the executors of the initiatives must share the same vision. The founder must ensure the vision is *practical*, above all else, and ensure that the executors of the vision are faithfully doing their job.

Table 14: Breaking the Falsehoods of Poverty

Fiction	Fact
I say it cannot be done: Diarrhea, Pneumonia, Malaria – the list is endless. We cannot possibly save the poor from the diseases they face within a reasonable time span; it's too costly and it's too much of a hassle.	Many of this diseases already have affordable and effective treatments: diarrhea has ORS; Pneumonia has a vaccine; Malaria has bednets. And you're definitely right – there is an endless string of diseases that the poor are afflicted by, due to their sad living conditions. But that is not the whole truth – indeed, most of the poor are infected by just a handful of these diseases. In addition to having treatments for all these diseases, we also have the idea of 'herd immunity', right? All we need to get is a 80% vaccination rate (WHO Guidelines) in every state or country – and the other 20% will be accounted for, by virtue of herd immunity.
The poor man bases all his decisions of public health on faith because he has no high school education.	That's true to an extent. Indeed, faith is one's only compass when there's no government, doctors, private clinics, or education to support you. But the poor man also relies on faith – in part due to the negligence of the health care system, public and private alike. Public being unreliable and private being incompetent. And so, who can the poor man turn to but faith? He runs around between spiritual healers and herb-producing magic in a hope to cure his chronic and life-threatening illnesses – analagous to how we run around between chiropractors and our own healers in an effort to cure symptoms of diarrhea or chest pain.

Refath Bari

Table 15: Breaking the Falsehoods of Poverty

Fiction	Fact
Cost alone, no matter how small or big, distracts the poor man, and convinces him that he should not buy a product, no matter how life-saving it is.	Actually, that's right – to an extent. Human Physchology is hard to decipher, but recall the idea of the sunken cost effect and the human tendency for 'time inconsistency'. These two phenomenon combine to make the poor man – or anyopne, really – avoid the smallest cost, even if it means incurring that cost means saving their lives down the line. Recall the example I gave earlier: going for a jog every day, but feeling lazy, despite knowing it will save me a heart attack down the rope.
Private Health Care workers are more motivated to save lives, which is why they have much lower absenteeism than Public Health Care Workers, who are paid by the government upfront, and they feel no investment in public health, which is why they're not commited to the people.	The truth is that the private doctor won't be paid unless he's on his post – that doesn't neccesarily imply high-quality service, however (much like purchasing a product doesn't imply using it). The public doctor, however, is paid upfront, and therefore has much less incentive to actually be at his post – he can be absent half the time, still receive the same salary, and still claim he's saved some lives (whether that claim is valid or not). In a way, incentives are the name of the game at the end of the day. Buereacts, Politicians, and Supervisors all play a role in what happens on the ground – as such, it is up to their responsibility to ensure that qualified doctors have the incentive to come in to work in a reliable manner.

Table 16: Breaking the Falsehoods of Poverty

Fiction	Fact
It's just too much – look at it: troubled bureaucracies, assent health workers, and incompetent doctors make ending worldwide poverty impossible.	I ask you to look no further than Jim Grant. I already shared with you some of his amazing work, but now I share his methodology: Jim would get personal and persistent. As Executive Director of UNICEF, he had access to heads of states around the globe, and he would often ask them about their own children – and lead the conversation into the children of their state or nation. Jim would often stay up late in the night, examining suggested initiatives for getting vaccines to every child in a state, and shaking his head and laughing "It can be done, it can be done." Jim sometimes carried an ORS packet in his pocket and pulled it out, telling a head of state that this five-cent solution could save five million lives. This was Jim's methodology.
The absenteeism problem in the public health care industry can be solved by setting up governmental boards that serve as elective bodies that monitor the attendance and performance of the health care workers.	As we've seen from Seva Mandir's intitiative, this is far from the case. Indeed, these kinds of monitoring programs persuade, and perhaps make it more likely, that health care workers. The fact of the matter is that these monitoring programs may in fact persuade health care workers to revolt, or be more absent from their work than they were previously, another telling sign of the Seva Mandir program. As such, we must carefully consider the nuances of these systems if we truly seek to set up a monitoring program for them.

Chapter 6

Education

Refath Bari

55 Days in Dharavi

Education is the poor man's stepping stone onto the ladder of socioeconomic de-velopment. We began with Baudghiri as a case study in Education, after which we explore 13 key themes: (1) The State of the Poor Man's Education (2) Private Schools are better than their Public Ones (3) The Supply & Demand of Education (3) Top-Down Education Policy (4) A Capital Boost to the Poor (5) Private Schools (6) Pratham & Co. show Education Reform (7) The 3 Key Players of Education (8) Why the Poor Man's School fails in it's premise and methodology, (9) Industry Has Found Talent, Not School, (10) Reforming Education, bottoms-up (11) A Class-room's resources, from textbooks to cirriculums (12) Understanding Jean Paiget and William Perry's Theories of Cognitive Development (13) An examination of various teaching advances

Keywords: Early Algebra, Flipped Classroom, Peer Collaboration, Polya's Prescrip-tion, Problem Posing, Bloom's Taxonomy, Peer Scaffolding, Tracking, Differentia-tion, Homogenous/Heterogenous Grouping, Abstraction, Numerical Development, Pratham, Supply & Demand, Top-Down vs Bottom-Up, (Un)Conditional Cash Trans-fer, No-Excuse Schools

1 Case Study: Baudghiri

He insists he only has one name. "Baudghiri, bhai. Or if that's too hard for you, Badu bhai, ay?" We agree on Badu. Badu bhai looks 60 or older, but he he insists on 40. "I don't know when I was born, but around the green revolution", he says. "Oh so you know Swaminathan (Father of Green Revolution)". "Oh yes yes", Badu says nodding in agreement. But I was here for no revolution – I was here for Education, indeed the very education that has kept classrooms the same for the last hundred years. Badu says he has four children, but only two go to school. "How old are they?" "4 of them: Polamma is 5, Sanoj is 8, Vanita is 14, and

Refath Bari

Salvi is 16" he says, nodding off into space. "Polamma goes to Bharatiya Vidya Bhavan and Salvi goes to Ansar". I stand confused for a minute: "Are they public or private?" "Polamma goes to private and Salvi goes to public." "Why only two?" I ask. "Sanoj is old enough to work, and so is Vanita. Salvi only goes to school one or two days and the other days he works. So he get both, money and school" I was starting to understand – this was a crash course on Risk Management. Badu continues, "the last one, Polamma is the smart one, so we have her go to private." "Why did you put Salvi in public but Polamma in private?" Badu strokes his long and not-imaginary beard. I realize he looks like a Mystic, with his cloudy beard, pink shirt, and blue *lungi.*

Figure 1: Were they staring at me or Badu *bhai*? It was midday sun in Kerala and the weather definitely wasn't on to me

I try to ignore the stares in my direction as we sit on the bench. "Salvi was our first one, and we thought we won't have any more." I was going to ask, but

I stopped. A simple few sparkles embezzle his necklace: "These are for prayer; I give people God and they give me money" Not a bad exchange, I say. "No, not at all. I get $1.50, but all the poor have to spend on food. Not me." Badu says, defiantly. I'm a bit skeptical, though. "How?" "Bhai, I go temple to temple, door to door, house to house. Where there is people, I go. I give my prayer to every one, and sometimes they give me food." He goes on, "Every day in the Guardwara [what we call, in the local parlance, Hindu Temples of Worship], they have the metal plate with little dal, little *Dosa*, little chutney, one somassa, everything you want, they have;" Badu says. "I just go, take some for me, the wife and go. That's it", he slaps his palms and gets up. "Oh no no, Badu *bhai*, little more, please. I'm almost done," I fish for some money magically find 50 Rupees. Badu's eyes widens, but he shakes his head. "I cannot take the free money, *bhai*. Let me give you my prayer, then I earn the money." What can I do? So I say yes, and Badu *bhai* gives me his prayer. He finally takes the 50 Rupees. "OK, OK. Back to school. First One's in public, smart one's in private." I say, hoping for Badu's approval. Instead, he's staring blankly into space, his eyes half-dozing. "Badu. Badu *bhai*", I say. Finally he wakes up: "Is the private school better than the public?" "Well, we are paying money, right? So it better be good. It takes out 10% of our money every month, so it's no joke. Please," Badu says. He murmurs a little something, and I hope its a prayer in my name. "How do you they're giving education and not just taking money?" I say, hoping to instill some doubt in his mind. But he'll have none of it: "Salvi tell me his teacher is absent almost every day. But Polamma, she never complains. That sound like just taking money to you?" I don't get Badu's point, but I nod anyway. "10% of your money every month. That's a lot of money" I persist, "Yeah, Books, Uniforms, this, that. Thousand things, but I don't care, as long as she learns" Badu says. "But how do you know if they're learning?" I shoot. It was the exact same question I'd asked an American Specialized High School teacher a couple weeks back. Now here I was on the flip side, asking the parent. Badu leans back, almost uncomfortable. His face, so calm for so long, twists and his shoulders slump under the blazing sun. He breathes a long and deep sigh, "I really hope she learns. The kids don't know how to lie, so I believe her." He crosses his arms and looks away, "You know, us old people from these places, ..." he looks at me, hoping I can finish the sentence. "You know, it doesn't have to be this way" I suggest, but Badu shakes his head. "What other way can it be?" "Sorry". "No, no, you gave me enough, *bhai*, and now I must go" But for all his talk, Badu *bhai* stays awhile and finally we talk without the guise of a interview. He reluctantly gets up to go, and I follow his lead. We both hesistate awhile and when Badu sees my tear, he offers not his prayer, but a hug. And I accept.

2 Badu's List

I need not speak to the importance of Education: higher thinking and creativity are the obvious benefits, but there are far subtler returns, unexpected to both the poor and rich man alike. We explore some of these returns in this chapter. But I go farther – this chapter is wholly devoted to four key goals. Here they are:

(I) The Poor Man's School

(II) Supply-Demand, Top-Down Approach to Education

(III) Pratham leads Education Reform in Developing Countries

(IV) Looking to a 2020 View of Education

Each key goal will have a set of associated questions, which will be explained in detail. We conclude the chapter – as always – by establishing the line of demarcation between the fact and fiction of poverty. There is much to cover, so let us commence.

3 The Poor Man's School

We begin by establishing the state of the poor man's education. Over the last quarter-century, largely due to the initiative offered by the Millenium Goals, the poor man has access to a wide variety of schools, both public and private alike. So the quantity is definitely there. But the quality? Now that's a much harder question to answer, and it is one we hope to understand throughout the chapter.

Table 1: Schools: Quantity or Quality

1 What is the status of the poor man's education?

2 Doesn't high enrollment mean high learning?

3 Do the poor have access to school?

3.1 What is the status of the poor man's education?

First and foremost, let me speak to the fact that the world is getting smarter. As Primary Education becomes a staple throughout developing and developed nations alike, so is literacy.

Literate and illiterate world population
Population 15 years and older.

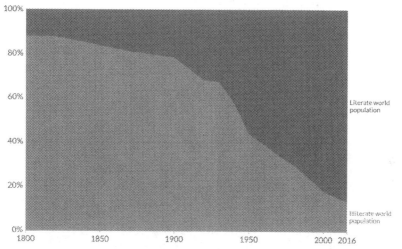

Figure 2: In just a matter of 200 years, mankind has made significant strides in universal literacy – and this is no statiscal gimmick, at that.

Before we get to the state of the poor man's education, we look to what our goals are.

Definition 3.1: Millenium Development Goals

At the start of the new millenium, every nation in the world agreed to achieve eight key goals in 15 years. Needless to say, many of them haven't kept their promise. Nevertheless, the Millenium Development Goals, established by the United Nations, have served as a key initiative towards global progress and has spurred action on the international stage to defeat the likes of Child Mortality, Extreme Poverty, and Lack of Primary Education. The Second and Third MDGs concern education, them being "Ensure that, by 2015, children everywhere, boys and girls alike, will be able to complete a full course of primary schooling" and "Eliminate gender disparity in primary and secondary education, preferably by 2005, and in all levels of education, no later than 2015"

Let me start with Pratham. Pratham is an Indian-Based NGO that collects data on the literacy of Indian Children based on a representative sample size. They

Refath Bari

do so via the ASER – Annual Survey in Education Report. Pratham begins with some 600 volunteers, each of whom they disperse to a few hundred villages – these volunteers then make the rounds, testing a random group of children in the village on their mathematics and reading skills using the ASER Assessment. Volunteers then compile childrens' results based on their grade standard and send them to Pratham. Here are the results of the 2020 ASER Survey.

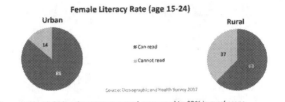

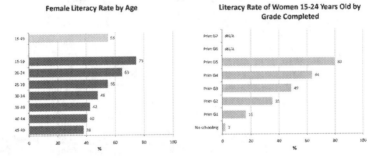

The data was paradoxical, if not strange. Good news first: over 90% of 4-8 years old are in school, and school enrollment actually increases in a certain age range: 91.3% among four year olds and 99.5% among eight year olds.

And yet, even among these first and second graders, cracks were starting to show – gender inequity resulted in more girls in public schools and more boys in private schools (this begs the question: are parents discriminating between their children?; after all, private schools are more expensive and India has a cultural, generational, and sometimes religious preference towards boys). 61% of girls ages 6-8 go to public schools, whereas only 52% boys do. There is also a huge disparity in what children are actually doing – 70% of 5-year olds are in Anganwadis, which are essentially rural day-care centers that also double as health care clinics in rural villages. These Anganwadis provide immunisation, health-checkups, Oral Rehydration Salts, Reproductive Care, and other basic health services. Here's a look at the three main types of schools children attend – Private, Government/Public, and Anungawadis:

Primary school enrollment, 1870 to 2010

Estimated enrollment ratios for total population aged 15-64, primary education level. Estimates adjusted with repetition ratios.

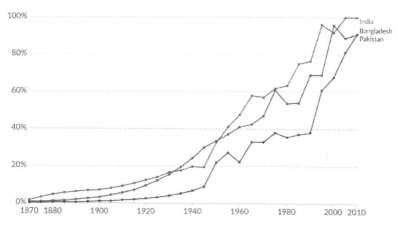

Figure 3: Primary School Enrollment has steadily grown in the thee trios that make up Southeast Asia, all hovering near total enrollment.

State	Anganwadi centers		Private preschools		'Known4 Practice' centers		Government Primary School		Total Sample	
	Progr ams	Child ren	Prog rams	Child ren	Prog rams	Child ren	Progr ams	Child ren	Prog rams	Child ren
Assam	101	602	10	58	6	16			117	676
Telan gana	54	257	54	402	13	91	6	26	127	776
Rajas than	10	48	33	369	9	76	2	14	54	507
Total	165	907	97	829	28	183	8	40	298	1959

Figure 4: The Distribution of Primary-School Aged Children Across Different Types of School

22% of 5-year-olds are in Standard 1, and for 6-year-olds, Anganwadi enrollment drops to 33%, and 46% are in Standard 1, with the rest in Standard 2.

And yet, despite the high enrollment rates in primary education, not many kids are learning: across all of India, only 26% of enrolled schoolchildren ages 5-16 can do simple division. This is not good. Reading isn't much better: 48% of schoolkids ages 5-16 can read a second grade paragraph. India is no isolated case

Refath Bari

Table 2: A Brief Overview of Indian Primary Schools

Type	Overview
Gov't Anganwadis	Limited class aids for learning; Most children below 4; Low Participation and small classes mean small student:teacher ratios; No defined schedule; Some formal teaching, but mostly play with prosocial activities; Local community worker with little training
Private Schools	Better infrastructure, but very few resources; most children are same age, and high student to teacher ratios (sometimes enrollment exceeds 100% as both under and over-age children attend overcrowded schools); fixed daily schedule with supervision; mostly formal teaching, rote memorization, no age-appropriate activities (i.e., manipulatives/pictorials) and teachers remain untrained in early childhood education
NGO/Local Schools	Limited infrastructure, but appropriate learning materials; heterogenous age groups; optimal student to teacher ratio; flexible cirriculum, adjustable in case of miststeps or otherwise unexpected hiccups. Community teacher with professional development and age-appropriate aids are available.

– we observe the same phenomenon in Pakistan, Kenya, and other developing nations around the world. In Pakistan, for instance, 80% third graders couldn't read a first grade paragraph. What's going on? Why are enrollment rates so high and yet student achievement outcomes so low?

3.2 Doesn't high enrollment imply high learning?

And here comes the kicker: just like purchasing a life-saving bed net doesn't mean you use it, enrolling your child in school doesn't actually mean you send them every day. Even worse, for the many kids who do attend school, the quality is subpar and far from what one would expect from a nation of one billion that is home to 5% of the world's billionaires. So, what's the catch? Do the poor have access to school? Are parents resistant to putting their children in school? Is there even a demand for a skilled labor force? We begin by adressing the latter two questions. There is certainly no willful parental resistance to putting kids in schools. Not only is student enrollment high, attendance follows closely: 95% of of children attended primary school at some time in 2006. So the hiccup definitely isn't in the parental resistance, as we clearly see from both the data and Badu's experience as a father of two school-children, one of whom he sacrifices 10% of his monthly income for.

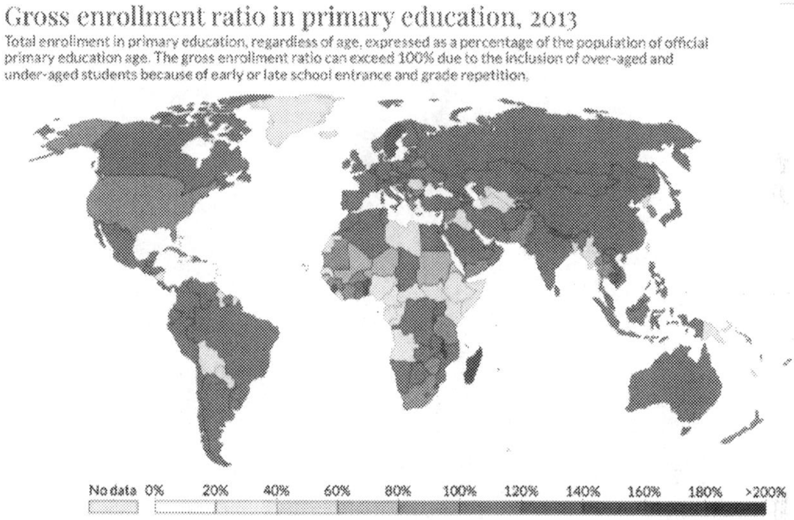

Gross enrollment ratio in primary education, 2013

Total enrollment in primary education, regardless of age, expressed as a percentage of the population of official primary education age. The gross enrollment ratio can exceed 100% due to the inclusion of over-aged and under-aged students because of early or late school entrance and grade repetition.

No data 0%   20%   40%   60%   80%   100%   120%   140%   160%   180%   >200%

Figure 5: Perhaps due to the UN's MDG initiatives, Primary Education has spread throughout the vast majority of the world; If over or under-age students are also attending primary classes, enrollment can exceed 100%

What about the labor force? Is there a demand for an educated labor force? Every Indian industry you look to will answer yes, most important of which is the Indian Technology Sector. Take Infosys, the second largest Indian Information Technology Company. Their Recruitment Process values unorthodox, creative thinking over rote, meomrized textbook knowledge. Their recruitment process begins with a test that anyone can walk in to a hiring center and take. It consists of three sections: Arithmetic Reasoning and Analytical Thinking (Quantitative ability), Communicative English (verbal ability) and Mathematical Critical Thinking and Logical Reasoning (logical ability). Applicants that pass the initial stage will be guided through a tehnical interview on their knowledge on software and hardware development. Look no further than home of India's IT Capital, in Karnataka Bangalore, where there is a high demand for Software Engineers, Product

Refath Bari

Managers, and Hardware Developers. All these jobs require significant educational attainment, but also compensate with a hefty salary, which is by all means an incentive to the poor man. So: there exists a demand for an educated work force. And Parents are willing to educate their children. What's the hitch?

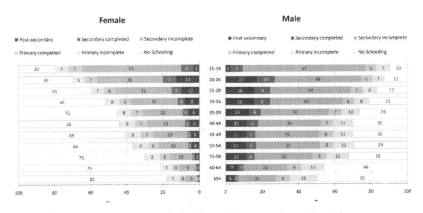

Figure 6: Large Gender Disparities still plague the Indian Education System, leaving a lot to be desired

3.3 Do the poor have access to school?

There's no excuse for this one: Urban and Rural poor alike, most have access to a school within a kilometer. Since India promised free education to all children up to age 14 in 1950, and made education a mandatory and fundamental right via a constitutional amendment in 2002, the number of schools have exploded: Primary Schools jumped from 530,000 in 1986 to 770,000 in 2005 and Secondary Schools jumped from 130,000 in 1986 to 280,000 in 2005. By 2003, 88% homes, huts, and shanties alike had a school within a kilometer. Schools are certainly available and many of them are free and accessible to the poor. So what's going wrong? This is the question we intend to explore this chapter.

4 Supply-Demand, Top-Down Approach to Education

Here comes the big idea: Education, like any other product, is an investment. We buy it and we expect there to be returns to it, preferably in the near future. Like any product, education must deal the question of equilibrium – the harmony between Supply and Demand.

Table 3: **Schools: Quantity or Quality**

1 What is the Supplier-Demander Approach to Education?

2 Do we prioritize Quantity over Quality?

3 Does Absenteeism Plague the Education Industry?

4 Why does Demand for Education matter?

5 What does the Parent see Education as?

6 Are incentives the key to fundamental education reform?

7 Does Top-Down Education Deliver?

8 What about Private Schools?

4.1 What is the Supplier-Demander Approach to Education?

Let me explain: Let's take the position of the Suppliers for a minute. These are International Organizations like WHO, UNICEF, and heads of state that argue that there simply isn't enough schools to go around. There must first exist schools for there to be an education in the first place, they argue. But the Demanders content something different – the best education is no education at all, they say. Instead of forcing education upon the people, making it constitutionally compulsory to put your child in school, incentivize education. Produce a job market that requires significant educational attainment to enter, and people will naturally want their children to become better educated so that they can capture those jobs. Parents will then pressure teachers to teach better, and schools to increase engagement. Soon, the private market will start competing over parents for their children, and the result will be ideal schools, each of which – in competing with each other – create the ideal educational environment for their students. Who's right? The supplier who argues we must create schools and impress upon parents the importance of education? Or the demander, who argues we must incentivize education and let parents do the rest of the work (i.e., lobbying, petitioning, pressuring schools and administrations)? This is a fragile question, one that can slip into both the demander and suppliers' territory, so we hope to examine it by experiment instead of conjecture.

Refath Bari

4.2 Do we prioritize Quantity over Quality?

Let's start with what they have in common: Suppliers and Demanders alike agree that schools must exist. Indeed, that is the basis of their whole argument: the existence of schools to proliferate literacy among the masses. And yet, in both the international and local circles, suppliers and demanders alike miss a basic requirement: quality. What use is educating children if all we're teaching them are rote algorithms? To understand just how low a priority quality seems to be to policy-makers, we only need look at UNESCO's Education for All Summit at the turn of the millennium, where out of six initiatives, improving the quality of education was the last. By this measure alone, we begin to understand the cracks in both the Supplier and Demanders' claims: having schools isn't enough; we must ensure they're providing children a quality education, a goal far easier said than done.

Population breakdown by highest level of education achieved for those aged 15+, India, 1970 to 2050

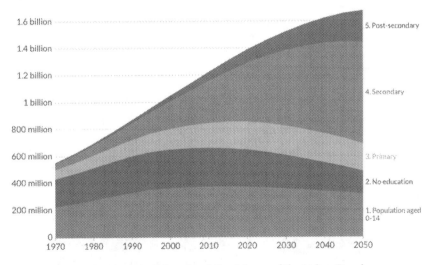

Figure 7: By 2050, the Educational Breakdown of the Indian Populace above 15 years old is expected to be mostly secondary education.

4.3 Does Absenteeism Plague the Education Industry?

Here the cracks start to show: we've already seen lack of initiative of improving education, but ... who says education needs improving in the first place? The data:

we need only look to the World Bank, who sent agents to schools around developing nations unannounced. When agents scattered class to class, and school to school, they found one common denominator across schools in Bangladesh, Indonesia, Ecuador, and Peru: teachers miss one out of every five days of work. The absenteeism rate in India was even worse, at about 25%, as of 2014. One teacher with a 'long and distinguished career' was absent 23 of her 24 years. And since teachers are by far (rightfully) the largest expenditures of India's education initiative, these absences are costing the government more than $1.5 billion every year, the equivalent of the infrastructure damage caused by a Category 1 Hurricane. The absenteeism rates varied between 15% in Maharashtra to 42% in Jharkhand.

Total government expenditure on education, 1971 to 2016

Total general government expenditure on education (all levels of government and all levels of education), given as a share of GDP.

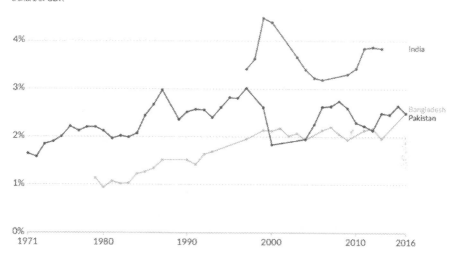

Figure 8: Of the three trio Southeastern Countries, India spends the most on education, at almost 4% of its GDP. Bangladesh has recently begun increasing its expenditure on Education, and Pakistan is starting to steady.

Salary or Qualifications has nothing to do with it – experienced and educated teachers, who are paid more, were just as often absent as their less qualified and less well-paid counterparts. Believe it or not, it gets worse: even when teachers are in the classroom, they're not teaching half the time. In fact, independent researchers have found that teachers, public and private alike, spend half their time drinking tea, reading the newspaper, talking to colleagues, or some doing

Refath Bari

some otherwise non-teaching activity. This should read like a Satirical Piece, and yet this is the true reality in many Indian schools. Now the question changes from "Why aren't children learning despite enrollment? to "How can children possibly learn?"

4.4 Why does Demand for Education matter?

Demand is key to Education. We see this from the data: school enrollment is highly sensitive to parental perception of educational returns. To understand this, we can examine two phenomenon: (1) The Green Revolution; and (2) Business Process Outsourcing (BPO) Call Centers – both of which occured in India.

(1) **Green Revolution**: The Green Revolution jumpstarted in Mexico during the early 1950s, but then spread to India by the '60s.

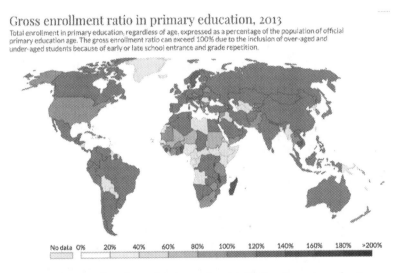

Gross enrollment ratio in primary education, 2013

Total enrollment in primary education, regardless of age, expressed as a percentage of the population of official primary education age. The gross enrollment ratio can exceed 100% due to the inclusion of over-aged and under-aged students because of early or late school entrance and grade repetition.

No data 0%   20%   40%   60%   80%   100%   120%   140%   160%   180%   >200%

Figure 9: Due largely to the demand and initiative for universal primary education throughout the world, primary education has become a staple through developing and developed nations alike.

At the turn of the new decade in 1960, India's Agriculture Minister Dr. M. S. Swaminathan invited American Agronomist and Father of the Green Revolution Norman Borlaug to assist the nation with its food supply. Borlaug introduced high-yielding varieties of wheat (dubbed 'Miracle Rice' by Indian farmers) to India, which greatly increased the food security of the nation, enabling it to feed the rich and poor alike in much greater quantities. In turn, the Green Revolution asked for much greater skill in farming to achieve much greater returns. As such, educated farmers were often more profitable during the revolution than their unschooled peers. When families realized schools now had a much higher value (since increased the students' technical capacity in farming and agriculture alike), school enrollment and educational outcomes increased in the areas where the Green Revolution was taking place (primarily Punjab). This phenomenon demonstrates the high sensititivity parents have towards the perceived returns from Education

(2) **BPO Call Centers**: Do Labor Market Oppurtunities affect young women's oppurtunities in India?

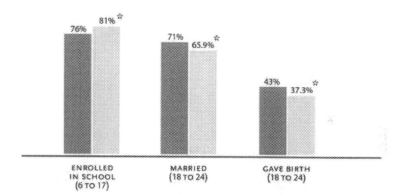

Figure 10: (Yellow = Treatment/Blue = Control) Jensen's BPO Intervention had wide-ranging effects on women fertility, and education.

To answer that questoin, UCLA Economist Robert Jensen embarked on a three year journey to the BPO Call Centers of India, a still-new, yet relatively flourisihing market. We all know the image of the young girl dropping out of school to marry and have many children. This unfortunate outcome is a common developmental indicator of low socioeconomic status of women. But can this outcome be changed? In other words, can we somehow persuade women to stay in school by incentivizing education? This is the very question that Jensen proposed, and he set out to test it in Delhi, India. By advertising and guiding young women to this new market with the added restriction that they must have the educational qualifications, Jensen single-handedly

Refath Bari

demonstrated the power of incentivizing education: during the period of the study, women were less likely to drop out of school, and in fact had less fertility rates as a result, along with increased career aspirations and desires to work in the labor market or enter post-school vocational training.

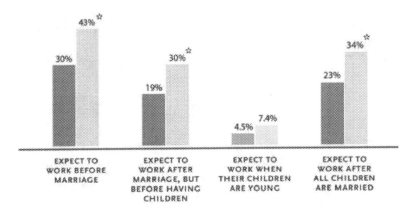

Figure 11: Jensen's BPO Intervention made the women in the treatment more ambitious, as evident from their desire to devote more of their lives to their careers, and not marriage

Figure 12: The Intervention had significant effects on women's employment; some women resorted to migration for the sake of work.

At the same time, Jensen found that girls in the experimental group were 5% more likely to be enrolled in a school than their control counterparts; girls also weighed more in the experimental regions after the study, perhaps because parents were taking better care of their investments. Therein lies the power of incentivizing education: one can fundamentally change the educatoinal outcomes of a population, no matter how resistant or unlikely they are.

Those two phenomenon alone demonstrate the efficacy of incentivizing education, and play to the demander's argument that education need not be forced. Instead, parents must understand the financial benefits of education, as in both the case of the Green Revolutoin and the BPO Call Centers – where praents realized education would have higher economic returns, school enrollment increased and parents began investing more into their chlid's learnning, demanding that government schools be of higher quality and admitting their children into competitive institutions.

4.5 What does the Parent see Education as?

But while parents certainly want the best for their children, they may not achieve it through the same means. In effect, Parents may see education as either an investment (as the Suppliers and Demanders propose) or a gift, or perhaps both.

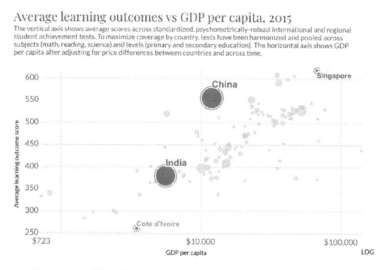

Figure 13: And how does the Government view Education? As a worthwhile investment, no less: countries with higher GDP per capita also have more student achievements in intellectual tests

Parents who see education as a gift may invest much into their childrens' education only for the benefit of telling their neighbors about it, or feeling proud of their childs' learning – even though they may not receive any actual financial benefits from their child's education. And then there's the all-too-true fear parents have that despite their dedicated investment in their child's education, their child will neglect them in old age, and the investment will effectively have been wasted. For that reason alone, some parents refuse to educate their children, who they fear will move out of their homes once reaching sufficient age. And then there's the parent with the idea that they must receive tangible, financial benefits for their investments in their child's education; such parents may fail to see any benefit to education after a few grades, and thus send their children to the fields, from which they can actually earn income. And here comes the suppliers' argument: such parents would ravage the future of their children simply on a whim or a flick. As such, the importance of education must be thoroughly impressed upon parents – an ideal already implemented in every developed country from the United States to Europe, where children must be placed in school for a certain age range, or otherwise be proved to be in homeschool. But realize that implementing such school policy requires a certain order of financial security and educational infrastructure – the two very things that developing nations don't have. So how can poor countries do what the rich are already doing (ensure all children attend school, parental-consent or not)? The key is incentives, or as Santiago Levy proposed, "Conditional Cash Transfers."

4.6 Are incentives the key to fundamental education reform?

For Poor and Rich; Developing and Developed; Third and First World alike, Conditional Cash Transfers are the answers to all their prayers (or most of them, as Badu reminded me). Conditional Cash Transfers, or CCTs, are effectively a monetary incentive – think of it as a capital boost to get the poor up and climbing the socioeconomic ladder – designed to persuade the poor to do things they otherwise wouldn't (think sending all their children to school, or having less children). The idea of CCT began with one man: Economics Professor Santiago Levy of Boston University. As Deputy Minister of the Mexican Ministry of Finance from 1994 to 2000, Levy wanted to create an effective, long-lasting intervention in the lives of the poor that would entice them to seek preventative health care and send their child to school via postiive incentives. Guising it as compensation for forgone labor (income lost as a result of sending children to school instead of work), Levy initially implemented a pilot program using Randomized Control Trials. Following a successful evaluation, Levy implemented the intiative as OP-URTUNIDADES, which turned out to be a hit among the poor: Secondary School Enrollment increased by 8% for Girls and 2% for boys, and increased educational outcomes for the poor all over Mexico. The initiative was such a success that in the years thereafter, govrenments around the world began using randomized control trails and conditional cash transfers to coax the poor to attend schools and seek health care services. This begs the question, then – is the contract part really neccesary? In other words, will this type of transfer work?: Promise the poor man money, but don't make education a mandatory requirement as part of the transfer. Will the poor man still send his children to school? The common sense answer is no. I mean, if going to school isn't part of the contract, why would the poor man do it? But as a matter of fact, in a study conducted by the World Bank, the conditoinality in CCT wasn't really neccesary – conditoinal or unconditoinal, the key point was this: if the poor man received money, he would naturally do what every reasonable person would do, which is seek out schools and health care (in the study by the World Bank, school dropout was reduced from 11% for families who did not receive money to 6% for families who did). It turned out that the poor man already wanted to do those things, but did not have the capital to do them. The moral of the story is this: both conditoinal and unconditional cash transfer programs can persuade the poor to educate their children, because the poor man needs capital, not incentive (i.e., they may not be able to afford school uniforms, textbooks, fees, or forgone labor). In effect, CCT and UCTs alike give parents breathing space – an opportunity to examine their lives on a broader scale, instead of being forced to think on a day-to-day basis. Parents may realize the importance of education is in paying the costs early in life so that children realize the benefits later once they go into the labor market or agricultural industry. In sum: parents pay for their children's education early, and education pays back far more in the form of greater job prospects, financial security, and agricultural know-how. Now here comes a key idea: Household income greatly influences a child's educatoinal attainment. We look to a family who earns a dollar a day versus one who earns $6-$10 a day – since fertility rates are inversely proportoinal to Income (as we examined in the previous chapter), families have more of their income to spend on less children, thus resulting in higher investment in any one child. It is because of this exact phenomenon that the rich get smarter and the poor don't – rich kids who may not be talented get more access to higher-quality education services than the poor child who receives – at best – a low-quality public school education that does nothing to highlight their talent. And here is where the demander's argument fails. Where the demander is true that education must be incentivized so that parents demand better educational outcomes from their children, we must realize one thing: if we leave it to the free market to identify talent, the poor will never be recognized for the talent that they inevitably have (look no further than the many poor social entrepenuers or billion-dollar IT companies with high school dropouts on their board or as CEOs). If we do listen to the supplier's argument that every village should have a school that provides quality-education, we can make the dream that "every child gets a chance" a reality.

4.7 Does Top-Down Education Deliver?

But first of all, what is Top-Down Education? Top Down Education Policy begins with reforms at the top level – it begins with the Government, descends to the Schools, adopted by the teachers, and implemented in the classroom. Top-Down Education Policy has some drawbacks – first and foremost being a sense of compulsion, in that teachers feel that their hand is forced on these reforms. Furthermore, many of these reforms are implemented hastily, so that teachers and students alike don't have much time to process changes to the curriculum. Then there's the reverse idea: the Bottom-Up Theory, which is that change begins at the grassroots level, with the teacher. Teachers are the ones who initiate changes to classroom learning, which ascends to changes made to school structures, which eventually influences government policy. There is a sense that this is much harder because it begins at the grass roots level, but the bottom-up theory may have its pros. Perhaps the best educational polices are those that combine the best of both worlds – top down and bottom up, which we denote as Integrated Theory. But Top-Down rebounds! The demanders claim that where there exists no schools, that must be the consequence of no demand for schools by parents. But the Top-Down approach proves otherwise. We now examine various countries, from Indonesia, to Taiwan, to Malawi, to Kenya, all of which were able to succesfuly increase students' educational outcomes in school through a top-down approach:

(1) **Indonesia**: 1973 was a jumpstart year for Indonesia. It was the year of the Oil Embargo, after which Indonesia's role in the world economy switched from that of an oil exporter to importer, and has experienced steady economic growth since the Oil Boom. At the time, Indonesia's Second President, Suharto, began a development project that initiated the rapid construction of schools. It was very much inspired by the top-down, supplier approach: districts that had the most number of illiterate children was where construction began. Now, from the demander's perspective, this is a disaster-in-progress, a failure waiting to happen. For if there were no schools, it was because the market didn't create them; because parents did not demand them! And yet,

the *INPRES* program proved them far wrong – the program was a definitive success, increasing primary school enrollment ratios up to 90% in just
a decade and drastically reduced the educational disparity between boys and
girls. The educatoinal dividends were clear. What about the financial? It was
even better: Nobel-Prize Winning MIT Professor of Economics Esther Duflo
conducted a study in Indonesia on the returns of education in these Indonesian schools, and found the financial returns to be statistically significant:
For every extra year of primary education that these children received, their
wages increased by 8%, educational returns similar to those of the United
States'

(2) **Developing Countries:** Indonesia is no isolated case – developing countries
around the world have implemented this supply-based, demand-driven approach. We take Taiwan as an example, where the nine years of compulsory
schooling was signed into law in 1968. Now – assuming the terrible innefi-
ciency of buraeacries, the complaints regarding the top-down approach, and
the demander's claims that the best school is no school, such a legislation
would seem doomed for failure. As a matter of fact, it proved all the critics otherwise: that law alone reduced dropout rates of 4-15 year olds by 4%,
and increases the # years of schooling by 0.22. But the benefits are far from
just educational: the law motivated girls to stay in school for longer, made
it less likely that they would become pregnant, reduced fertility rates, and
thus also reduced child mortality rates, all the while girls had greater status
due to their higher educational attainment and greater skill. Malawi, an East
African country, implemented the same approach using Conditional Cash
Transfers and found similar results, and so did Kenya.

At the end of the day, it comes down to this: every drop of education is crucial, primary, secondary, or otherwise – simply because you don't know when
you're going to use it. Grant Sanderson, a Stanford Math Graduate and an all-
around Math Recreationalist once walked into a room of Pixar Engineers and
asked "How many of you use the Quadratic Equation more than once a month?"
Of course, looking back, he regrets he asked the question in a room full of engineers, because the answer was that animation – Pixar's Specialty – requires lots
of mathematical hardware, from Quadratic Equations to Ray-Tracing to Linear
Algebra. The point is that you never know what concepts you learn in school
you'll run into in real life. If you say my example too far-fetched, many of the
children of poor social entrepenuers or buisnessmen are their in-home accoun-
tants, managing business transactions or other behind-the-napkin calculations

Refath Bari

at the speed of light. Even more practically, in the case of natural disasters or otherwise unexpected incidents, the poor man can usually advantage of some government programs, which are advertised via newspapers or bulletin boards, neither of which the poor man can read if he doesn't have the baseline education. Even being a good farmer means understanding the ins-and-outs of agricultural practices, fertilizers, and pesticides – all of which, again, require a basic baseline education. Now I want to look at the bigger picture. We've seen many examples of the supply-driven education infrastructure at work and we've seen their succesfful implementatoin through a variety of developing countries. Now we turn our attention from supply to demand. And what is the most prominent example of demand in the poor man's education? None other than private schools. Are private schools the answer to the poor man's prayer (Badu *bhai* says yes)? India sure thinks so: in fact, the Indian Legislative Bodies passed the India Right of Children to Free and Compulsory Act in 2009 to guarantee free education to all children between ages 6 and 14.

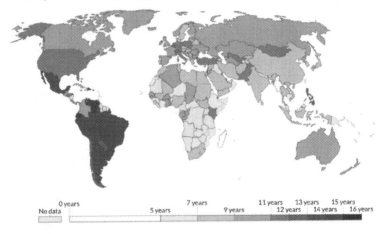

Duration of compulsory education, 2013
The number of years that children are legally obliged to attend school.

Figure 14: India is far from the only country to implement supply-driven mandatory schooling. More developed countries like the US and Europe have implemented the exact approach.

In addition, the Right of Children Act provided the poor vouchers to subsidize the costs of private schools. When first introduced, the Right to Education Act was launched under the guise of a huge advertising blitz, as India joined the 134 other countries (out of 195) that made Education a right for all. Sad to say it didn't work out. As Times of India itself found in a 2016 investigation, the Right to Education Act failed to translate enrollment numbers to achievement outcomes. The facts were these: after the RTE Act was introduced in 2009, % third graders who couldn't read words jumped from 24% to 38% in a matter of two years. The % fifth graders who couldn't do basic subtraction jumped from 29% to 47% in two years. You get the picture: student educational outcomes actually got worse under the act. Why? What was happening under the scenes? Corruption? A failure of the top-down approach? Did rigid cirriculums and hasty administrators cause the downfall of a promising legislation? Is there even a solution to the absenteeism problem in Public schools?

4.8 What about Private Schools?

They're good, but not good enough. The facts are these: they're cheap (as low as $1.50 a month, presumably due to private market competition between parents), they're modest – usually operated as a home-based business with family members and teachers are usually frustrated from finding no jobs, and thus start their own.

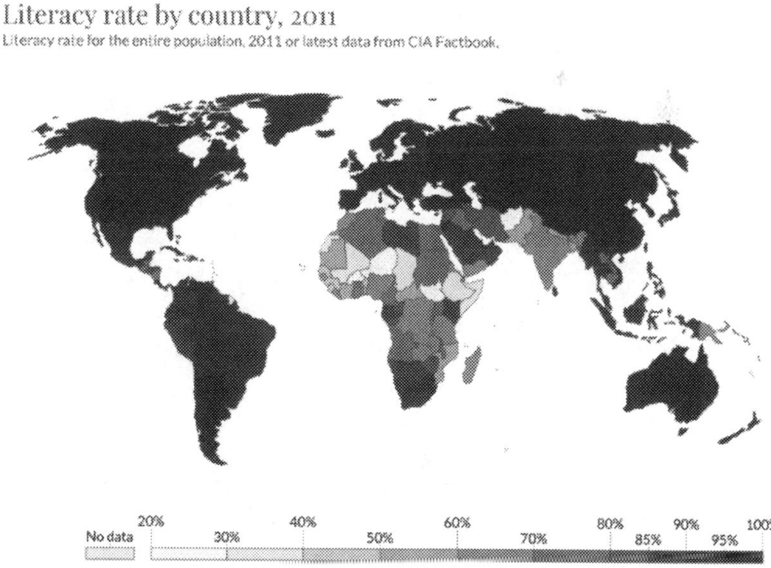
Literacy rate by country, 2011
Literacy rate for the entire population, 2011 or latest data from CIA Factbook.
No data
20%
30%
40%
50%
60%
70%
80%
85%
90%
95%
100%

Figure 15: Countries with higher GDPs seem to have higher Literacy Rates, but this is by no means a rule, as we can see from exceptions in Africa and other developing countries.

Private Schools are hailed by the demanders as proof that where there is a need, there is a school. And indeed, this need is very strong in areas where there does not exist public schools (i.e., in the case of Kaistan, where independent researchers found that private schools are much more likely in places like rural areas where public schools do not exist or are too low-quality). Because their salary and job depends on their attendance, the absenteeism problem in the private education sector is much smaller than that of the public – the World Bank sent unanconued agents to Indian private schools and public schools and found that private schoool teachers were 8% more likely to be in school that their public ocunterpsrts. What's more, Privately Schooled Students have better Educational Outcomes for children than their public counterparts, in both math and reading literacy. We see this in the 2008 ASER, which found that 47% of public school fifth graders couldn't read at the second-grade level, whereas only 32% of private school students couldn't. And India isn't alone in the Private School revolution: Pakistan has employed it to a similar effect – the Learning and Educational Achievements in Pakistan Schools survey (akin to the ASER in India) found that third graders in private schools were 1.5 years ahead in English and 2.5 years ahead in math than their public counterparts. Certainly makes one wonder about the efficacy of their own public education (although I can, and do solemnly testify to the efficacy of my own). Now here's the caveat: is this large student achievemnet difference between public and private schools the result of income? As in, is it because publics attract poor and privates attract rich students? It couldn't be: the difference between the privates and publics is ten times that of rich and poor. The point has been made: private schools are in many respects better than their public counterparts. But for all their success, they leave a lot to be desired. To find true schools operating at maximum efficiency, we need look no further than Pratham.

5 Pratham leads Education Reform in Developing Countries

Indian NGO Pratham teaches us the right way to do Remedial Education. In this chapter, we hope to explore how Pratham makes these education miracles work – using essentially free interventions to make life-long differences in the education of the poor man.

Table 4: **NGOs pave the way to a 2020 Vision of Education**

1 What programs are Pratham implementing to address Remedial Education for the poor?

2 What is the poor man's illusion of Education?

3 What role do teachers and administrators play in perpetuating the deficit education of the poor?

5.1 What programs are Pratham implementing to address Remedial Education for the poor?

Their interventions are affordable (to the tune of essentially free), effective (large increases in student achievement outcomes), and simple (often require no more than a few volunteers). They are the ideal mode of long-lasting interventions, and they pave the way for reforming the future of education. We begin by examining three of Pratham's most successful remedial education programs for children:

(1) **The Balsakhi Program:** It worked like this – low achieving third and fourth grade students were identified in school (four hours a day), and assigned to a Balsakhi, a local woman who typically had no more than ten years of school. The program was located in Mumbai and Vadodara. The Balsakhi works with a group of 15-20 students, working on remedial concepts for two hours a day outside of school. The Balsakhi received no professional development other than a week of training with Pratham, and they received a very low fee. The results were significant: the students achieved twice the average gains of their private school counterparts.

(2) **Volunteer Training Camps:** Pratham recruited various volunteers all over univeristies and colleges, most of them who were not paid. These volunteers agreed to help out their young brothers and sisters by going to villages and making the rounds, going home to home, tutoring children in their specific area of weaknesses. The results were dramatic: comapred to their control counterparts, of whom only 40% could read letters, 100% – literally all of the students – of the the treatment group could read letters. In additoin, students who could already read letters by the beggining of the program were 26% more likely to be able to read a story than those who did not participate in the program.

Refath Bari

(3) **Remedial Summer Camps:** I'll admit, this one's supposed to stir some contro-
versy. Pratham recruited government school teachers, many of them who had
the neccesary qualifications, but refused to teach to remedial students during
the school year. And yet, during Pratham's Remedial Summer Camp, the public school teachers actually taught so much so that students achieved much
of the same gains as in the Volunteer Training Camps. As such, it wasn't
the teaching *style* of the government teachers, per se, but their beliefs; their
ideology that was at the heart of their neglect of the poor man's education.

Now nations all around the world are taking note of Pratham's initiative from
Ghana to Mali to Senegal, all of whom are attempting to implement the same
cost-effective, long-lasting interventions in their own countries, mostly to the
same effect.

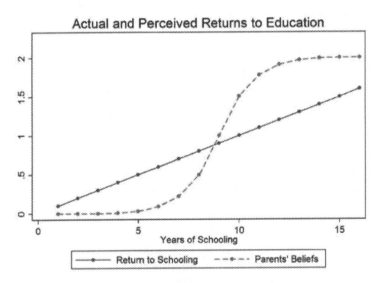

Figure 16: The consequence of misperceiving returns to education can
be fatal for a child's education

But we've spent so much time on the work of Pratham – what about the work
of the parents? After all, the most important stake-holder in a child's education is
their parents. As such, it is crucial that we understand the poor parent's illusion
of education.

5.2 What is the poor man's illusion of education?

Here it is: the poor man takes education as a gamble – a lottery, if you will. Analytically, that means that he perceives the returns to educations to be much like the S-Curve we encountered earlier – except this time, the parent believes that the first few years of primary education are meaningless, after which students will greatly benefit from secondary and higher education. The reality is that the returns to one's education is simply proportional to the # years he is in school. Recall, then, that is why every bit of education matters – because every additional year of education produces an equal and consistent amount of financial return.

The poor man also has an almost-rigid tendency to believe that a simple primary education alone would enable their children to qualify for government jobs or to the very least, some office jobs. Reality does not agree with the poor man's belief: In Madagascar, researchers asked parents what profession they expected their post-primary educated children to go into. 70% of the parents thought their children would get a government job, when the reality is that only 33% actually do (a combination of most not making it to sixth grade and failing the examination required for such posts). In reality, even if post-primary-educated students go into the informal labor market or agricultural section, they're likely to find large benefits to their education, and thus fare better than their non-educated peers.

Understanding the consequences of the poor man's vision requires us to go back to the drawing board. We look first to his belief that education is a lottery – you either it make it past the "bump" or you don't. The poor man in Madagascar sas that every additional year of primary education would increase their child's income by 6%; post-primary education by 12%, and secondary education by 20%. This is no isolated case – we observe the same case in Morocco, India, and developing countries throughout the world. In Morocco, for instance, parents believe just a year of primary education would increase their son's earnings by 5%; a year of secondary education by 15%, and so on. Parents thought primary education was basically worthless, coming in at 0.4% increase in salary. No ifs, buts, or whats, says the poor man. The reality, however, is that education is not a lottery, and it doesn't have any bumps. Instead, it is a proportional give-and-take, where the returns are proportional to the # years one is in school. But the poor man does not know this. And so, his lottery-picking mindset convinces him that as breadwinner, he must pick the next 'winner' from his family – a winner who can, in his view, overcome the bump of education. This winner would later qualify for a government post later in life, and take care of the parents in their rich home.

Refath Bari

That is the poor man's ideal vision. We know this from the many studies done on parental perception on Education, including one in Udaipur, India, where parents had to make drawings of what they thought the results of education would bring them, with their children. Most of the parents agreed that education would bring them wealth – in the form of gold-studded earrings, saris, and cars.

It is this precise mindset that makes the poor man seek a 'winner' from his own household. Based on a few whims and flicks, the poor man chooses the smartest of his children – these whims can be anything from what their child did on the first day of school (if they come back with a broken eraser, you know that's a bad sign). This is especially dangerous because a child's entire education may be lost simply due to parental intuition or misperceptions. Some of the poor man's ilk realizes that such off-the-hat guessing can seriously risk identifying the true potential of a child. So they turn to intelligence tests. We see this in Burkina Faso, where the high-scoring children were more likely to be sent to school, but less likely if their siblings scored higher than them, creating an interesting sibling-rivalry, if you will.

In my own case, reality did meet expectations, and indeed, these are exactly the phenomenon I witnessed when I went to Badu's field. He showed me his three working children. When I inquired about his eldest son, the one who used to go to public school, Badu responded "Yeah, now and then, I send him, but usually he stay with us to work on the field. Sometimes the neighbors ask about him, and then I send him to school so I can say he goes to public. The truth is that he's just not the level of Polomma, you know?" Badu's full transparency of (perception of) his childrens' own intellectual abilities reflects the "Breadwinner backs winner" argument – the idea that the head of the family, or perhaps the family of their own violition – picks the smartest of their children to go to private-schooled education, and sends the rest to the fields, or only occasionally sends them to public schools.

Here's a scary picture: CCTs (Conditional Cash Transfers) actually fail here. A CCT Program in Bogota, Colombia, found that the poor man tended to focus all his resources on just one child, to afford them the best educatoinal and health oppurtunities. Centered in Colombia, the program had only so much capital, and offered parents to enter their children into a lottery. If parents won the lottery, their children would be able to attend school, whilst they receives a monthly bundle of cash (advertised as 'compensation for foregone labor'). Good part first: lottery-winning children were more likely to get promoted and actually attend the next school year, and much more likely to attend college (for the modified CCT that was conditional on college enrollment). The bad part was that in families with more than one children, if both were entered into the lottery, but only one won, the other child would be less likely to go to school than if both children lost – even though family income increased, thus enabling families to (potentially) pick multiple winners, although we know that increased income for the poor doesn't necessarily translate to the most obvious expenses (we need only look to alcohol and tobacco expenditures among the poor to see this). And now, I end with the big idea: there is no education poverty trap. Every bit of education is valuable to the poor man. But the simple *belief* – the belief alone – makes parents behave as if there was a poverty trap, thus creating one out of thin air. What an idea. And what an outcome.

5.3 What role do teachers and administrators play in perpetuating the deficit education of the poor?

Corruption, Bribery, and Malfeasance alike plague schools, administrations, and faculties through any education system, but this is especially true in the case of the poor man's school in India. The Indian Culture alone emphasizes the need to prepare for end-of-year exams over actual comprehension of content. As such, the Indian teacher looks to the students who can enable him to achieve that goal the fastest – the top 10%. It is to these top students that the typical Indian teacher caters to, leaving the other 90% of average or low achieving students to fend for their selves (or more likely, drop out). A classic example is when researchers from Pratham made an announced visit to a school in Vadordara, a city in Western India. The teacher had made an all-too-obvious effort to teach a difficult topic, and it became clear that he was explicitly negligent to the bottom 90% of the class, and was catering knowledge solely to the highest-achieving learners. This is no exception – the same trend can be found in classrooms all over India, and indeed classrooms throughout developing countries. Furthermore, these classrooms have a tendency to emphasize rote memorization and mindless application of algorithms over comprehension and intuition, thus effectively damaging the young impressionable minds that enter the classroom. Economists weren't satisfied with these classrooms. Nobel-Prize Winning Economists Esther Duflo, Michael Kremer and Stanford Economist Pascaline Dupas hoped to change this all-too-common trend in Kenya. Their idea was simple: split classes in half by student achievement, and randomly assign teachers to either the low-achieving or high-achieving class. The results were unexpectedly large. It began like this: teachers who were assigned to the lower-achieving class relunctantly began teaching, but because the achivement gap between the high and low-performing child in the lower-achieving class was much smaller than the achievement gap between the high and low-performing child in the standard classroom, even the lowest-performing students could benefit from this simple manuever. This reluctance is far from uncommon; in fact, it has spanned generations of classrooms, going back as far as the 1990s, when a team of economists led by Jean Dreze found the following: "Many teachers are anxious to avoid being posted in remote or "backward" villages. One practical reason is the inconvenience of commuting, or of living in a remote village with poor facilities. . . . Another common reason is alienation from the local residents, who are sometimes said to be squandering their money on liquor, to have no potential for education, or simply to "behave like monkeys." Remote or backward areas are also seen as infertile ground for a teacher's efforts." It goes further (and deeper, too): in a study designed to identify teacher discrimination towards lower-caste students, teachers were divided into two groups – an experimental and control. Teachers were first given papers without student names and with student names (which revealed students' castes, as well). Here's the kicker: it wasn't the higher caste teachers discriminating against the low-caste students. In fact, it was the low-caste teachers who discriminated against their low-caste students. This was effectively self-discrimination in practice. And teachers aren't alone in discriminating against children like this – parents and children alike do the same thing. They tend to self-discriminate, believing themselves unfit or otherwise incompetent for a school education. If the son of a wealthy academician were derided in school for low performance, the parents themselves would come to school and demand their children receive a quality education, even though the low-performance may be on the child. We then look to the case of a poor farmer, who – in the exact same scenario – would backfire on himself. He would believe the teacher, the administrator, and principal alike. He would persuade himself that – yes, indeed – his son is unfit for a school education and maybe its a much better fit for him to work on the fields whilst simultaneously making money for the family. All the poor man needs is a little push. And the school is there to give it. And the poor man and his children are there to support it. We can see the same self-discrimination in the poor man's children, as well: in a study conducted by the World Bank to identify self-discrimination amongst students, a group of students were separated into a control and treatment group. Both groups were given mazes, and the experimental group children were asked to identify their caste (by way of explicitly asking for their names), whereas the control group students just had to complete the maze. It was expected, but at the same time perplexing: whilst in the control group, the low and high-caste children were performing essentially on-par with each other; the experimental group told a different story: the low-caste group – upon having to identify their caste – performed much worse than they originally had, now far below their richer and now, better-performing peers. The poor were discriminating against themselves, and all the schools had to do was support it. Indeed, that is exactly what many schools in India do – dropping out the lowest 10% of the class to claim a 100% graduation rate when it comes to the final standard.

6 Looking to a 2020 View of Education

The year is 2020 and the world has weathered a global pandemic. Yet our goal stands same: reform education. Reforming Education not only has the potential to give the poor man the intellectual and capital boost necessary to begin climbing the ladder of socioeconomic development, but can also propel a developing nation as a whole towards to economic prosperity, as its workforce becomes more skilled and smarter.

Table 5: **Looking Forward with Pratham**

1 Why does the poor man's school fail in both premise and methodology?

2 How do we ensure every child learns in school?

3 What are some classroom-enhancing techniques?

4 What Learning Theories can teachers implement in class?

6.1 Why does the poor man's school fail in both premise and methodology?

Many of these schools – while they claim to have been built to satisfy the nation's Right to Education act, offering every child an equal and comprehensive education – were actually founded on the principle of distancing the top 10% of society from the rest of the peasants, merchants, and beggars. And to this very day, many of the teachers in this school practice the same kind of methodology, going out of their way to cater knowledge only to the highest-achieving students. We see the consequences of this behavior in action in Michael Kremer's 1990 introduction to Randomized Control Trials, in which he sought to prove that adding inputs to a school in the form of textbooks would greatly boost student achievement outcomes. After all, textbooks are universally agreed upon to have large effects on students achievement. And so, Kremer did just that, introducing hundreds of textbooks to a randomly selected group of 25 schools in Western Kenya. And yet, the results were null. There was no result to be had. And why is this? Because the schools were serving the elite (who had a good grasp of English), they had neglected to account for the fact that the textbooks were written in English, which was the third language for most of the average and low-achieving students. As such, the textbooks proved useless for most of the kids, who couldn't even read them in the first place. We see the same phenomenon with other additonal inputs, like visual aids in the classroom and better student-teacher ratios. The key idea is that if pedagogy does not adapt to additional resources, neither will the students. Students will receive no benefit from additional inputs if teachers don't adapt to teaching the class better using the extra resources, whether by means of professional development, or simply experience. Now it becomes clear why private schools, for all their success, remain a definitive work-in-progress: their entire goal is to cater to the top 10% of high-achieving students, in the way neglecting the bottom 90% of students. In this way, the very premise upon which these private schools are founded is wrong – and government does nothing to help. Recall the Right to Education act implemented by the Indian Government in 2009 to make education free and compulsory to all children ages 6-14, effectively a card in the supplier's hat. And yet, the Right to Education accomplishes the exact opposite, by way of forcing schools to adapt a rigid cirriculum, the entirety of which teachers must cover during the academic school year. These rigid cirriculums and inflexible rules make it almost inevitable that poor students will fall through the cracks of the traditional education system. Under the Right to Education act, covering the entirety of the cirriculum is mandated by law. The net result of such negligent school systems that demand test prep over content comprehension; rigid cirriculums over flexible material is a waste of talent. It's inevitable. As the poor children are neglected more and more, they themselves add on to their self-discrimination and the result is a negative feedback loop that results in many talented poor people dropping out of school, even though their potentials were enormous. School cirriculums were designed by benevolent buerecrats who had nothing but the best intentions in mind: identify talent, increase critical thinking, and provide students a basic foundation of skills. And yet, these overambitious cirriculums, unwilling teachers, and broken incentives work to perpetuate a dangerous cycle of non-education for the poor man and his children, failing the very reasons for which they were created. Does the rabbit hole ever end? Or are we doomed to fall forever?

6.2 How do we ensure every child learns in school?

I propose six steps to reformation. These are by no means comprehensive, but at least offer a guideline as to the goals we can achieve, and the means by which we can achieve them.

(I) **A Combination of Top-Down and Bottom-Up Approach**: Top-Down has its pitfalls, and so does Bottom-Up. The Top-Down approach has been widely criticized by teachers and students alike for being beuracratic, overly political, and rigid, not giving schools enough time to adapt to revised cirriculums. The Bottom-Up approach, which has been praised for being designed with the teacher and student's best intentions in mind, is much less pragmatic to achieve. As such, it is perhaps best that we take a healthy combination of both approaches to form an integrated approach to education reform. Top-Down and Bottom-Up Approach also arrives in the classroom, where the teacher may choose to provide students a breif overview of the entire subject, immersing them in the big picture before delving in to the smaller details (this works best, in mathematics, for instance, in providing students intuitiion when problem-solving or in history, where historical context is obviously needed). The Bottom-Up approach to teaching takes the microscopic view of the subject, and gradually builds up to the bigger picture. Think an English Class full of ESL Learners, where the teacher begins by establishing basic components like phonics, vowels, syllables, and letters before charging to the bigger picture of reading stories and interpeting author intentions.

(II) **A Healthy Mixture of Supply and Demand**: We've seen from an ample amount of historical and research evidence that both the Supplier and Demander argument of Education has its pros and cons. We look to the supplier argument, one shared globally by international organizations and nongovernmental organizations alike. Indeed, it is the argument most developed countries implement when they make education mandatory for children in a certain age range. We've also come to the see the advantages of the demander's argument, which comes in the form of incentivizing education for the poor man so that he understands its benefits of his own violition, and is not forced his hand in any way to admit his children to school. In retrospect, seeing the pros and cons of both approaches persuades one that a healthy mixture of both the supplier and demander's argument must be taken. In this way, parents will not only understand the benefits of educa-

Refath Bari

tion (while not supersizing their expectatoins), but also have significantly more access to them.

(III) **A Lesson from Israel**: Where do I get the audacity for such hope? None other than Israel, land of the sacred. A 1991 Social Experiment from Israel shows us the potential of schools to act as *catalysts*, essentially eliminating gender disparities, high fertility rates, child mortality rates, dropout, and grade repetition even among the most disparate populations. We need look no further than the difference in education between the Russian children, whose parents had twelfth years of school and the Ethiopian Jews, whose parents had at most two years of schooling. The educational attainment between the two populations – quite literally – could not have been greater, not to speak of their cultural differences. And yet, these 15,000 Ethiopian Jews and their children made it. By the time their children were about to graduate high school, 65% of the Ethiopian Children reached twelfth grade without repetition, compared to 74% of their Russian counterparts. It was remarkable: Schools alone had narrowed the significant educational attainment gap from one generation to the next in a matter of years.

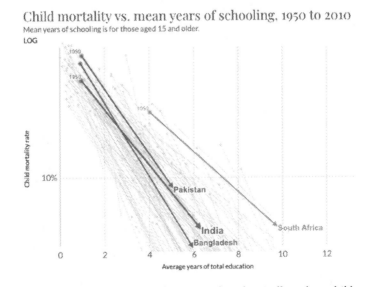

Figure 17: School alone has the potential to drastically reduce child mortality due to reduced fertility rates as women gain greater career aspirations, as shown here from the examples set by Bangladesh, India, Pakistan, and South Africa.

(IV) **A Lesson from No-Excuse Schools:** It is no excuse that some children are innately unable to master material, or incompetent for school. Indeed, we will see this idea as the very guiding principle of a set of charter schools known as "No Excuse Schools". These Charter Schools have been widely praised (and equally disparaged for their strict behavioral codes) for their consistent ability to take low-income populations and provide them significant, high-quality education. These schools are comprised of the KIPP (Knowledge is Power Program) schools, Uncommon Schools, Success Academy, YES Prep, the Harlem Children's Zone, and Achievement First are just a handful of these no-excuse schools. Instead of catering to the top 10% of the rich, elitist, high-performing students, these schools were founded on the premise that the poor – the low income students – can achieve significant, and high-quality educational attainment. Their bare-bones cirriculum focuses solely on the knowledge acquisition of fundamental skill and there are a continous assessments on students' ability to retain material. In this simple, yet focused methodology, these No-Excuse Schools have found much success. A study of Boston Charter Schools found that with the same demographics, but four times the # of charter schools, the achivement gap in math test scores between black and white children would be cut by 40%.

(V) **No Training or Pay Needed, Just Volunteers:** As we've seen from many of Pratham's Remedial Education programs for the poor, there is no need to pay expensive Summer School teachers or educators from government public schools. All one needs is a volunteer – this may come in the form of a young local woman, like the *Biskhala*, or even a local university or college student who wants to help their younger siblings. Professional Training isn't even neccesary – most of these volunteers spent a week, at most, training with Pratham and then were sent to the villages to make the rounds.

(VI) **Reforming Cirriculum for Self-Paced Learning:** By changing unrealistic expecations, setting pragmatic goals for teachers and children alike, and reforming rigid cirriculums, we can make vast strides in self-paced learning, and ensure that every child – poor or rich, urban or rural alike, get a chance to prove their ability.

6.3 What are some classroom-enhancing techniques?

For the teacher already equipped with the mindset that he must cater knowledge not to the best high-achieving students, but every student in the classroom, this section serves a brainstorming session if you will, of possible pedagogical tools and practices that can be implemented in the classroom. All of these practices have been demonstrate to increase student achievement outcomes in a variety of classrooms, from public to private; rural to urban; from specialized to remedial. We examine them below:

6.4 What Learning Theories can teachers implement in class?

Let me introduce the six learning theories that have dominated discussions of pedagogy over the last century. In addition to these learning theories, I will supplement them with the cognitive development theories of Psychologists William Perry and Jean Piaget. We begin by the six fundamental learning theories every teacher should incorporate in their classroom:

(I) **Introducing Early Algebra**: Despina Stylaniou of the City College of New York and her colleagues pioneered the idea of an early algebra intervention in grade three to five classrooms. The key question was whether students would be able to handle the abstraction of Algebra at such an early age. The study divided a set of 46 participating schools from three different districts into two groups: Control and Treatment. The control group were taught regular, third grade mathematics, along the lines of multiplication, division, and other basic ideas. The treatment group, however, was taught Algebra by the intervention teachers, who were taught and trained in professional development seminars by the researchers. The results were significant: the treatment students in grade three improved significantly in critical mathematical thinking and demonstrated marked improvement in subsequent assessments. However, the key to an effective intervention is in the curriculum. Stylianou knew this and she and her colleagues set out to create a flexible curriculum that could be adapted by a wide range of classrooms. The goal of any curriculum is to increase students' mathematical thinking, which is reinforced by problems that encourage students to represent, reason, and justify mathematical relationships. These practices can be applied to a wide range of content areas, from concepts associated with expressions, equations, inequalities, arithmetic, and equivalence.

(II) **Flipped Classrooms**: With the ever-increasing resources of the classroom, flipped classrooms may be the future of education. The goal is that students learn the content material in home, and apply the concepts they learned in class. This is especially applicable to mathematics, where theory can be kept to home, and problem sets can be done in class. Students can of course extend their learning and check their udnerstanding via online assessments conducted out of class. In this way, all class time is wholly devoted to students' mastery of content. Flipped Classrtooms (1) enable students to learn content at their own pace, (2) provide teachers better insight into students' difficulties in learning ideas and their learning styles, (3) the flipped classroom (FC) style makes cirriculum flexible, as it can be updated quickly online, (4) teachers using the FCs report increase in student achievement outcomes, student engagement and participation, (5) Giving quick quizzes online just before the class enables the teacher to adjust the lesson on a need-to-know basis, thus ensuring all students' questions and difficulties are dealt with. Let's not get too hasty, however – Flipped Classrooms have their own pitfalls. In a survey of 15,000 STEM teachers from the National Center of Case Study Teaching in Science Listserv, STEM teachers identified two major pitfalls of the FC: (1) Students may be resistant to learning new material at home, and may easily give up. Teachers resolve this by giving a quick in-class quiz to assess class readiness (2) Teachers spend time finding or creating high-quality videos in line with the curriculum;

(III) **Peer Collaboration**: Grouping students is far more than a pedagogical practice. It has definitive impact on students' achievement in the classroom. This begins, first and foremost, with a teacher who sensibly groups students in mixed or homogoenous groups. In a 2016 study by Veronica Morcom of Murdoch University, Morcom investigated the effects of Peer Collaboration on students' acquirement of social and academi responsibilities such as work ethic and integrity. Through routine reflective activities such as Daily Social Circle, Weekly Class Meetings, Reflection Logs, and Interviews, teachers encouraged prosocial values through the mode of Peer Collaboration. The outcomes demonstrated that peer collaboration can be effective not only in improving student achievement outcomes, but also in enabling students to acquire a values education.

(IV) **The Art of Problem Posing**: Increasing Students' Problem Solving abilities is a major goal of most cirricula. But here's one most neglect: Problem *Posing*. In a 2009 Study conducted on 76 Senior Teachers at the Department of Elementary Math Teaching in Erzurum Ataturk University, it was found that a students' ability to pose creative, difficult problems in a certain area of mathematics is highly indicative of their problem-solving abilities. The paper esatblished a parallelism between the number of problems posed by

Refath Bari

a student given a few restrictions, and said students' success in problem solving. Even though it is more difficult to create and grade assessments that concern problem posing, it may be worth the difficulty if one wants to truly measure the creative potential or critical thinking of one's students.

(V) **Tracking**: We've already seen some of the benefits of tracking through the division of Kenyan Classrooms by student achievement by Pratham, which found huge success, as increased both student achievement and engagement in classrooms. Tracking even plays a role inside classrooms, as many teachers mix low and high ability students in heterogenous groups, average students in homogenous groups and free-pick where high ability students go. As a matter of fact, since by definition most classrooms consist of average students, not adapting ability grouping may in fact inhibit the achievement of most students (Saleh, De Jong 2005). But tracking is clearly not a universal solution: in a 2008 study of struggling readers in mixed ability groups, low-performing readers encountered the same problems they did in other groups – as a matter of fact, they read less in mixed groups and were interrupted more often than their peers. This begs the question, *does heterogenous grouping create the same stigma of the low-achiever that it was designed to avoid?* Indeed, this may be the case as low-achieving students become intimidated the participation of their higher-achieving peers. So, if ability grouping and tracking is not the perfect solution, what is? The answer truly depends on the exact resources, state, and cirriculum afforded by one's classroom. As such, there is no "one size fits all" model, but a different prescription for every classroom.

(VI) **Polya's Prescription**: I actually have Polya's *How to Solve It*, an absolute staple for any math teacher. Polya's famous book identifies four basic principles for solving problems: (1) Understand the Problem (Metacognitive questions such as "Do I understand all the words in the problem", "What am I being asked to find?", "What is the condition?", "Are there restrictions?", "Is there enough information for me to find the solutoin?" may assist with this stage), (2) Devise a Plan (this comes in many forms in mathematics, including guess and check, working backwords, using symmetry, just to name a few), (3) Execute the Plan (you've got an idea, or a path towards a solution – now it's just a matter of doing the numerical computations; if the path is false hope, turn to another plan; were there any similar problems you solved in the past? Can you connect this one to them? Create backups of your original plan in case the first one does not work out; persist in solving

– that is the key), (4) Look Back (reflecting on a problem is key; did you use your intuition? Were there any misteps? If so, how could you have avoided them before going through the computatoins?)

(VII) **Differentiation**: In the case of the poor man, differentiation may come in the form of providing remedial support for low-achievement students. However, differentiation is just as useful for high-achieving students, many of whose needs are not met in the traditional classroom. Differentiation come in many forms – introducing challenge problems into the exit slip for advanced students, offer low-achieving students tutoring after-school, and so on. The possibilities are endless and one must find the best means of incorporating differentiation in his own classroom.

(VIII) **Abstraction & Numerical Development**: In math classrooms especially, numerical development is the key to grasping more advanced topics in mathematics. Educational Physcologist Dr. Robert Siegler of Columbia University is a prominent advocate of this phenomenon and proposes two forms of numerical development: (1) understanding the magnitudes of individual numbers, and (2) learning artihmetic. The former comes from deadling with increasing ranges and types of numbers, from rational to real to whole to integer. A strong foundation in understanding the magnitudes of numbers has been demonstrated to be correlated with and predictive of students' profeciency in whole number arithmetic. As such, it is the goal of every primary school math teacher to ensure that students receive a strong foundation in the scale of numbers before they begin handling arithmetic.

We now begin to consider some of the seven crucial learning theories that teachers public or private, rural or rich alike may seek to implement in their classrooms. We begin with the famous Lev Vogystky.

(I) **Lev Vogytsky**: The best problems are the problems just out of your reach – problems you will spend a considerable amount of time trying, but may fail to solve. To find these problems, Educational Psychologist Lev Vogytsky suggested the Zone of Proximal Development (ZPD), which consists of skills just beyond the reach of one's students. This can be applied to reading literacy, as well – when forming a reading group, pick a book that students will not be able to immediately pick up and need support to read along the way. As students master more content areas, their ZPD expands to accomodate their growth. This naturally leads the idea of scaffolding, a means of educational support by which a teacher provides students assistance to complete a task that they couldn't otherwise. Scaffolding can be gradually reduced as students master the content area better and their ZPD expands.

(II) **Jean Paiget**: Swiss Psychologist Jean Paiget introduced the idea of the Four Stages of Cognitive Development, which essentially divided a child's lifetime into four stages, with each preceding stage leading to more abstract reasoning. The first stage begins with Infants (0-2 years), and is dominated by sensory explorations of the infant's physical world. We ascend to the Preprational Stage when we're toddlers, using symbols like words and images to represent object. We also have the ability to pretend, but we're still unable to transcend from Dualistic Thinking (which we'll expand on with Perry's Scheme of Cognitive Development). Once we become Young Adults, Paiget terms this the Concrete operational Stage, at which point we can logically manipulate symbols and begin thinking abstractly. The final stage, the formal operational, is the point at which adults can fully think abstractly and hypothetically. Paiget's Four Stages can be implemented in any classroom to great effect in student achievement outcomes. Paiget also coined the ideas of Schema (student's preexisting knowledge, which they build upon by connecting new knowledge to existing schema) and Constructivism (Students learn best by kinesthetic learning and practicing material)

(III) **William Perry**: Cognitive Development is the name of the game when it comes to educational psycology. Perry took this to the next level, proposing that students progress through four stages of mental and moral development: dualism, multiplicity, relativism, and commitment. These four stages are further divided into nine sections of cognitive development. Dualism is essentially children and young adults' tendency to be egocentric, in that they believe ridigly in their ideas and refuse to acknowledge its limitations. Dualism extends to the belief that every problem is solvable, students must learn the right answers, and one must be defferential to his elders. Multiplicity acknowledges that there exist problems which cannot be solved, by virtue of their difficulty or our lack of tools to solve them. Relativism, the third stage, views problems intuitively, in-context. The final stage, commitment, is essentially the exact opposite of dualism: the student understands life is not black-and-white, solutions are not yes-and-no, and accepts an inherent uncertainty in all things.

(IV) **B. J. Skinner**: Skinner's idea is evident, and is really just a formalization of a basic idea: the idea of Behaviorism – that if a teacher positively reinforces the good behavior of one student, the rest of the class will naturally follow. On the other hand, negative incentives like punishments discourage students from behavior. Main Idea: use positive incentives to pull students to a behavior; negative ones to push students away from a behavior.

(V) **Jerome Bruner**: Here comes the cirriculum man – one who simply formalized the idea that ideas should build upon one another and that a students' mind is essentially *tablau reseau*, as John Locke put it, waiting to be nourished with good ideas; this is the perspective that the teacher is a giver of knowledge and the student is a receiver. Bruner proposed the idea of a spiral cirriculum in 1977, essentially stating that before mastering content areas of a subject, students must have expertise in the prerequisites.

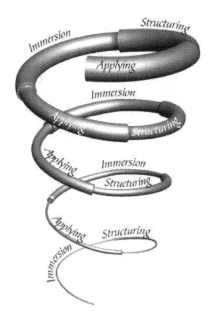

Figure 18: Bruner's Spiral Cirriculum is founded on three core prinicples: Immersion, Structure, and Application, all of which are essential to the development of a holistic, flexible cirriculum

(VI) **Benjamin Bloom**: The Common Core are a set of educational initiatives that are founded on the premise of Bloom's Taxonomy – essentially a Maslow's Hierarchy, but for learning. Bloom claims six steps to the goal of higher level thinking, begginign with the lowest stage.

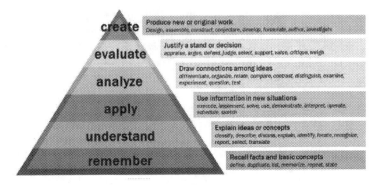

Refath Bari

Figure 19: It can be found hanging from most classroom walls; Blooms Taxonomy has become the Maslow's Hierarchy for Education

First is memorization/retention of basic facts; understanding follows as the next stage, which is one's ability to explain ideas to another peer (think mathematical discourse, translating problems, etc.); applying problems is the next stage (recall Polya's Prescription, in which recalling similar problems was a key step in making a plan to solve a problem); analyzing problems takes it a step further (can you draw a line between past problems and this one? can you distinguish their differences, perhaps in their restrictions or givens or unknowns?); evaluating problems comes next (can you justify why you chose to solve the problem method A, instead of method B? can you reflect on your line of thinking and propose a more efficient route to the solutoin? In essence, can you critique your own thinking process?); lastly, we come to the apex: the create stage (can you pose your own problems? Create your own conjectures? Investigate or prove your own ideas?)

(VII) **Howard Gardner**: Gardner proposed the idea of Multiple Intelligences – the idea that humans have multiple ways of processing information (i.e., visual, verbal, logical). Indeed, this is the very basis for the different types of learners (i.e., kinesthetic, auditory, visual). This may seem obvious today, but many developing nations still prize the notion that intelligence is an inherited trait that is born at birth. And further still to this point, many educational physcologists such as Perry and Piaget believed could occupy only one cognitive developmental stage at a time, which Gardner refused, stating that children could occupy multiple stages at once – children could, all at once, have any combination of linguistic, mathematical, musical, bodily/kinesthetic, spatial, interpersonal, or intrapersonal intelligence. Gardner makes the case that these seven forms of intelligence enable teachers to adopt a wide variety of means to teach their students.

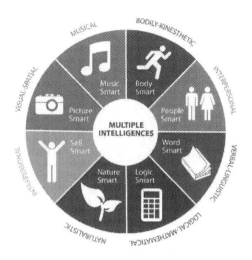

Figure 20: Gardner's Theory of Multiple Intelligence actually opens doors for teachers, as they can now address the same concept from multiple perspectives, each suited for a different type of learner

7 Moral of the Story IV

I hope you grasped the key idea of this chapter – that being that there is a significant deficit in the poor man's education. But, let it be known that there does exist an ideal education for the poor man and his children, as we've seen from the many cost-effective, long-lasting, and simple interventions by the Indian NGO Pratham. We've also come to understand that the first step to reform is diagnosis, as a nation must first understand the extent of its educational deficit – this diagnosis typically comes in the form of an NGO like Pratham conducting the ASER in India, or LEAPS in Pakistan. Now let us begin and establish the line of demarcation between the fact and fiction of the poor man's education.

Refath Bari

Table 6: Breaking the Falsehoods of Poverty

Fiction	Fact
The poor man is forced to discriminate amongst his children	But I ask you now: does he have a choice? He had limited capital, we know that, and he has many children. Because of his misconception of education as a lottery ticket to a government job and as a luck-based path with a bump that only the smartest can overcome – it seems like the only sensible option for the poor man is to discriminate between his children, especially because of the foregone labor costs that he'll miss out on. It's not even discrimination, really – it's simply natural selection, except by hand of the parent this time, not mother nature.
Good education is expensive. By this notion alone, an Ideal Education for the Poor Man is just impractical. An ideal education means ideal teachers (such skilled teachers cost a lot of money), perfectly retentive students, not to mention adequate resources.	Pratham has proved such pessimists wrong, by pure virtue of its persistence in the field of education. Ever since it's founding in 1994 by Madhav Chavan, Pratham has established various long-lasting, cost-effective interventions that demonstrate the essentially free path to education reform. These interventions are often implemented by local college volunteers, or young school dropouts; They receive a week of professoinal development and yet create remarkable strides in student achivement. If Pratham can create such effective interventions with unpaid volunteers, private and public schools should be able to do far better with their resources. Pratham is proof that education reform can be simple, affordable, and effective. Pratham leads the way.

Table 7: Breaking the Falsehoods of Poverty

Fiction	Fact
India's Right to Education Act has enabled it to join the other 135 countries in offering free, quality compulsory education to all children 6-14.	Yes, that would be the ideal scenario. Unfortunately, reality disagrees: the Right to Education Act, despite all its advertising blitz and claims to secure a higher education for all Indians, has failed to do so. The Annual Survey in Education Report still finds the same deficits in mathematical and reading literacy of students, a trend that has actually gotten worse since the establishment of the RTE Act. This is in part due to the uncompromising, top-down approach of the RTE Act, which has made it a legal mandate for schools to cover the entire cirriculum in the academic year. Schools have been unable to accomodate the cirriculum, for various reasons ranging from lack of resources to administrative inertia.
The best education policy is top-down: it ensures schools are kept in line and follow beauracratic orders from the top.	RTE is a prime example of top-down education policy gone wrong. True change may indeed be a healthy combination of top-down and bottom-up education reform. We need look no further than the No-Excuse charter schools for evidence of them – they were the result of teachers agitated for change in the classroom; in fact, the KIPP Program was founded on UPenn Graduate Michael Feinberg's hope to promote a higher standard of learning for minority standards, and has achieved significant success.

Refath Bari

Table 8: Breaking the Falsehoods of Poverty

Fiction	Fact
Schools are no more than a product; as such, they should adhere to the laws of supply and demand. Where there is no school, there is no demand. Likewise, where there is a demand, parents will advocate for better education from private – if their public counterparts fail – schools, which will compete for the children, thus creating the ideal education for the poor children.	Here comes the demander's argument. And indeed, it is far from wrong – it has found significant success throughout many countries by incentivizing education. Two cards in the demander's hat are the prominent examples of the Green Revolution and BPO Call Centers. During the Green Revolutoin, as parents realized the value of a technical education in learning the ins-and-outs of agriculture, they began enrolling their children en-masse in schools. But if we dualistically believe the demander's argument to hold true in all respects, that would mean Indonesia's massive gamble in building hundreds of schools during the INPRES program in the 1970s would have been a failure. History tell us it wasn't – the program was a hit among poor parents who did not find any nearby afforadble school to send their children to (which is exactly the need the program was designed to cater to). Indeed, the demander does not find many friends among internatoinal policy circles, or even developing nations, many of which enforce a compulsory educatoin policy (implying that the value of education must be impressed upon parents – whether by force or not) The moral of the story is that we need a little bit of both the supplier and demander's arguments to achieve the apex of education.

Table 9: Breaking the Falsehoods of Poverty

Fiction	Fact
Education is worthless. When will I ever use it?	This is a common complaint among the youth. Where does the need for education come in reality? When will one actually use anything more than basic addition or subtraction? In truth, education is a shifts realities in the developing countries, not neccesarily because it has higher returns there (although it should, since a high school education in Bangladesh is far more valuable than it would be in the US), but because of its seismic effects: reduced fertility rates, pregnancies, dropout rates, and mortality rates. Education is a secondary means to achieving public health: by requiring students to have full vaccination packages before entering school, governments ensure their populations are up-to-date on their immunizatoins. By means of preparing students for future job prospects or industry, even ineffective schools provide students with aspirations for a career, which naturally results in reduced fertility rates, and the rest follows like stacked up dominoes. We saw this in the Malawi CCT Interventions, and we see the same effects in Pratham's Cost-Effective Interventions throughout India and BRAC (Bangladesh Rural Advancement Committee) in Bangladesh. These two NGOs alone reach over 200 million people, effectively a third of all the extremely poor people in the world.

Refath Bari

Table 10: Breaking the Falsehoods of Poverty

Fiction	Fact
If everyone's in school, literacy will increase.	India teaches us the danger in making these large statements. The # schools in India have no doubt increased since 2000, and even more so after the 2009 RTE Act. And enrollment has followed foot, with over 96% school-age children in India estimated to be enrolled in school. And yet literacy hasn't increased – what's more, the % children 6-14 who can do simple division has been on the fall. We cannot rest easy upon finding such high enrollments (sometimes dangerously high, as teacher to student ratios are so high that students are often left with no textbooks or other classroom resources; some schools in India actually have over 100% enrollment). If India has taught us anything, let it be that we must prioritize the quality of education as much as we do its quantity.
Private schools are better than their public counterparts. After all, private schools students are literally years ahead of their public counterparts (look no further than Pakistan, where private school students lead by 1.5 years in English and 2.5 years in Math).	They are, but not much better. It is true that in developing countries, private school teachers do have less absenteeism rates than their public counterparts, but this is really a matter of how their paychecks are distributed (public teachers are paid upfront, so any absences are on the school; private school teachers get paid based on their attendance). There goes the issue of attendance. In comes quality. Private school teachers are typically less qualified than their public counterparts (since they're essentially locals who had too little capital or skill to do anything else). The second point is true.

Table 11: Breaking the Falsehoods of Poverty

Fiction	Fact
Education has a logistical rate of returns, in that primary education is essentially worthless, but secondary and higher education is extremely valuable, after which the financial returns just plaeatu.	Thank you for bringing that up. I had the very same belief when I was younger – that the elementary grades were useless in all respects and it was truly higher education that one should aim for. I now find myself thoroughly corrected, as universal primary education is truly the focus of all international educational circles to this day. Indeed, the UN's MDGs are centered around primary education; the true reality is that primary, secondary, and higher education are all equally valuable. Every single bit of education matters, especially for the poor man, who never knows when it may become applicable. Attending and dropping out of fifth grade could mean the difference between knowing how to read paragaphs – this could factor in, for instance, when a farmer must apply his fertilizer, yet does not know how to do so effectively, because he cannot read the directions. These simple daily hiccups become a ritual for the uneducated poor man, who often suffers in the form of lower financial returns in contrast to his more educated peers. Nevertheless, the key point is this: returns to education are proportional to the # years one is in school. As simple as that. That's a card in your hat, Occam.

Refath Bari

Table 12: Breaking the Falsehoods of Poverty

Fiction	Fact
There's no way to change the gender disparity in education (i.e., much more boys in private schools than girls; in contrast, more girls in public schools than boys)	That's just flat-out wrong. First, I should say that this is precisely the goal of the third MDG, which seeks to eliminate all gender disparity in all levels of education by 2015. Clearly – writing about this half a decade later – that hasn't happened. But that doesn't mean it's difficult to curb gender disparities. In fact – far from it: Robert Jensen's BPO Call Centers Study in India demonstrates that creating an educational incentive only for girls naturally encourages parents to care for their girls better, since their daughters are the key to better financial prospects for the entire family. Recall that as a result of the three year study, which placed a minimum educational qualification to be hired in the call centers, girls were more likely to stay in school, and in fact gained weight – evidence of a positive parental presence in light of a positive economic incentive. And keep in mind that this study was conducted in Delhi, Northern India, where there has been a historically strong familial preference for boys (look no further than the child gender ratio of boys per 100 girls; Delhi has the second highest gender ratio in all of India, second only to Kashmir, for Children Ages 0-1, as per the 2011 Census)Therein lies the power of economic incentive: the power to shift traditional behavior.

Table 13: Breaking the Falsehoods of Poverty

Fiction	Fact
Conditionally matters! Without promising the poor man money upon the condition that his children go to school, he will be reluctant to educate all his children.	I wouldn't be too hasty – it depends: Recall the Bogota, Colombia instance which involved a CCT program via a lottery. Despite successes in students' engagement in school, the program discouraged unaccepted children whose siblings got in from going to school. CCTs have unintended effects, and may backfire on their original intention. As such, it helps to consider all aspects of the program.

Chapter 7

Food

Refath Bari

55 Days in Dharavi

Chapters 3 and 4 on the Problem of Poverty only scratched the surface of the food expenditure and consumption of the poor. Here we go more in-depth, hoping to formulate relationships between the poor man's food consumption, undernourishment, his performance in both work and sports, and his natural tendency towards entertainment. I will not reveal the key ideas of this pivotal chapter in this short abstract. Instead, I encourage you to embark on a journey with me to understand how the poor man decides what he will eat. We begin with the case study of Ramchandran Ravidas.

Keywords: Purchasing Power, Micro-nutrients, Healthy Diet, Poor Man's Olympics, Witch Hunts, BMI, Malnutrition, Undernourished, School Meals, Deworming Pills, Barker Hypothesis, Law of Common Knowledge, Engel's Law, Maslow's Hierarchy

1 Case Study: Ramchandran Ravidas

I don't know what to write. It's too hot to think. Delhi can be a real heater, especially in rush hour. Now I know. Calling for a auto-rickshaw can be a death sentence. I hope from one side of the street to the other, hoping one of these capsule-crammed locomotives can notice me. Finally one of them pulls over, nearly running over me in the way. He flips the FOR HIRE sign upside down and starts the meter, like clockwork. Ideas start coming to me – this is the man I for my next survey. But first, did he even qualify? "How much you make?" I asked. "You don't even know my name. Why you asking me for my money?" the guy slapped the meter and I saw the narrow eyes in the rearview mirror. "I'm doing a study – its on how people live. Here, in Delhi." He didn't respond, but it was far from silence. The damn honks every second from the passing auto-rickshaws was giving me headache enough. "Can I interview you Sir?" He slaps the meter

Refath Bari

back on. I take that as a yes. Alright, alright. Making progress: "OK, Income?" "Still no name?", he asked, brows furrowed. Cut me some slack, for God's sake. I've been drowning in work all day. "OK, OK, name, go." "Ramachandran Ravidas" After struggling a few seconds, he cut in: "Just Ravi, that's it. Ravi, Ravi, Ravi." he started chanting. We slipped into a narrow alley and came so close to a man that his arm actually came through the rickshaw's opening. "Hey, hey, we OK?" I knew better than to grab his shoulder. Instead, I clapped next to his ears. "Sorry. Gnuh. I didn't eat anything."

Figure 1: The Rickshaw man and his meter, standing by. "I'm sacrificing ten customers talking to you, man" he claimed. I don't take that

He must have seen my wide-eyed shock, and even declines my small parceled granola bar. "No, no. Don't worry, this is how I do it. First work, and then food. Because I only eat one time a day. But the one time is enough." I feel bad for Ravi, but here was a man who stuck to his morals and no one could budge him. Maybe. Anyway – third time's the charm: "Income?" I asked, hoping for an answer this time. None came. All I had to do was look in the mirror: there he was again, overcome by sleep, hunger, and possibly thirst. This time I took my offer: one solid granola bar, which I proudly kept in my pocket, but was happy to loan to a man in need. "Income?" "On a good day, ..." he said, his voice trailing off, but he jerked back up: "On a good day, its something like $6, if I have a lot of energy. But its hard to do it every day, you know?" "Sorry," I said.

I realized my trip today was done. "Ravi, 100 Rupees, if you can just let me take your interview here". "So you telling me to stop the meter?" I thought he was angry, but instead slapped the meter off. The rickshaw stopped next to the AirTel store. I saw Ravi staring at the people in the store, maybe hoping for a phone. Instead, I saw him pull out what looked like a Cell Phone from his pocket. "I need a new SIM," he explained. "Alright, let's go. But, the deal is this: I pay for your SIM, you stay for my interview." It took no time – Ravi swiped the card from my hand and the profuse thanks began. "What plan?" I said, "Family, I brought my new son a phone long time ago, and we're still paying for that." he said. Was this man really poor? I began questioning myself. "Wait – so let me get this straight: you can buy phones but not food?" Ravi hesitated – maybe at first guilty – but then roared in laughter "*bhraata*, you don't get it" he slapped my shoulder the same way he did his meter. "I make, maybe, $2 most days, and I told you $6 because that's the most I ever made in one day. It was Dilwali, that's why I got some many customers. But not today. Not any day." "No, but that's not my question", I repeated. "The point is – you have $2 to spend today, let's say. What you buy? The whole-wheat bread and bananas, or some sugar *Jalebi*?" I could see Ravi's mouth watering, but he defiantly shook his head. "Your rupee will give me hundred *Jalebis*" I shook my head – the guy didn't get the point: "Ravi, look – the *Jowar* and *Bajra* are the obviously the cheapest and they have the most calories. Why don't you get those instead of the *Jalebis* and *Haleems* and everything expensive?" I sensed something wrong. Ravi's jaw clenched and he squint his eyes, red and glistened in the flourescent store lights. He flinched his lips into a tight-lipped look. "You're all the same. I see people like you every day on the TV, preaching you have some ideas for us. But are you us? Do you live in the slums? Do you walk in the mud? Go, go, go back to your country, man, I don't need you." he shouted. He threw me out the store, with all eyes watching.

I don't know if Ravi ever got his SIM Card or the *Jalebis* he wanted. Here was the first time I met a poor man with a TV, and two Phones, but no food. I couldn't think in the searing hot sun, and I wasn't able to leave Ravi the little note and and Rupee I usually give to all the people who tell me their stories – Babu, Mo, Badu, Arjun. But I could do something: I went back to the AirTel store after I saw Ravi leave. I found all the eyes staring at me as I entered the store. "How much does he come here?" I asked the clerk. "He is a regular, *bhai*" I had an idea. *574-245-9983 – Refath Bari – 01/06/20 – Thank you for everything Ravi, I hope you get your Jalebis and the SIM card. I keep you in my prayers every day. Please, be well and stay safe.* I scribbled the best I could. "Do you have an envelope?" The clerk stared at me before blurting out a nod. The note went in, but I had one last thing: "How much for a Sim – family plan?"

Ravi was the first poor person I met in India with not one, but two phones. It's all the more surprising given his average wage of $2 a day. I hope he and his family are safe, wherever they are, in this dangerous time. I know his heart, mind, and strength alone are all he needs to overcome this scary time.

2 Ravi's List

Ravi teaches us an important lesson: what is logic to the rich man is simply common sense to the poor. In this chapter, I want to give background, maybe even reason to Ravi's perplexing story. Here are the major themes of the chapter:

(I) 1 Billion Hungry and Counting

(II) The Poor are eating less

(III) A Poor Man's Reason

(IV) Olympic Medals & Nobel Prizes: What the Poor Man doesn't have

We commence now.

3 1 Billion Hungry and Counting

This is a commonly cited statistic by the UNICEF. But have we ever questioned it? What does it mean for over 1/7 of the world population to be hungry? These are the forms of questions we hope to answer in this pivotal chapter. In Chapter 5, Health, we extensively discussed the effects of malnutrition on a population.

Now we go further – examining the definition of Hunger through the perspective of Biology, Pscyhology, and perhaps most importantly – Poverty.

Table 1: **A Tall Order of Magnitude**

1. What is the state of the poor man's hunger?

2. Are the poor actually *feeling* hungry?

3.1 What is the state of the poor man's hunger?

First, let me say this: hunger rules above all; Hunger is the breaking point between life and death, and it is a sad reality for the subjects of this book. So, we begin first by diagnosing the state of the problem: How many people are hungry? Is it really a billion? Well, the reality is this: as of 2016, there are 815 million hungry people, as per the World Bank and FAO. But that's the classical definition. If there are so many hungry people, is it because they can't afford food?

Food is a complex reality for the poor. And it is one we must tackle step-by-step. First – if the poor were so hungry, they would spend every nickle they had on food, and food alone – save, of course, for other expenses (i.e., housing, medicine, etc.). But this is not the case – far from it, in fact: the average poor man in Udaipur, India could spend up to 30% more on food instead of expendable, non-essential goods such as alcohol and tobacco or even festivals and theatre. That leaves a lot of slack for the poor man. And it leaves a lot of questions on our hand. Why does the poor man behave the way he does? Is the poor man's reasoning poor?

An individual's reasoning can be poor at times, due to impulse decisions or spontaneous consumption, but an entire population's behavior is rarely flawed. As such, we must resort to another possibility: what if, the poor are not actually stuck in a hunger poverty trap?

Here it is: an L-Shaped Definitely-Not-A-Poverty-Trap. What's happening here? Simply put, as income in the present increases, so does income in the future, albeit plateuing some time in the future. In other words, as your present income increases, your future income follows rapidly; then it comes to slowly trickle off. What a rosy picture – but is it true? Are the poor really not stuck in a poverty trap? Is there even any food available for the poor?

Refath Bari

A Not-Poverty-Trap

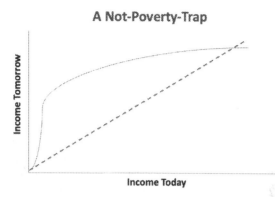

Much like education, the food is certainly there. There is no shortage of food for the poor. This is no small part due to the supply-driven work governments have dedicated to ensure subsidized food gets to the poor – although there are shortcomings of that system, as noted by Ganesh-Kumar, Ashok Gulati, and Ralph Cummings Jr., who found that in India, a third of rice and a half of wheat get lost in delivery. In fact, the logistical problems associated with food delivery afflicts not just India, but developing countries around the world. These logistical problems are akin to the 'absent teachers' or the 'unreliable doctors' existing in the education and health industry, respectively. Indeed, there is a lot of bureacratic slack in Health, Education, and Food alike that we can cut. Let's look to a success story, Indonesia, which proposes a solution to this wasteful crisis: postcards.

Here was the problem: the government was delivering subsidized rice from government faciilities to peoples' homes. But for every 100 kilos of food that left the storage sites, less than 50 actually got to people's hands. And so, as the government tried its best to provide nutrition to the poor through a supply-driven ideology, more than half of the food ended up nowhere – this was in a nation of 270 million, over 3.5% of the world population, and only the fourth largest country in the world after India. The crisis was real: the government was spending $1.5 billion on the Raskin Program, Indonesia's largest social support mechanism for the poor, through which it delivers thousands of tonnes of food to millions of households. In 2008, the Raskin Program delivered 10 kg of rice at a fifth of the market price, at 1,000 Rupiahs per kg. In 2012, the Raskin program provided 3 4 million tons of subsidized rice to the poorest 30% of Indonesia's population, over 17 million people. The program was intended to work like this: the inodnesian government ships rice to thousands of government storage sites, each of which then takes over rice distribution by handing off the rice packages to officials at each center. Poor families were supposed to receive 33 pounds of rice a month at a fifth of the market price. But obviously, expectations did not meet reality at this point: well over half of the food didn't end up in the poor families' kitchens. The Indonesian government was well aware of the crisis undergoing in the Raskin Program, as over half of the food wasn't reaching its intended beneficiaries. In 2008, Economists Hastuti Hastuti, Sudarno Sumarto, Asep Suryahadi, Sulton Mawardi conducted an investigation into the state of the Raskin Program, via document review, meta-analysis, and field studies. The investigation identified that the low effectiveness of the Raskin Program was due to a lack of publicization of the program (many poor people didn't even know the set prices of the rice set aside for them, even though the price remained fixed for seven years). There was also a lack of transparency (Indonesia ranks 85/180 on the Corruptions Perception Index 2019) – beneficiaries were often found to have received the wrong amount of rice upon closer inspection, and there was no complaint mechanism or monitoring agency set to track the rice shipments. Here was a program ripe for corruption: (1) Lost Rice (intended benficiaries received only a third of their entitled rice) (2) Awareness (despite prices being fixed for sven years straight, the program's eligibility requirements weren't well known) (3) Targeting (63% households were able to purchase Raskin Rice, despite being unqualifed for the program), (4) Pricing (Officials at government distribution centers inflated prices, and eligible households were forced to pay 42% more than the actual price).

And corruption could have been the downfall of Raskin. But it wasn't, largely due to the intervention efforts implemented by J-PAL's Abihijit Banerjee, Benjamin A. Olken, and Rema Hanna in their Study "Improving the Transparency and Delivery of a Subsidized Rice Program in Indonesia". The facts were these: officials at the government distribution centers weren't giving the food subsidies to those on the government poverty roll, but those they believed were in need. Even worse, many of the officials set subsidy prices themselves and intentionally gave poor families less than their due amount of rice. This corrupt behavior essentially wiped out more than half of the food coming from Raskin. Now here's where the tables turned: the study implemented a yearslong intervention from 2012-2014 that studied ways to repair the program. The team realized that all they needed to do was change the tides; turn the tables; flip the switch; call it what you will, but the name of the game was giving the poor man power by way of knowledge. Here's how they did it: the team sent every poor Indonesian beneficiary of Raskin in every one of the 500 villages a postcard. The postcard explcility stated

Refath Bari

that the individual or his/her family were eligible for the program and entitled to so-and-so many pounds of rice at so-and-so price. It was a game-changer, to say the least. Just sending out the cards, a minimal expense, increased the rice received in experimental villages by 26%. But the team went further, posting flyers in villages declaring eligible recipients of the Raskin program. At the end of the day, this was the Law of Common Knowledge in practice – ensuring that the poor man is aware of his rights, and cannot be cheated of them by corrupt bureaucrats; in effect, the poor man knows the rules of the program, and he knows the bureaucrat knows that the knows the rules and in sum, everyone knows that everyone else knows the rules.

Additional impact of price cards and public information treatments on total households, on average

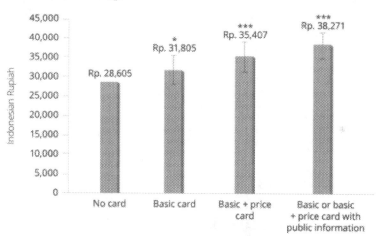

Figure 2: After a huge successful intervention, the Indonesian Government decided to take JPAL's work and put it in further practice by providing over 15 million Indonesians an ID Card entitling them to various social programs and services

We come back to India: The Indian Government alone manages the world's largest food welfare program, and has set aside $25.3 billion aside for food subsidies for the 2019-20 fiscal year, a 6.5% increase in food subsidies. The Indian Government's biggest expense after military are food subsidies. Since Prime Minister Modi's ascension to power in 2014, Modi raised food subsidies by 47%, up to 1.69 trillion rupees as of 2019. India's Nonprofit Food Corp Organization buys Rice and Wheat from farmers at a set price and state agencies sell the goods to the people at a tenth of the market price. Much of these food subsidies goes to to the poor at reduced prices. But much like Indonesia, India suffers from a food distirbution problem, as much of the food doesn't end up in the hands of those who need it most. India is not alone in food welfare programs: Food Subsidies are commonplace throughout developing countries such as Indonesia (which has the food subsidy program Raskin, which means "Food for the poor", first established after the Asia Financial Crisis of the 1990s) and Egypt alone sent almost $4 billion in food subsidies in the 2008-09 fiscal year.

So in essence, the poor man seems not to be taking much of the food avialable to him. If the poor man was truly starving, would he not take every chance to eat food? And yet that's exactly what the poor are not doing: food represents only 36%-79% of household consumption for the dollar a day poor in rural reas, and 53%-74% for the urban poor. And remember, this is not because the poor are stretched thin by other neccesary expenditures – they spend a lot on specialized adult goods such as Alcohol and Tobacco; they spend a considerable amonut on nonessential assets such as Televisions and Phones; they spend a lot on Festivals, Weddings, and Funerals (so much so that in South Africa, the government actually had to restrict how much the poor could spend on funerals, especially because funeral homes were essentially coaxing the poor out of their essentially non-existent income).

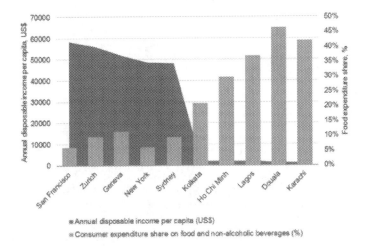

■ Annual disposable income per capita (US$)

■ Consumer expenditure share on food and non-alcoholic beverages (%)

Recall that in Udaipur alone, the poor could spend up to 30% more on food. And you would expect that the more rich the poor become, the more food they would

Refath Bari

consume. Not so: even for the poorest of the poor, a 1% increase in spending re-sulted only in a $frac23\%$ in food expense. This isn't just in India – throughout developing countries and developed countries alike, food expenses are decreas-ing as incomes are rising. In sum, the richer a country, the less it seems to spend on food; the United States, for instance, is projected to spend 18.2% of the bud-get on National Defense, 17.4% on Medicare, 16.9% on Social Security, and 11.6% on Health for the 2020 Fiscal Year. We can in fact describe this counterintuitive phenomenon by way of Engel's Law, which states that as an individual's income increases, so his food expenditure decreases.

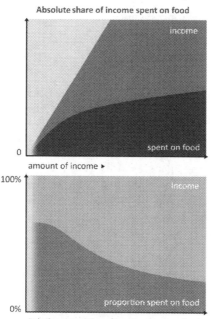

Figure 3: Engel's Law (named after Statiscian Ernst Engel) finds that as an individual's income rises, the propotional expenditure on food decreases. We see this in stark action in the case of the United States, which has the lowest household expenditure on food of any country

Let's take an example from Ravi's story – Ravi had a salary of $500 per year, and spent $300 on Food, let's say. If his annual salary increased to $800, his food expenditure would become $400 – an increase, no doubt, but a smaller proportion of his total income. We see this phenomen in effect right here in the US, which has the smallest household expenditure on food, standing at 6.5%. In effect, your grandparents spent more on food than you did, and this is simply a result of Engel's Law. We see the same consequences in the life of the poor.

3.2 Are the poor actually *feeling* hungry?

It seems not. After all – as we said previously – the poor man would devote every dime and a nickel to recuperate their hunger if they were actually starving. So what is their true endgame? To understand the poor man's reasoning, we must look at hunger from the poor man's perspective – does he actually *feel* hungry? Due to increasing automation, the poor may actually need to spend less energy – and thus calories – on laborious work.

4 The Poor are eating less

What do you see when you look at Poverty? Hunger – you see famines, like the one that ravaged Bangladesh in 1974; hurricanes, like the one that's killed more than 80 people in Kolkata, India and Bangladesh, leaving millions more left to suffer. This is what we see when we see Poverty. And it's no mistake. Natural Disasters can press impossible standards upon the poor. But Natural Disasters are only the exceptions, not the rule. So how do we understand the rule and not the exception – that being that the poor are naturally attracted to the quality of food, and in result sacrifice its quantity.

Table 2: **A Decline in Consumption**

1 What is the trend in food consumption of the poor?

4.1 What is the trend in food consumption of the poor?

The trend is that the poor are eating less, day by day. And why is this? The goal of the poor man is to treat himself rich. He does not want to *feel* poor, much the same way he does not want to fall socially behind, which is why he spends so much on festivals and funerals. But the act of food may transcend any marks of peer pressure; it may simply be human nature to treat oneself well and not get bogged down in the reality of being poor, which can naturally lead to depression

Refath Bari

or an otherwise unfortunate mental state. What I may say next may seem counterintuitive, but the name of the game when it comes to the poor man's world is this: what is logic to us is simple common-sense to the poor man. The poor man spends more on getting *tasty* calories, instead of the maximum amount of calories. It goes all the way back to 1983, in India, Maharashtra, when for every 1 Rupee increase in food expenditure, half went to getting more calories, but the rest went to getting more *tasty* calories. And what does this mean? Well, once again, we need look no further than India, where the best bargain on wheats is none other than the *jowar* and *bajra* (kind of brown *porothas*). I should have known this from Ravi's behavior. Even he, instead of buying what gave him the most amount of calories, brought Sugar instead, which is more expensive than any grain and has basically no nutritional value. Ravi's not alone: the average poor man spends over 5% of their total budget on sugar alone – more so than even Tobacco or Alcohol. In addition, only 66% of the poor man's expenditure on grains were on *Jowars* and *Bajras*, with another 30% going to rice and wheat, which are double the expense when it comes to calories per rupee.

I will say this: Relativity is to Physics as the Poor are to Economics. The poor bring the unreal to reality. Just one instance of this is Robert Jensen and Nolan Miller's social experiment via Randomized Control Trials: they offered subsidized rice to the poor people in China. Naturally, as price goes down, demand should go up. I mean, it should be like Walmart on a Black-Fridays. Its just basic Supply and Demand, you say. Not so: people atually ate less of rice and wheat and ate more shrimp and meat (even though those cost more). In effect, even though their purchasing power increased, they sought epensive foods devoid of any nutritoinal value. The same thing's happening all over India: the poor become naturally attracted to tastier, not healthier calories. Despite sustained economic growth in India (which is now inevitably slowing, not just due to COVID19), more than 75% of the population live in households that live below the recommended daily calorie consumption. Even when food prices declined, the poor kept flocking to the good stuff, expending more of their incomes on less nutritional goods, and thus eating less.

The moral of the story is this (exceptions are in the cases of natural disasters that naturally lead to food depletion): starvation exists today not because of a lack of food, but because of an unequal distribution of it. The poor have every reason to buy cheap food – it can help against malnutrition, raise labor productivity, and even increase wages. And yet they do nothing of the sort (or at least, not to the extent that they can). At 21 cents, the cheapest and equally nutritious diet is affordable for even the poorest of the poor, who live on a dollar a day. We've now eliminated two possibilities as to why the poor do not consume as much food as they can: cost and supply. Now we turn to the deeper, perhaps more psychological than economic question: why?

5 A Poor Man's Reason

Let me begin by establishing the Millenium Development Goals of the first 15 years of the 21st century, and their subsequent Substainable Development Goals. The first MDG (of eight) was to Eridicate Extreme Poverty and Hunger. Similarly, of the 18 goals, the second millenium development goal is Zero Hunger; The first target of SDG2 is "End hunger, achieve food security and improved nutrition and promote sustainable agriculture. By 2030, end all forms of malnutrition, including achieving, by 2025, the internationally agreed targets on stunting and wasting in children under 5 years of age, and address the nutritional needs of adolescent girls, pregnant and lactating women and older persons."

Table 3: **Poor Reasoning**

1 Why is the poor man eating less?

2 What is the reality of food consumption?

5.1 Why is the poor man eating less?

Many reasons: automation has paved the way for less man-made labor, as in the case of even the most remote villages in the poorest countries, many of which have farming technologies like motorized mills. There's also the case that educational interventions, medicinal strides, and public health advancements alike have reduced the incidence of diarrhea in many poor countries, which has the effect of reducing the # of calories lost in severe diarrheal bouts. But then, there also comes a hidden, perhaps less obvious reason: money.

5.2 What is the reality of food consumption?

John Strauss, Professor of Economics at the University of Southern California, looked for a way to demonstrate the inevitable link between calories and productiviy. Obviously (or so it would seem), as the number of calories one consumes

Refath Bari

increases, so does one's labor productivity, and thus so does one's wages. He set-
tled on Sierra Leone farmers, poor people who tried their best to work hard (but
really, how hard can you work when you've only got so many calories left in your
system?). What he found was surprising: when their calorie intake increased – in
fact, when their calorie intake doubled, the farmers' wages rose only 40%. In fact,
the largest strides in productivity were made at the lowest rungs of the calorie
ladder, after which the effects simply plateued off. This is the L-Shaped Not-a-
Poverty Trap we saw earlier. So we can defiantly rule out food consumption as
the reason why the poor stay poor. But the allure of the S-Shaped Poverty curve
stands.

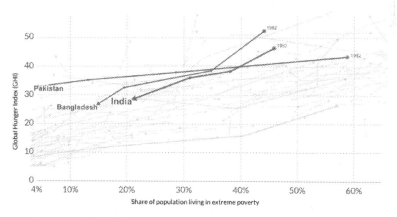

Figure 4: The Global Hunger Index is measured in part by the amount
of people in a region who live in extreme poverty. The GHI is measured
on a scale of 0 to 100, with 0 being the best (translates to no hunger),
and 100 meaning a lot is left to be desired. Most countries today have
considerably improved in their GHI ratings over the past few decades

And it is, by no means, a wrong intuition: Nobel-Prize Winning Economoist
Robert Fogel found that in the medieval ages, when food production was particularly low and population particularly high, the population would resort to
violent measures to eliminate population, and thus lessen the strain on the food
supply. This is far from history – it's happening right now in countries like Tanzania, where the occasional "Witch Hunt" happens, when unproductive mouths
are eliminiated in the name of "Witchcraft". These unproductive, and equally un-
forunate mouths are typically old women, over 20,000 of whom have been killed
over the last two decades in the name of these "Witch Killings" – which, in effect, seems to be a convenient means of population control. But in our world

today, full of technological advances and agirucultral revolutions, this simple explanatino simply does not fit the picture – there's enough food to go around for everyone. Amartya Sen caught a notable exception, which is in the case of natural disasters or famines, but even in the case of famines, most are the case of food mismanagement or a wealthy country witholding food from a poor one (think Bangladesh Famine of 1974).

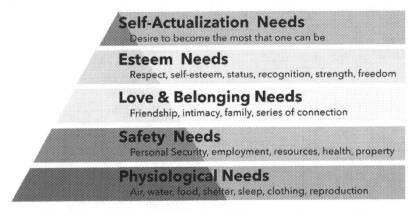

Figure 5: It's basically Maslow's Hierarachy in action: one must first receive the basic necessities to subsist human life to then be able to concentrate on other matters. In other words, one must ascend every single ladder of Maslow's Hierarchy of Needs, from receiving the bare basic needs of food, water, and housing to Esteem Needs such as societal respect and peer encouragement. Abraham Maslow coined his hierarchy in 1943, and to this day it has served many applications in both education and psychology.

We apply the same thinking to schools. Here is where Education and Nutrition intersect: by providing poor children school meals – breakfast, lunch, and in-class alike – we can afford them a better future. Exactly such an intervention was implemented in Pakistan from 2002 to 2005 through various districts, in which a team of five researchers collaborated with 11 NGOs, the Pakistani Government, and Rural Women to effectively train and mobilize them to manage a school nutrition program. The Tawana project-school nutrition program was an outright success: providing children cheap, locally sourced food increased school enrollment by 40%, Wasting decreased by 45%, undernourishment decreased by 22%, and stunting decreased by 6%. The message is clear: give students the adequate nutrition they need, and they will do better both cognitively and physically – and this will last in lifelong gains both economically and on the international stage, as we will see in the upcoming section.

Refath Bari

6 Olympic Medals & Nobel Prizes: What the Poor Man doesn't have

The facts are these: Bangladesh is the largest country in the world without an Olympic Medal, and the lowest Nobel Prize Winners per capita (Exception: Nigeria). Most will attribute that to Bangladesh's low-quality primary and secondary schools and the equally low-quality Madrasah schools in the nation. There's also the issue of many of the private schools not having adequate resources to meet student needs (the consequences of which we discussed in the previous chapter). And while these propositions are by no means outright wrong, they do not highlight the full facts of the story. The answers seem deceivingly simple, but as a matter of fact, lead to a rabbit hole of uncomfortable facts and disturbing truths. Will you jump in?

Table 4: A Lack of Achievement

1 Why does the poor man win no Olympic Medals?

2 Why does the poor man win no Nobel Prizes?

6.1 Why does the poor man win no Olympic Medals?

Height. Height makes all the difference between a poor man and a rich man. Here's why: the poor man often suffers from malnutrition, diarrhea, and other nutritional diseases, which stunt him at an early age, effectively making him shorter and less productive in his labor. This means that his annual wage for the rest of his life will be less than a poor person who does receive the appropriate micronutrients. In effect, Childhood malnutrition at an early age stunts not only physical growth, but also cognitive development. This is exactly what the Barker Hypothesis states: the conditions in which a uterus is born can have life-long impacts on the child's life chances. We see this in full force in Tanzania, where mothers who were given Iodine capsules had children who completed half a year more of schooling than the children of mother's who didn't take Iodine Capsuls. A single pill can be the make-or-break of a child's life – who would've thought? This is all the more important because the poor often complete only four or five years of schooling, and half a year more can be a game-changer. This extra educational attainment alone can provide the child an upper hand in whatever labor profession he chooses. The study even found that if every mother in Central and

South Africa took these capsules, the total educational attainment of children in these regions would increase by 7.5%. What a wonderful finding.

Here's another: the poor may not eat more (or more healthy, perhaps) maybe because of Spooky Action at a Distance. First off, even if a poor laborer makes $40 more in a year, his income fluctuates so much day to day that he might not realize he a net increase in income by the end of the year. Even worse, money is not so easy to come by, even if you work harder.

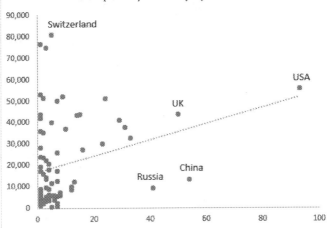

Figure 6: It's clear that GDP and Olympic Rankings per capita have a correlation: richer and bigger countries not only have more of a population to choose from in the frist place, but can also afford full time training.

Let's now change the subject to Micronutrients – an essential life-saver for the poor man. They're affordable, healthy, and effective; here we list just a few:

(1) **Deworming Pills**: Coming in at $1.36 USD PPP, these can be an incremental life-saver for the poor. A study in Kenya demonstrated that deworming children for two years instead of one would lead to a lifetime income gain of more than $3,300. Deworming pills essentially work against the worms in a undernourished body that fights with the host for calories and vitamins and nutrition.

(2) **Iodized Salt Packet**: At $0.62 in India, these simple packets can mean the difference between a bankrupt farmer and a profitable one. Why so? We need

Refath Bari

only look to Indonesia: farmers who are well-nouirsed (by means of Iodine or otherwise nutritional good) worked harder, but their employers didn't know that. As a result, when these farmers were employed under someone else, their incomes stayed frozen, but when they were self-employed, their incomes obviously shot up. We see the same in the Philliphines, where workers who were given food on a per-labor basis ate 25% food when they were nourished.

(3) **Fortified Fish Sauce**: At $7 a year, these sauces are an excellent investment. Studies have demonstrated that they bring a $46 yearly gain in income, making them a must-have for any poor farmer or laborer

Is there a connection between stunted children and Olympic failure? Economists Anne Case and Chris Paxson argue yes, in their paper "Stature and Status: Height, Ability, and Labor Market Outcomes". Case and Paxson find that taller adults hold more prominent positions, and on average, earn more than their shorter counterparts (Unfortunate Exception: Napolon Bonaparte). Case and Paxson argue this may be the case simply because taller people make for smarter people. Even before mandatory schooling begins in any country, at age and throughout their childhoods, taller children score significantly higher than their shorter counterparts. The primary reason for this is that taller people are more well-nourished, and thus smarter, and it is for this reason that they are led to more prominent jobs and greater incomes. Thus, this may indeed be the true reason Bangladesh holds no Olympic Medals – Gold, Silver, or Bronze: a height, nutritional, and educational deficit all contribute equally.

Prevalence of anemia in pregnant women, 2016

Prevalence of anemia in pregnant women, measured as the percentage of pregnant women with a hemoglobin level less than 110 grams per liter at sea level.

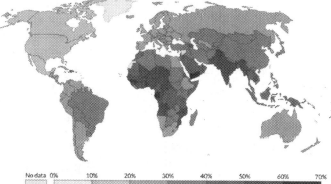

Many pregnant women in developing countries suffer from worms, which results in Anemia and Malnutrition, because worms are basically competitors in the child's own body, fighting for its own nutrients. These undernourished children grow to unproductive adults, end up with lower educational attainments, and in turn, give birth to their own small, nutritionally-deficient babies. And therein lies the invisible trap. And so it goes.

6.2 Why does the poor man win no Nobel Prizes?

Muhammad Yunus is the only Nobel Prize Winner born in Bangladesh. Before 2006, the eigth largest country in the world remained Nobel-Prize-Less. Why is this? Why cannot a country of 160 million produce a few bright minds? Why is it that it took nearly 40 years for the eight largest nation to win the Nobel? We've thoroughly highlighted the educational deficit that plays out in these developing countries in the previous chapter. But now I seek to change the subject to health, a perhaps equally-important player when it comes to intellectual achievement.

But perhaps its more important not to focus on the biggest population, but with one with the highest proportion of Nobel Leaurates: the Jewish Population. Despite being only 0.2% of the World Population, Jews make up the second-largest share of Nobel Leaurates, a remarkable achievement. And yet, Muslims make up more than 24.1% of the World Popiulation, but comprise only 0.8% of Nobel-Prize Leaurates. What's playing at this consequence are the exact same players as the Olympic Failure: It may be due to Bangladesh's nutritional, educational, and health deficit.

Let's first diagnose the state of the problem. It falls into two categories: (1) A Lack of Academic Achievemnt (2) A Lack of International Achievement. Let's look into the first case: there exists not a single tenured professor in an American University from either Pakistan or Bangladesh (a combined population of 350 million people). In other words, from a pool of 350 million people, not a single Bengali or Pakistani candidate has emerged to ascend to professorship in a top-tier Ivy League or even second-tier American State Universities. This naturally extends to the upmost recognition one can receive in one's field, which is the Nobel Prize. A single city in India, Calcutta, has produced twice the # of Nobel Leaurates that Bangladesh and Pakistan combined have ever produced. This is no fluke. We see the same phenomenon in professorships: there are two, three, sometimes four Indians in every department of top-tier American Universities. Indians have sent rockets to Mars, while we are still throwing rocks to the sky. What's going on? What's behind this intellectual deficit in the Pakistan and Bangladesh?

Refath Bari

Religion of Nobel Prize Winners 1901-2000

Global Population		Nobel Prize Winners
31.2%	Christian	65.4%
24.1%	Muslim	0.8%
16.0%	Unaffiliated	10.4%
15.1%	Hindu	0.7%
6.9%	Buddhist	1.1%
0.5%	Other	0.6%
0.2%	Jewish	21.1%

Figure 7: There are 2.3 billion Christains, making up a majority of the 7.4 billion of the World's Population.

I say two things: Education and Nutrition. First off, Education: the cracks begin at the root – at the foundation – and the problems show at the top. We need only look to Pakistan's HEC, the Higher Education Commision (responsible for higher education policy, the management and development of existing universities and provision of academic degrees). One of Pakistan's foremost academics, Dr. Pervez Hoodhboy, has called out the HEC's educational equivalent of fraud. The 9/11 Terror Attacks were a gift for Pakistan's HEC, as the nation joined the US in the War against Terror. Now here's where the story gets interesting: the US thought funding Pakistani Higher Education would be a small investment with huge returns – it would be the end of Islamic Radicalization as we know it! After US support, HEC budget increased 1200% in a single year. Well, this was no less than a miracle – a miracle that the then-chairman, Atta ur Rahman of the HEC sought to exploit. And exploit he did – in the span of a few months, the

PhDs awarded, papers published, and Pakistanis cited shot up. It was Opera, but for Higher Education: it seemed like everyone had a PhD now; in fact, some academics published more papers in a single year than a able Pakistani scientist could do in his whole lifetime half a century back. Rahman even claimed that Pakistani Mathematicians were cited 20% above the world average. Things were looking perfect – almost too perfect, for a country that was struggling with higher education just a few years back. It seemed like HEC had done the impossible: they'd not only fixed the existing institutions, but also drmatically increased the productivity of university academics in the span of just a few months.

And perhaps it was success that was their downfall – the speculative questions arose: Of that 20% statistic, were most of those citations self-citations? And if so many PhDs and papers had been published, where were all the applications – the new technologies, medicines, equipment? Why weren't other countries using Pakistan's advancements in math, medicine, and physics alike? As the questions tumbled in, so did the corruption. At the end of the day, HEC was shooting for meaningless numbers, when instead they could have focused on producing a steady stream of quality papers. Bangladesh is no doubt plagued by the same problem of corruption – at all levels, higher, primary, and secondary education alike.

We learn two lessons from this. And what are they? First and foremost, throwing money at the problem won't solve it. Money is to bueacrats as gold is to a robber: it encourages corruption. No – we need more than just money. We need equitable organizations that can be held responsible, and accountable for their behavior. A form of oversight that shares no national or politcal interest, but is solely devoted to the managmenet of the educational institution. We must adapt, and learn from our more successful peers in India, and the US. Second and equally important, this problem is not isolated to higher education. Nor is it isolated to Pakistan. Corruption is a powerful force that extends the borders of any one country – Bangladesh, Africa, India, Indonesia, among others, are all equally afflicted by corruption. The roots of this program stems further from higher education, all the way to primary education. The problem with primary education is that it is often so low-quality (and as we discussed, catered towards the most talented students) that poor students really have no incentive to learn in school. On top of that, being in school adds up to foregone labor for parents, and acts as "Informal Insurance" for the poor, many of whom face many financial shocks any given day. It gets worse: most students aren't even afforded nutrition at school. Most Bangladeshi, and Pakistani schools don't have anything in the way of school meals for children, even though it has been repeatedly demonstrated

Refath Bari

that school meals increases enrollment, engagement, and physical and cognitive development. And school meals can be provided easily, as demonstrated by affordable, long-lasting interventions by Pakistan's Tawana project-school nutrition program. By not providing children micronutrients in-school, children's parents are most likely not to feed their children any supplements such as Zinc or Iron-Fortified Fish Packets, mostly due to small costs that lead to procrastinative behavior (i.e., it's too expensive, I'll just buy it later) – even though that small cost results in a huge return on the investment in the form of additional labor productivity and physical and cognitive development.

To conclude: If they ever hope to be propelled to the International Stage in terms of both Physical and Cognitive Achievements by way of the Nobel Prize or Olympic Medals – Bangladesh, Pakistan, and (to a lesser extent) India, must implement nationwide school nutrition programs in primary schools and provide oversight comittees of higher education institutions so that (1) children receive the nutrition they need and grow into more physically and cognitively capable adults, thus able to perform better in academics and (2) higher education institutions will prioritize undergraduate teaching to foster and nature the curiosity of students, rather than emphasizing a rash of meaningless paper publications and PhDs.

7 Moral of the Story V

What are some of the foundational ideas we grappled with in this chapter? We saw that the poor man has a desparate need to enrichen his life, whether by means of spending more on specialized adult goods, nonessential assets, or festivals. We've applied this principle to food, as well. The poor man goes out of his way to find food of quality, not quantity. In this way, he ends up spending more on less healthy and more expensive calories. And even with essential micro-nutrients at his door, he refuses to take them – not because they're not affordable or nutritious – but because he prizes the pscyology of feeling rich rather than eating poor. And so, developing nations like Bangladesh end up disturbingly short on both intellectual (the Nobel Prize) and physical (Olympics) achievements. Now I hope to establish the lines of demarcation between the facts and fictions of poverty, and perhaps its most misunderstood cousin, Food.

Table 5: Breaking the Falsehoods of Poverty

Fiction	Fact
I see two spikes in the Religion of Nobel Prize Winners: Christians and Jews. The Christians are easily explained – they're the largest population on earth. But the Jewish – they're just an anomaly. How can they emerge so high on one of the largest intellectual achievements in the world? Perhaps it is education alone that accounts for this difference between the Nobel Prizes accumulated by the Jewish versus their Muslim Counterparts.	Education alone cannot be a sufficient explanation. I'm not the only one asking this question. Dr. Perez Hoodboy, a Pakistani prominent Nuclear Physcist, posed his own question "Can Pakistan expect to get its own Stephen Hawking?" Hoodboy was disturbed upon investigating the question further: Not a single Pakistani had tenure had a mathematics department in any Ivy League University. He expanded his search to include Second-Tier American Universities, and did not find a single Pakistani Mathematician with Tenure. This is not a problem isolated to Pakistan – the same problem afflicts Bangladesh. Let's analyze what the two countries have in common (believe it or not, much more than they have in difference): India and Pakistan are the biggest countries with the lowest Olympic Medals per Capita – India has one medal for every 45 million people, and Pakistan has one for every 18 million. Bangladesh isn't even on the list. That's Physical Achievement. We look at Cognitive Achievements (Nobel Prizes, Field Medals, etc.), and find the same story. Look at Professorships and once again, we find the same story. In the final section of this chapter, Nobel Prizes and Gold Medals: What the Poor Man doesn't have – I attempt to get to the basis of this phenomenon through a combination of Education, Nutrition, History, and Psychology.

Refath Bari

Fiction	Fact
A rich person would spend more on food than a poor one, which is why rich countries are devoid of health problems like malnutrition and anemic mothers.	Naturally, developing countries where the population does not receive much nutrients are at risk of these symptoms, and thus risk falling behind global economic competition and innovation. Micronutrients are the root issue behind lower labobr productivity, mental retardation, and stunted physical and cognitive development. The fact of the matter is that due to the high costs of most cereals, low-income households are forced to consume montonous diets (indeed, as I suggested above, the cheapest diet is only 21 cents, but consists only of eating bananas and eggs, as highlighted by Abhijit Banerjee). On the other hand, richer households are free supplement their regular food items with a variety of nutrient-rich foods.
Government Subsidy programs are the answer to providing the poor the exact nutritious food that they need.	Indonesia tells us this is not the case. Only after strict monitoring and the application of the Law of Common Knowledge did Indonesia's biggest food welfare program, Raskin, become a success. Before that, it was plagued by corruption, inaccuracy, and misinformation. And obviously, the poor are the most vulnerable to misinformation, a vulnerability corrupt bruacrats are eager to exploit. This may be the exact same scenario playing out in Bangladesh and India.

Table 6: Breaking the Falsehoods of Poverty

Table 7: Breaking the Falsehoods of Poverty

Fiction	Fact
The average poor man spends every cent and nickel on essential food and calories. His sole goal is to maximize his intake of calories, and his every meal goes to that goal.	This is counerintuitive, but the poor man's goal is not just to maximize calorie intake, but also to maximize the quality of his food. It's impractical to assume that the poor will willingly follow a rudimentary, monotonous diet that is nutritious. As such, we must find a way to put the micronutrients that the poor need to survive into their hands so that they naturally demand it. Perhaps the answer is a healthy combination of a supply and demand-driven approach, much like education.
It is impractical to truly eridate malnutrition. For one, it's just a logistical nightmare: how do you even distribute so much food on such a large scale? On top of that, its a complex policy: how do you convince the poor man that these nutritional packets and sauces are for his own good?	That's right. It is a long shot – for one, there's the issue of brucratic institutions slowing down the and often corrupting the delivery of food to the poor. But then, there's also the much larger issue of educating the poor of the importance of these nutrients in the first place. One way may be the supply-driven approach, which is to simply provide children school meals that come pre-loaded with micronutrients such as Iron, Zinc, and Vitamins. But then there's also the issue of pregnant mothers – in most cases, children who are born nutritionally deficient do not have a choice; in fact, their life quality is decided primarily by their mother's health. Thus, we must get the medicinal improvements over the last couple of years in nutrition into the hands of pregnant mothers in developing countries, many of whom who suffer from symptoms of anemia, and other malnutritional diseases.

Refath Bari

Table 8: Breaking the Falsehoods of Poverty

Fiction	Fact
Look, they're the one's working. We have no right to make decisions for them. After all, they probably know what's best for their own good. In that way, maybe eating less food *is* the way to go for the poor man. After all, less is more.	We know for a fact that the BMI (Body Mass Index) of the poor is severely under the recommended BMI for working adults. And we know that the poor consume less and less nutritious food as their incomes increase. So what are we left to but our own devices? Well, as I explained previously, we must find a way to incentivize micronutrients for the poor so that they are enticed to buy them, because their benefits outweight their costs. For the poor man, every decision is seen as an oppurtunity cost – whether they know this conciously or not. As such, we must make it beneficial for the poor man to invest in Micronutrients, much the same way Seva Mandir incentivized immunizations by providing Dal to the village residents of one Indian community, which shot up vaccination rates from 6% to 38%.
Aha, I've found an exception to your rule that there's enough food to go around in today's world. Paradox: if there's enough food, why's there still famines throughout the developing world?	As Economics Nobel Leaurate Amartya Sen noted, many of today's famines are the result of food mismanagement by the govenrment during a time of crisis. We've examined the Bangladesh Famine of 1974, but this is no isolated issue. "No famine has ever taken place in the history of the world in a functioning democracy," Sen states in Democracy as a Freedom. And while Sen's thesis stands the test of time (India has had no large-scale loss of life since Independence in 1947), there still leaves a lot to be desired in the way of steady rise in starvation and hunger (especially due to COVID19)

Table 9: Breaking the Falsehoods of Poverty

Fiction	Fact
Perhaps school meals can be an effective means of curbing malnutrition and other public health consequences of a lack of malnutrition in poor countries.	School meals have been proven to not only increase student attendance, but also increase student achievement in both the classroom and standardized exams and cognitive tests. For instance, even in America, some public schools have experienced an attendance growth of 30% to 90% just because of the introduction of free breakfast and lunch meals. In fact, attendance was highest on the first and last days of the weekday, when students were especially hungry going into the weekends, where they often had no food. The situation is no different in developing countries – and indeed, introducing free breakfast and lunch not just in cafetarias but even in classrooms may serve to produce even higher returns in terms of student achievement in the form of increased student engagement and development.
Here's the problem: there's not enough food reaching the poor man's open hands. Its obvious: just send shiploads of rice his way; Alternatively, lower the cost of subsidized nutritional goods so that the poor can buy more of them	As demonstrated by Indonesia's Raskin food welfare program, sending buckloads of food to the poor man's door doesn't guarantee he will actually receive it, due to the ever-consistent factors of corruption and buraracy. As such, if these large-scale food programs are implemented in developing nations, they must be accompanied by equally-adequate minotoring agencies that track the efficiency and success of these welfare programs.

Refath Bari

Table 10: Breaking the Falsehoods of Poverty

Fiction	Fact
A couple of pills and capsules can't eridicate malnutrition. If it were the case, it would have been done already!	There can't be a $100 bill on the street. If it were there, someone would've taken it already! This is a recurring theme in traditional economics, when the traditionalists claim that an approach will not work through simple theory or ideology. It is the same folly that failed Archimedes thousands of years before. Instead, we must make a broader shift to Normative Economics – towards policies and interventions that have actually been proven to uplift the lives of the poor. Indeed, this is exactly what Nobel Prize Winning Economists Abihijit Banerjee and Esther Duflo's JPAL (Abdul Latif Jameel Poverty Action Lab) does via Randomized Control Trails and definitive evidence. What JPAL has done is start an economic revolution that has geared economics as a hard science – making it based on actual trials (much like trials in Medicine), instead of foundationless ideologies and backwards arguments.
The poor doesn't consume micronutrients like Iron and Vitamins because they're inaccesible, expensive, or inconvenient for the poor, for any number of reasons.	The essentials are there and they are cheap, as in the case of Iron-fortified fish sauce, Iodized Salt Packets or Zinc. And yet, because of the poor man's resistance to buying these (which may be explained by the natural human tendency to procrastinate in the face of a small cost), malnutrition arises. It can arise in three ways: (1) hunger (2) obesity (3) micronutrient deficiency.

Chapter 8

Population

Refath Bari

55 Days in Dharavi

We examine the question of population at two scales: the Macroscopic and Microscopic. We begin at the macro level by investigating four famous population control programs in Asia: Bangladesh's Family Planning Program in the 1970s, Indira Ghandi's Agressive Popoulation Control Campaign, Pakistan's Recent Half-hearted Attempts with FP2020 and finally China's infamous one-child policy plan. But the macroscopic level only gives a diagnosis of the problem: a what, not why. To find the why, we must zoom in, into the microscopic behavior of families on an individual basis. We try to understand how families behave as both units and as complex hubs of decision-making between two individuals (husband and wife). We discover that macroscopic populations of communities are tightly linked with their microscopic counterparts by way of phenomenon such as social, religious, and cultural pressure. By carefully analyzing the relationship between these two population structures – families and communities and eventually, nations at-large – we are finally able to reach a definitive conclusion on the age-old question of population: "Why do the poor have so many babies?" (an answer I cannot reveal in the abstract)

Keywords: Missing Women, One-Child Policy, Bangladesh Family Planning Program, Becker's Theorem, Sex-Selection, Fertility, Contraception, Family Structures, Social Services

1 Case Study: Pomolla Singh

Thid time was *not* the charm – far from it. Seems like seventh time was the case for Pomolla Singh and her husband Haisan. Let me be honest: I didn't exactly end in Pomolla and Haisan's house by mistake. It was rather, an unfortunate series of events, as one might put it. "Just keep walking straight, you will know when you see it," the cab driver promised me. "You came in the busiest time of the day,

Refath Bari

so I need 50% tip". This was no auto-rickshaw, so I had no way of telling if I was getting scammed out of my hard-earned rupees. I ended up paying the guy 120 Rupees (which he was no doubt happy to see, judging by the childish delight in his face) for a 20 minute ride – half of that was being stuck in traffic. And his windows were broken, so I couldn't even roll them down. It was by all accounts a miracle, that I survived the car ride. Now all I had to do was find Lakshmi Market. Just go straight, he said. It felt like a war trying to even walk: cars and autorickshaws almost running over me on the left and hundreds of people jamming through me; I couldn't even ask for directions – everything was that hectic. By great will, or simply luck, I somehow turned the corner on God-knows-what road. All hell broke loose on the 55th minute. The blazing hymn of the people was replaced by a great fury of noise – what looked like a bunch of shirtless young men stomping the ground in great fury and ryhtm, banging their drums along the way. Their faces glistened with sweat, but they pounded like it was the end of the world. Here I was barely hanging on to life in my fifty pound heavy-weight black coat and I found my polar opposite on the other side, shirtless and all. But what I also found was a bunch of children, running around and celebrating with the young men. By the time I got to the other side (another story for another day), I found a group of kids huddled around a young woman and a considerably older man (presumably, her husband) – she was covered in a colorless purple sweater peckered with white snow dots and her hair was covered in a biege hijab, while a ring pierced her nose. The husband leaned back on the wall, what looked like a cigarette bobbing in his mouth – his skinny beard peckered below his nose as he wore a black-white checkered shirt. He pulled back one of his kids from getting too close to the parade of young men, but refused to do anything that would require spitting out his ciggarete. I knew better than to ask; instead, I showed them by ID, and Haisan grabbed all his children to him, spitting a broken stub. "No, no, I'm just an interviewer. I just want to ask some questions, that's all" After a few minutes of convincing that I was indeed a researcher, I checked off the usual qualifications. Income? *Check.* Shanty? Well actually, "House?" Hasian nodded. *Check.* A few hundred checks later, and I happened to know a good deal about Haisan, Pomolla, and their seven children. For one, the family actually had nine children, but one passed away due to consistent diarrheal bouts, and the other ran away from the home a couple of years ago. I saw Hasian's eye twitch as I mentioned the lost one, and he kept blinking in the harsh Pune Sun. Of those that remained, only two were boys, both of whom were dressed in matching brown t-shirts and light-up sneakers, probably for the parade. "The smarter one's in private. His *daada* pay for him to go Bishop's Private, best in Pune". There was a ring of pride in Haisan's voice, but it rang hollow when I asked him about his five older daughters. "How can send all of them to school? Please don't ask me that kind of question. It makes me think I'm not ... " Haisan paused, but shook his head, only to continue, "I send them to the fields, or I will lose so much money. And if I pay for their school now, how will I pay their dowry after they marry? After they marry, they gone! I never see them again, and you are asking me to put so much into them now, if it will mean zero later?" I scribbled all I could in the span of Haisan's short burst. "What about him?" I asked, looking at the other son. "He's in public, and we pay for him. He is good, but he is still small, so let's see what happens." Haisan said with a shrug. "Let's see what happens" I followed. And I'm happy to see we left on a good note (an literal good note – as always, I signed off my good will to Haisan and Pomolla and left them what little Rupees I had, even after being scammed by the driver).

Figure 1: Pomolla shows me the youngest of the seven, Akhilesa, named after the all-pervading, omnipotent Hindu God

Refath Bari

2 Pomolla's List

Pomolla's story teaches us the importance of big families to the poor, but it also struggles to communicate the dangers of big families from a national, administrative, and public health standpoint. What seems rational or downright inevitable in the microsocopic decisions of families may not be so in the larger context of nations, and states, and even communities. This chapter hopes to harmonize the relationship between large and small; macro and micro; high and low. And this is how we'll do it:

(I) High View: The State of the Population

(II) Low View: The Decisions of Families

3 High View: The State of the Population

The high level view only affords us so much clarity. But what it does offer us is a diagnosis – how bad is the problem? How many babies are people generally having? What is the replacement fertility rate and why have developing countries rapidly implemented family programs to quickly achieve it? What's the point of the fertility rate in the first place? These are all the forms of questions we hope to answer in this crucial section.

Table 1: A Pregnant Pause

1 What is the state of the fertility rate?

2 Why is fertility rate important?

3.1 What is the state of the fertility rate?

Because fertility rates are so innately linked to population, let's examine the population first. As of 2015, about 140 million children are born every year – 110 million of them from Africa and Asia alone, and the other 30 million from the remaining continents combined. Coincidentally, perhaps, the greatest poverty is in Southeast Asia and Subsaharan Africa, which have some of the world's highest fertility rates, mortality rates, and malnutrition rates.

The state of the fertility rate in many developing countries has been on the downward trend for much of the late 20th century and mostly plataeued for the early 21st century. No country has been immune to lowering fertility rates, especially due to advances in medicine, economic development, and technology alike – all of which has made it possible to offer greater security to mothers around the world. To understand the state of the reduced fertility rate, we need only look to its greatest beneficiaries, the old trio of Southeast Asia: Bangladesh, India, and Pakistan.

History and Future of the World Population by Total Fertility

Shown is the estimated total fertility rate – the number of children per woman – for each country in the world over time. Future projections are based on the UN Population Division Medium Variant projection.

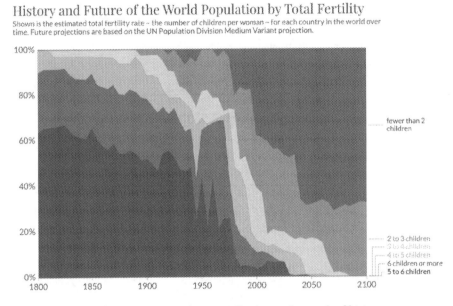

Figure 2: Oftentimes, we neglect to realize how – for much of history – the average woman had six babies, on average, many of whom she was forced to watch die due to malnutrition or other health problems, due to the high child mortality rates at the time.

After a bunch of economic shocks (what was an unfortunate combination of famines, extreme monsoons, and food misminagement) slapped the Bengladeshi government into reality, the Bangldesh government finally took action and implemented family planning programs, executed by young, educated, and assertive women from the most remote villages in Chittagong to the most dense districts of Dhaka. These young women made the rounds in villages, advertising the importance of sterilization and the Bangladesh fertility rate plummeted from 6.95 in 1970 to 2.06 as of 2017, the lowest of any of its Southeast Asian peers.

India had its own population control attempt under the reign of Indira Ghandi,

Refath Bari

to date the only Woman Prime Minister of India (perhaps that's why she had both the audacity and ambition required to implement such a large-scale program). Indira Gandhi, the "Iron Woman of India", was the second-longest serving Prime Minister after her father. Gandhi lamented that all of India's economic growth would be of no use if the population wasn't reigned in under control. She launched the campaign with the fire and fury that only the Iron Woman could have, and the picture of the ideal Indian family with two children became ubiquitous in the second largest nation in the world. Twist enough arms and you can get anything done – this was the methodology of Indira, who centralized power unlike any any PM before. The program was a success, largely because of the Law of Commmon Knowledge: everyone from the local officials to the home guard constable to the distrcit collector knew of the sterilization quota. What wasn't a success was the Iron Woman's political career. After the stringent population sterilization program, she was elected out of office after holding two national emergencies to postpone elections. When she finally did lift the emergency status, she did so because she badly misjudged her approval ratings (the heavily censored press that praised her rain-or-shine did nothing to help).

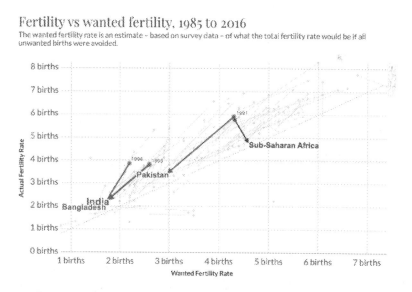

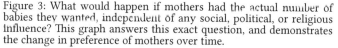

Figure 3: What would happen if mothers had the actual number of babies they wanted, independent of any social, political, or religious influence? This graph answers this exact question, and demonstrates the change in preference of mothers over time.

Pakistan is a different story – there exists explicit and implicit (we'll find out what that means later) demand for contraception and reproductive health care services, but a beauracratic, and shiftless government has managed to fail the public's demand. As the sixth largest country in the world and a higher fertility rate than both its southeast asian peers, Pakistan is in unique danger of a public health crisis (and COVID19 can only make that worse).

Fertility rate vs the share living in extreme poverty, 2015

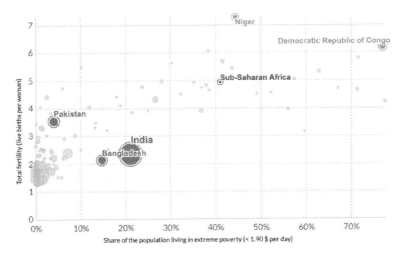

Figure 4: As the share of population living in extreme poverty decreases, the fertility rate plummets much faster. It is clear from above that the countries in Subsaharan Africa are not in good state, as they seem to have a fatal – combustible, in fact – combination of high fertility rates and extreme poverty, conditions that can only pave the way for high mortality in both children and mothers.

After the three trios, of course, we have none other than neighboring China, and its draconian one-child policy. The enactment of the One-Child policy in 1979 was a truly singular moment in human history when economics, politics, and humanity collided to create an unprecedented policy decision unseen in human history. While its consequences remain debated to this day, the one-child policy unquestionably altered the population's perception of Women in Chinese society. Prior to the one-child policy, educational opportunities were disproportionately reserved for men, as home-caring opportunities were for women. But with the dawn of the radical policy, families left with one girl enrolled their child into

Refath Bari

school more often, and with only one child to invest in, there remained no option but to fully invest in one child, rather than discriminate between multiple.

Birth Rate: The number of births per 1,000 people in the population, 1911 to 2009

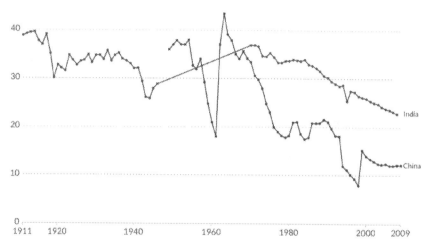

Figure 5: India and China, the largest two countries in the world, collectively make up 37% of the world's population and population control has been a major initiative that has shaped the histories of both of these countries.

Such educational oppurtunities resulted in a generation educated like never before; a generation acutely aware of the active legalized genocide against them. With the advent of the one child policy and a drop in fertility rates, greater job prospects opened up just as the most educated generation in contemporary Chinese history began participating in industry. With more families earning greater income, many families lifted themselves out of poverty. With such an educated generation engaged in industry, the Chinese economy surged, and Chinese families saved up more money, spending less on consumer goods to the point that as of 2018, China's personal saving rate is 25% and national savings makes up 47% of the GDP, compared to the United States' 0.5% personal savings rate and national savings make up 12% of the GDP (such a high savings rate for a rapidly developing economy such as China reflects a populace with either no faith in the government, due to lack of government-paid jobs, or very expensive living costs). This growth would have been impractical without the one-child policy; China's fertility rate has been projected to be 2.1 in 2006, compared to a rate of

1.6 due to the policy. Even this small change of 0.5 in fertility rates has enormous economic dividends for China, producing 24% more resources for familial and national investment. In fact, since 1996, the Chinese economy has grown almost 8% every year, an unprecedented economic growth credited with lifting over 150 million people out of poverty – an astounding achievement.

Children per woman, 1950 to 2015

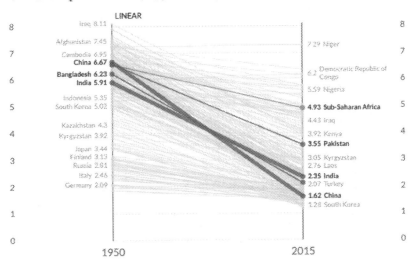

Figure 6: The Southeast Asian Countries have had the most drastic change in fertility rates, along with China. Countries in Sub-Saharan Africa, however, have not been so fortunate – we need only look to the Democratic Republic of Congo or Niger to see this effect in action.

In retrospect, the one-child policy may have been a necessary force of evil, a sacrifice millions of Chinese families took for the greater economic benefit of the nation. When the policy was first launched in 1979 – in the hope that "the rate of population growth may be brought under control as soon as possible," as declared by the Chinese State Council – it was backed by the most powerful force in China, Deng Xiao-ping, the renowned 'Architect of Modern China' who proclaimed that if fertility rates didn't drop, "we will not be able to develop our economy and raise the living standards of our people". Indeed, Deng's assessment may have been right, as China claims that its one-child policy has reduced their expected population size by more than 400 million people in less than 40 years.

Refath Bari

But even this figure is flawed; as countries develop, their fertility rates naturally drop. For instance, Japan, a rapidly developing country, recently announced a total reduction of 300,000 people in 2016, because there were less than 1 million births for the first time in the country's history. In comparison, even with the one child policy, China had one million greater births than deaths every five weeks in 2006.

Children per women vs. unmet need for contraception (% of married women aged 15-49), 2014

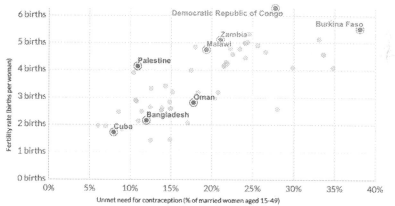

Figure 7: There exists a huge unmet demand for contraceptives in developing countries, as evident from the graph above. We find especially that developing countries with higher fertility rates may be the result of an unmet demand for reproductive health services.

But even China's singular objective of economic superiority came at a dangerous cost. The one-child policy may have been a necessary force of evil, a sacrifice millions of Chinese families took for the greater benefit of the nation, but a sacrifice is voluntary; and the one-child policy was anything but. To millions of Western bystanders, the one-child policy was seen as a uniformly enforced policy on each and every one of China's 1.4 billion inhabitants. In reality, such equity would have no place in China's cold bureaucracy. Of the 30% of the population on whom the policy was actually enforced, it disproportionately targeted poor families, enforcing fines and property penalties on families with multiple children; penalties that only the rich could afford to withstand. Fortunately, the free market has produced liberal views in the West that prioritize human rights more than any economic outcome. In fact, regardless of the market economy, most governments take a sacred hippocratic oath to preserve and protect the basic human rights of their people, including the right to reproduction and family planning. But China has outright violated this sacred oath to preserve the liberties of its people; in fact, the implementation of the one-child came with strict enforcement of brutal birth control programs that outright violated the basic human right of family planning, as declared in the International Conference of Human Rights a decade before the one child policy's implementation in 1968.

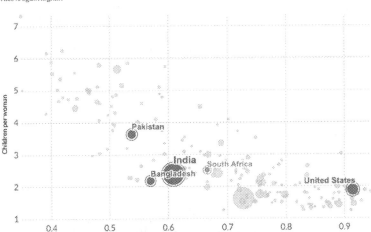

Children per woman vs. Human Development Index, 2014

The fertility rate is much higher in countries with low living standards. But at very high living standards the fertility rate is again higher.

Figure 8: At low standards of living, the fertility rates are high, and then ticks up again for very high standards of living, as evident from the example of the United States. Then again, fertility rates are highly subject to economic shocks such as the Global Pandemic we live in right now or Economic Reccessions or World Wars, so HDI isn't the only factor – economic shocks also play a role.

These birth control programs induced an increase in abortion and female sterilization in the 1980s, eventually culminating in the premature deaths of millions of women, and a culurual and generational preference for boys over girls. At one point in the 1990s in China, the birth cohort had a sex ratio of 1.17, with 117 boys for every 100 girls, in excess of the maximum ratio of 1.11 and the natural ratio of 1. The upshot is a sex ratio that clearly exposes the severe punishment the one-child policy afflicted on women, both culturally and socially. Even worse were those who suffered the collateral damage of China's one-child policy – the orphaned children, many of whom were girls left out in archaic state-run orphanages because they were either abandoned by their parents, or had no parents in the first

Refath Bari

place. Even when families abroad sought to adopt orphaned girls, China made it intentionally difficult for them to adopt Chinese orphans, raising prices so high that only the wealthiest could afford to adopt, resulting in millions of children left uncared for in neglectful state-run institutions. Perhaps the greatest victim of the one-child policy has been the children. With most households having one child, these children end up caring for four grandparents and their parents simultaneously, a heavy burden on their most productive labor years. The result was overburdened children hoping to outsource their duties to charitable supporters, most with no luck. As Sociology professor Feng Wang warns, "By implementing the one-child policy, China reaped the short-term gains, but by draining the pond, they ensured that there would no longer be fish".

Maternal mortality ratio vs. Fertility rate, 1990 to 2015

Maternal mortality ratio is the number of women who die from pregnancy-related causes while pregnant or within 42 days of pregnancy termination per 100,000 live births. 'Total Fertility Rate' measures the average number of children per woman.

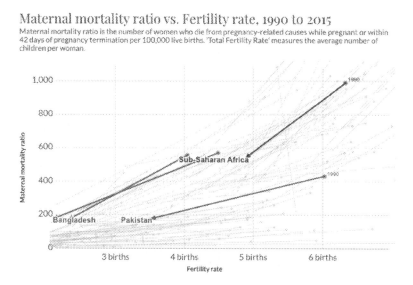

Figure 9: As fertility rates have been reduced due to population control campaigns and the millennium development goals, so has maternal mortality – recall that high fertility rates at a young age incurs most damage to the mother and child.

The richest parts of China have the worst crises in terms of child sex ratio, and with greater development, the problem is only getting worse. As seen above, most of the rich business and social districts have the worst sex ratios. Enter the One Child Act, an act notorious for limiting Chinese parents to only one child since 1976. Since then, however, slight relaxations have been enacted that allow Chinese parents to try again if their first baby is a girl, but these relaxations have had insignificant, if any, effects on the growing proportion of boys per every 1000 girls in China. Following the one-child act, China's sex ratio skyrocketed, reaching up to 1.2 in some regions.

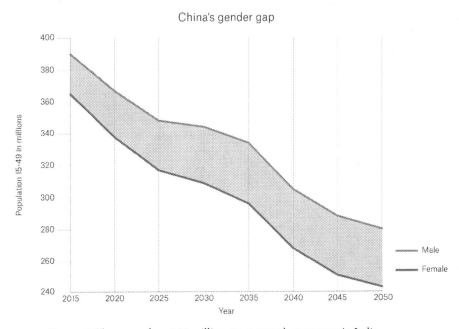

Figure 10: There are almost 70 million more men than women in India and China combined (a clear underestimate, since many districts in India and China alike are keen on underreporting the numbers). This creates a disturbing imbalanced gender ratio in the two largest countries in the world and sets the wrong kind of role model for other developing countries.

The above graph shows China and India, two of the most populated and rapidly developing countries in Asia, face dangerously high sex ratios relative to their western peers. As evident from the graph, India's worst exponent of a dangerously high sex ratio is Punjab, home to the Indian Agriculutral Green Revolution (which began in 1965). As they become richer and more developed, India and China continue to face worse sex ratios.

Why did the One Child Act increase China's sex ratio? To understand the question, we must first understand why the expected sex ratio is one. Given n births, what is the expected value for the number of male births? Since the probability that any birth will either be a boy or girl, there is a 50% chance the baby will be

Refath Bari

a boy and a 50% chance it'll be a girl. Instead of focusing on individual babies or families, we examine the population at large, realizing that out of n births, exactly half should be boys and the other half girls. Even if individual families vary in the gender of their babies, when considered as a whole, there will be an average of $\frac{n}{2}$ girl babies and $\frac{n}{2}$ boy babies in the population. So why doesn't reality conform to our biological expectations? Perhaps the answer is development; in some way, there are birth complications occurring disproportionately when a baby is a girl, and all it takes to reform the problem of "missing women" is development. As it turns out, development is far from the answer. In fact, looking at the following map of China, we note that the sex ratios are the greatest in the most developed regions (Shanghai being a notable exception) of China, including Beijing, and Ho Chi Min. Moving farther to the northwest to the poorer regions of China, sex ratios decline to the point they simply become one. The same problem is prevalent in India, where — once again — the richest areas have the worst sex ratios. In fact, the two richest states of India — Punjab and New Delhi have sex ratios above 1.2, higher than anywhere else in the country. Naturally, the emergence of selective sex technology has enabled parents to abort a female fetus. Although the service is illegal by name, it is a common practice throughout India and other developing countries. Otherwise, parents can simply neglect their unwanted to children to get rid of them – a disturbing thought that nonetheless explains the "Missing Women" phenomenon.

When expectations do not conform to reality in Economics, there is always a human factor that must be considered, however sadistic. As is the case with Missing Women. On July 16, 1986, Nobel Laureate Amartya Sen saw a dark matter existing within Africa, China, and other Southeastern countries in Asia. Unbeknownst to the public or those countries, this dark matter was leading to an alarming outcome in these countries, all of them characterized by disturbing sex ratios in which men outnumbered women by the thousands, if not millions. This was the dark matter that Amartya Sen had found – the matter of missing women. Sen calculated that over 100 million women were missing from the world as of July 16, 1986, a number that has only grown worse over the coming decades. And yet, 34 years after Sen's startling assessment, the matter of missing women remains missing from the minds of many. This ignorance is unacceptable, as it justifies a horrific phenomena and enables those who seek to profit from the trend of missing women. Missing women are by definition, a contradiction – women who should exist, but don't. The story of missing women is a story of nurture versus nature; a story of individuals actively and culturally acting against the forces of mother nature. Economics predicts that every country in the world should have a greater number of women than men. While girls have greater mortality rates than boys, on average, they also have greater life expectancies than men in nearly every country in the world. By 60, most men, especially those living in third-world countries, suffer from respiratory diseases as their arteries clog and tighten and often lead to cardiovascular complications. As such, economic models predict that every country in the world should have a greater number of women than men. In other words, the sex ratio (ratio of men to women) of any given country in the world should be greater than or equal one. And sure enough, theory meets reality nearly perfectly in the west: the United States has a sex ratio of 1; the UK has 1.05; all of Latin America has a ratio greater than 1, and Australia has a ratio of 1.022. But then we turn to the east; more specifically, Africa and South Asia. The results are astounding. Southeast asia has a sex ratio of 0.94; Bangladesh has a ratio of 0.95; India has a ratio of 0.93; and Pakistan has 0.96, all below the expected ratio of 1.

The countries with a greater number of males than females are in blue, stretching from northeast Africa, around Morocco, all the way to China.

These numbers tell a frightening story – that something is either actively or indirectly leading to the disappearance of millions of women around the world on a daily basis. To find the number of missing women, we use Amartya Sen's formula total population * (number of males/number of females) - current # females. Where would be expect the sex ratio to be the worst? An area where poverty disproportionately affects women more than men: Africa. Africa has the highest fertility rates in the world, and the highest rate of birth complciations in the world, as a result of reduced access to contraceptives such as surgery or pills, which results in one of the worst sex ratios in the world. That's the worst-case scenario. Now what if we took that and applied it to China, the largest country in the world? The result is an astounding 44 million missing women – and that's in 1986. By now, the number must be far worse. Applying Africa's sex ratio to all the developing countries in Southeast Asia including Bangladesh, India, and Pakistan, they have missing women of 4 million, 37 million, and 7 million, respectively. Doing the same for all countries with sex ratios smaller than one, we get a total sum of 100 million missing women – an astounding result.

Money is the key to health, economy, and education. And we expect it to be the silver bullet for the missing women crisis. There are few crises in the world on the scale of missing women and fewer still that stand the test of time. For the last 40 years, numerous socio-economic factors have contributed to the premature death of women in the above countries, fueling the crisis of missing women. We expect the answer to be money, whether in the form of development aid,

Refath Bari

or rising economies. As countries become richer, they gain access to the tools that should enable them to cure the crisis of missing women. But that's exactly the problem. Development is not the answer, and in fact has made the crisis far worse. As developing countries continue to grow in GDP and enjoy economic growth, the problem of missing women has gotten worse. In fact, development is inversely correlated with the number of missing women; as countries grow more developed, their sex ratio continues to decline, and the number of missing women expands. The crisis of missing women is perhaps most evident in China, the one-child nation, and the largest country in the world, home to 1.4 billion people. China is uniquely burdened with the crisis of missing women, a crisis that threatens to overpower its status as an economic stronghold. In fact, the number of men outnumber women by so great a margin that there are 30 million more men than women in China, as of December 2018. Recent outbreaks such as the SARs virus in 2003 and the novel Coronavirus of 2020 has slightly balanced the gender gap, as they tend to afflict men more than women. Furthermore, these outbreaks discriminate against the poor, who have less resources to defend themselves in the case of medical emergencies.

4 Low View: The Decisions of Families

Fertility Rate is one of the most crtical development indicators. Reduced fertility rates have been associated with rapid economic growth, as in the case of Korea and Brazil in the 1960s. But its not as clear-cut as it seems: these lower fertility rates may instead be the result of families being more financially content and thus having less babies. Perhaps parents have more financial freedom as a result of economic growth and feel empowered to make other investments. Replacement Fertility Rate (around two kids per mother) is the minimum number of children required for the preceding population to be of equal size to the current one.

Table 2: **A Pregnant Pause**

1 If Education implies Health, does the converse hold?

2 What are the supply and demand debates of Population?

4.1 If Education implies Health, does the converse hold?

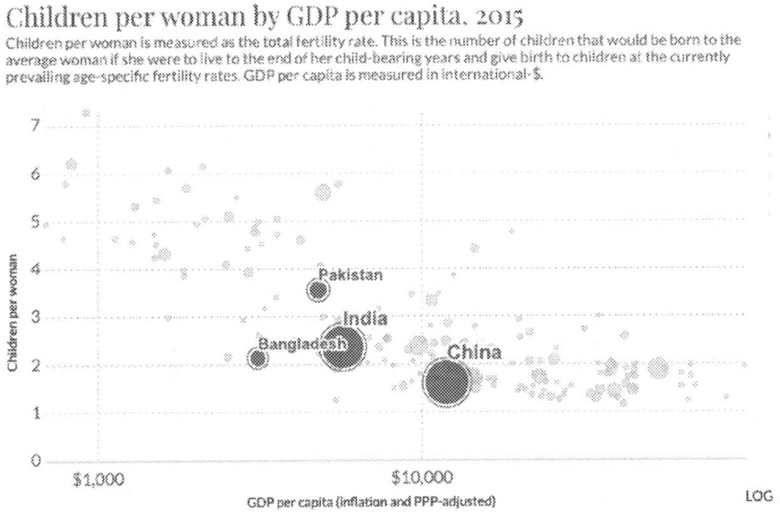
Children per woman by GDP per capita, 2015
Children per woman is measured as the total fertility rate. This is the number of children that would be born to the average woman if she were to live to the end of her child-bearing years and give birth to children at the currently prevailing age-specific fertility rates. GDP per capita is measured in international-$.
Children per woman
7
6
5
4
3
2
1
0
Pakistan
India
Bangladesh
China
$1,000
$10,000
GDP per capita (inflation and PPP-adjusted)
LOG

Figure 11: The poorest countries have the highest fertility rates, but fertility rates again peak/steady once we arrive at the richer countries.

We've seen the power of education reflected in many sectors – perhaps most important is that of Health. Education alone lowers fertility rates, likelihood of early marriage, early pregnancy, and child mortality. School, in other words, can do more for a child's health than any life-saving medicine or pill can. But the converse does not hold – lower fertility rates would intuitively to better education for each invidual child, no? After all, if a parent conceives less children, they have more capital to invest in each of them. But all is not what it seems. We need only look to Bangladesh to see proof of this in action: in the family planning program's roots in Matlab, Bangladesh, despite lower fertility rates, there was an absolute null effect on the educatoinal attainment on mothers and their children. Enrollment did not increase, and neither did the # years spent in school. So if children are not benefiting from lower fertility rates, who is? As it turns out, the benefits of lower fertility rates (i.e., less money needed to invest in a child), are reduced with its disadvantages.

Parents in the treatment villages where contraception was made avialable received 2500 taka less from their children, on average. Nevertheless, their quality of life – or at least the quality of their assets – seemed to increase: parents in the treatment village had 55,000 taka more in assets than their contraceptive-

Refath Bari

deprived counterparts. And in fact – more than just null effect – the educational attainment of children actually improve after higher fertility rates, a totally counterintuitive idea found by Nancy Qiang in her paper "Quantity-Quality and the One Child Policy: The Positive Effect of Family Size on School Enrollment in China". Qiang's finding flew in the face of decades of contemporary belief – that decreased fertility rates implied greater educational attainment and that the opposite would not hold – Becker's Theorem in a Nutshell.

Fertility rate vs. mean years of schooling, 1870 to 2010

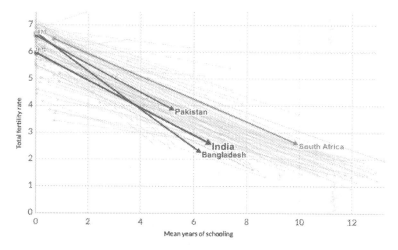

Figure 12: It seems that as the fertility rate decreases, the mean years of schooling that a child/woman receives increases. As such, we may conclude that fertility rates and education have an inversely proportional relationship. But the deeper question to ask here may be if this effect is a correlation or a causation.

4.2 What are the supply and demand debates of Population?

But the question of population is difficult – and once again, it endorses two views: that of the supplier and the demander. The supplier says that all we need are contraceptives. Establish clinics all over rural and urban developing countries alike, and provide contraceptives to every remote village, and the issue of population and reproductive health will be all but solved, the supplier claims. This is not so. Even though contraceptoin has proven to increase women's height and weight and career aspiratoins, many women in developing countries instead opt to have babies, which can be damaging to a mother's health – especially to a young mother (often the case in arranged early marriages, as in the case of Pomolla, who told me that she was 19 when she married to Haisan). The question now becomes if having so many babies at a young age is damamging to the mother, why does she still have them? Is she pressured by society? By her husband? By her religion? How much power do she actually have in determining her child? These are the questions we must reckon with if we hope to solve the crisis of population growth.

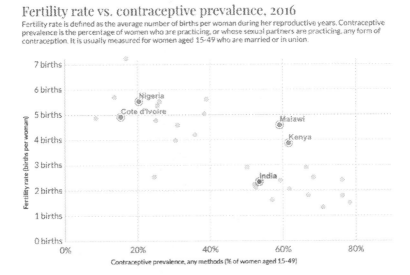

Fertility rate vs. contraceptive prevalence, 2016

Fertility rate is defined as the average number of births per woman during her reproductive years. Contraceptive prevalence is the percentage of women who are practicing, or whose sexual partners are practicing, any form of contraception. It is usually measured for women aged 15-49 who are married or in union.

Figure 13: Just like Education, the answer to reduced fertility rates may be a healthy combination of the supplier and demander's approaches. In effect, these two approaches in conjunction with a top-down and bottom-up approach may result in the lower fertility rates that developing countries seek.

In developing countries where women often drop out of school and marry young (either by arranged marriage, or by social norms), they often cannot stand up for themselves in the face of a more educated or older man (as may have been the case with Pomolla and Haisan, unfortunately). As such, husbands have a huge influence over their wives in these developing countries. These husbands in developing countries are the ones who tend to want more babies, usually because there is a generational preference towards Boys, not just in India, but in many developing countries. This can be because boys are expected to take care of their

Refath Bari

parents when they get old, as in the case of China, where over half of parents live with their children. Then again, in India, Bangladesh, and Pakistan alike arises the unique concept of Dowry – that the wive's family is expected to provide money and other assets to the groom's family. Many families begin saving up for a daughter's dowry as early as childhood – no wonder many billboards in India advertise "Pay 500 Rupees now and save 50,000 later".

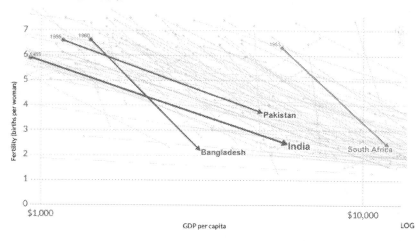

Children per woman (fertility rate) vs. level of prosperity, 1955 to 2015

Fertility rate, measured as the average number of births per woman versus gross domestic product (GDP) per capita, measured in 2011 international-$.

Figure 14: We find that (almost) no developing countries is an exception to lowering fertility rates, which naturally results in higher GDP (once again, we ask – causation or correlation?)

But we have yet to examine the macroscopic scene of population – at the community level. At this level, two main things play out: Peer Pressure and Religious Norms. First and foremost, it seems that individuals follow 'herd behavior' when it comes to reproductive health. We see this in action in the Matlab villages in Bangladesh, where Hindus took contraceptives if other Hindus did; likewise, Muslims ask for birth controls if they know other Muslims in the village do. This is almost a form of reverse peer pressure, as individuals learn that an unorthodox behavior is increasingly becoming the norm and they are more comfortable in accepting it. In regards to religious norms, we see the consequence of this in Pakistan, the only country in Southeast Asia which has yet to even try to implement a family planning program (the FP2020 Initiative to increase contraceptive usage from 35% in 2012 to 55% in 2020 was only recently launched at the London

Family Planning Summit). Dr. Ansar Ali Khan, an advisor to the UN on Reproductive Health in Pakistan lamented, "A combination of factors like non-availability of services, baseless traditional beliefs and misconception play a big role [in Pakistan's low conctraceptive use] ... a fairly large number of the population believes the use of artificial contraceptives for family planning is against nature and also against Islam." As such, we find that religion and community alike influence a mother's decision to take contraceptives. However, just because religion makes contraceptives taboo doesn't mean fertility rates must stay high. We need only look to the case of Brazil, a Catholic country that has largely strayed away from explicit family planning programs. However, Spanish TV offered a path to lower fertility: Soap Operas advertised families with at most one child, in stark contrast to spanish families at the time. As television ownership increased, so did engagement with these soap operas, as parents began naming their children after characters in the soaps (often portrayed by young, liberal actors/actresses) and emulating their behavior. often In addition, her own household plays a major role – when husbands were present, women were less likely to accept family planning practices. In Zambia, economists Nava Ashraf and Erica Field gave vouchers guaranteeing free access to a variety of reproductive services via a private meeting with a nurse. The sample size was 850 married women in Lusaka, Zambia; some of the vouchers were given in private, others in front of husbands. When women were given the vouchers in private, they were 23% more likely to go to the nurse; 57% less likely to have an unwanted baby 9-14 months down the line; and 38% more likely to accept a contraceptive.

To conclude: poor women have many babies due to a combination of societal factors, ranging from religious norms, peer pressure, spousal influence, lack of contraceptives, and future planning (i.e., more sons so that at least one of them cares for me in the future). We must thus take all these factors in consideration upon devising a population management scheme, so as to afford the poor the maximum flexibility.

5 Moral of the Story VI

What are some of the foundational ideas we grappled with in this chapter? We saw that the poor man has a desparate need to enrichen his life, whether by means of spending more on specialized adult goods, nonessential assets, or festivals. We've applied this principle to food, as well.

Refath Bari

Table 3: Breaking the Falsehoods of Poverty

Fiction	Fact
Poor Women have more babies because they don't understand the importance of population growth. What we really need to do is educate them on thse matters. As of 2016, the Rohingya refugees have a fertility rate of 3.8 – more so than most developing countries. This is unacceptable – these illiterate poor must be educated on the dangers of a high fertility; otherwise, they will continue to exacerbate their own suffering.	The Rohingya are a stateless population of refugees that have fled their home state of Myanmar because of the genocidal campaign launched there by Nobel Prize Winner Aung Sun Suu Kyi. The Rohingya's (who cannot afford to be educated or eat properly, because as of 2017 – aid to the Rakhine State was suspended) lives are ripe for belief and superstition, and perhaps they have the old agrarian belief that more babies mean more labor productivity and income for the family.
Low Fertility Rates will result in high economic growth and development for any country. That is the desired outcome, and that is why Low Fertility Rates are such an important developmental indicator.	Low Fertility Rates does not automatically guarantee high economic growth, and indeed it may be the other way around – perhaps great economic growth provides more capital for every parents, and these parents feel free to make investments in places other than more children. One may pull up the examples of Brazil and Korea, but these are dubious at best, and give birth to the same questions I've proposed above. However, Fertility Rates are important not just for dubious economic growth, but definitive social progress – women have higher career aspirations, and greater educational attainment upon receiving contraceptives. Furthermore, lower fertility rates are often a signature of improved social standings of women in developing countries.

Table 4: Breaking the Falsehoods of Poverty

Fiction	Fact
When economic shocks occur, fertility rates probably won't change, as in the case of COVID19.	COVID19 has turned the tables on the eridication of poverty. As a result of international lockdowns in nearly every country, domestic abuse is grown, as spouses are forced to live with each other for extended periods of time. This may completely change the bargaining dynamic in a family, as to who gets to decide to have a baby, and such. However, we should also pay close attention to the demographics structure. Most of the COVID19 victims are older men in the 50-80 age range who are afflicted with preexisting conditions. And many young women in developing countries are married to older men, many of whom may now be sick from the disease. As such, there are many factors to take into consideration when making the argument that fertility rates will change in the face of a global pandemic. For instance, after the sociopolitical shock of World War 2, the United States' fertility rate was at an all-time high during the baby-boomer period.
For countries like Brazil and Pakistan where religion make contraception and reproductive health taboo, it is impossible to create change or lower the fertility rates.	Ironically enough, it is not the government – but the citizens themselves who have taken upon the issue of reduced fertility rates in Brazil: a clear contender for the bottom-up apprach. Much of the Brazilian population at the time were actually emulating the behavior of famous soap opera characters they watched on increasingly common home television sets.

Refath Bari

Table 5: Breaking the Falsehoods of Poverty

Fiction	Fact
Sure, Education results in lower fertility rates, pregnancy rates, etc. I buy that. But, the converse is not neccesarily true – in fact, it's just common sense that greater fertility rates will lead to less education, because parents have fixed assets and now they must divide it among more dependents. Boom – just do the math.	Actually, increased fertility can actually increase the educational attainment of the poor under the right conditions, as demonstrated by Nancy Quian in China. However, more importantly perhaps, lower fertility rates frees up more capital for parents (although they do receive less in transfers from their children), which they can invest as they see fit.

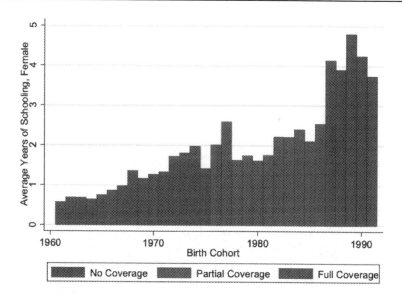

Figure 15: Education is an important determinant in the fertility rates and reproductive health of women in developing countries, as seen by the different cohorts above. As a matter of fact, in 1994, Ethiopia enacted education reform that increased the average schooling of girls by 0.8 years. The reform was successful in part to the many incentives promoted by the government, including no school fees for first to tenth grade, teaching in the local language, introducing school meals as food incentives, a reformed curriculum (i.e., textbooks that support local languages), and an increased educational budget to accomodate professional development for teachers.

Table 6: Breaking the Falsehoods of Poverty

Fiction	Fact
As the world population nears 9 billion by 2050, fertility rates will only grow. We must reign the population in under and ensure that we have enough food for everyone on the human table.	Fertility Rates have actually been decreasing for the better half of the last four decades, although that reduction is now slowly plataueing. As such, we must be careful not to 'tip over the pot' and dive beneath the replacement fertility rate.
I don't get it. Every country, developing and developed alike are only reaching a fertility rate of around 2.3; If reduced fertility rates are so important, why not just go all the way and achieve a fertility rate as close to zero as possible?	I don't blame you – I had the exact same conception when I saw Bangladesh's Family Planning Initiative. Why go for a fertility rate of 2.5 or 2.4, when you can go for zero? It turns out that a fertility rate of zero means there is no next generation – in fact, the minimum replacement fertility rate is 2.1, which is the number of babies the average woman must have so that the preceding generation is just slightly more populated than our own.

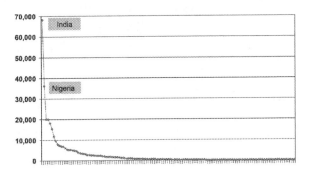

Figure 16: We graph here the Maternal Deaths of all 135 countries on an annual basis. The crisis is evidently concentrated in just a few countries, among them India and Nigeria, which account for 70,000 and 35,000 maternal deaths per year. Coincidentally perhaps, these two sets of countries have the most poor people in the world.

Chapter 9

Money

Refath Bari

55 Days in Dharavi

"As my father used to say: "There are two sure ways to lose a friend, one is to borrow, the other to lend.", said one Patrick Rohouss. This is sound advice, as we will learn from this chapter. Here we unravel, most importantly, the power of Microcredit – the all (supposedly) powerful tool of alleviating poverty. We diagnose the financial problems in developing countries, where the poor are often left to their own devices. We then examine the utility of Microfinance at both the macroscopic and microscopic level, and the effects of Microcredit Institutions on the LIves of the Poor.

Keywords: Default, High Interest Rates, Microcredit, Grameen Bank, Muhammad Yunus, Spandana, Collateral, Down Payments, Promoter's Contribution, Multiplier Effect, Monopoly Power, Babuliwalas, Eunuchs, Banks, Moneylenders, Adverse Selection, BRAC, Spandana Sphoorty, SKS, Graduation Programme, Financial Independence, Sustainable Livelihood

1 Case Study: Raul

Raul was his name and I did not object. What I did do is buy a couple of his dal puris, a kind of beef patty of the east (without the beef, of course). I like it. I munch on it for awhile before hearing the drumming of the fingers. 10 Rupeesfor a bunch of dal puris. Fair to say, I was not gonna be conscientous objector for this one. It was a good day: the driver didn't scam me, the sun didn't set me ablaze and hey, there was nothing to complain for. But not Rao. No, no, no: there wee exactly five things on the man's mind. And here they were – in his own words – "Number 1", gesturing in his thick Indian accent and rubbing his thicker beard. "Jaswal." he cursed deep in his thick breath, coughing in the thicker Palakkad air. "I ask him for five Rupee today, he ask me for six tommorow" "Local moneylender?" I asked. "Yeah, but that is not the problem. It look small, right? Fix, six rupee, nothing for you, right?" Didn't want to be rude, but fact of the matter was yes, as a matter of fact, I get scammed ten or twenty rupees any given day by any given profession. But now – now was good, not for Raul, but at least for me. "You hear me, or not?" I must have dazed off and Raul clapped his hands in front of my face. Wow, talk about agressive. I nodded – a potentially dangerous tactic when you don't know what you're agreeing to. And in this case, I clearly didn't. "Dear KARAGRE VASATHU LAKSHMI, KARAMADHYE SARASWATHI, KARAMOOLE STHITHA GOWRI, PRABHATE KAA DARSHANAM." It was a quick prayer to the hindu God Lakshmi, one I happened to have in my pocket for occasions like this. "But it gets big so fast. Let me show you." He picked up one of the dal puris. "I don't make these. They're from Palakkad Deli and Sweets." OK, sounds good. I think Babu did much the same. "But, how do I get them? Magic?" he waved his hands in my face. I would tell you how they smelled, but I think won't – they smelled of crackling oil and fine powder dust. Probably from handling all the dal puris, if not making them. After all, I saw no mini-kerosence stove as I did in the case of Babu. Anyway – back to Raul and his magic hands. "No! Not magic – that's exactly what I'm telling you, I get them with a loan from Jaswal, that little pig smelle-" My head picked up at the insult. "Jaswal, you say." Raul nodded fast, at the first hint of recognition in my voice. "Ah yes, yes, Jaswal. Tell me a bit about him." What can I say? It's one of the many interviewing tactics I'd learned over countless rejections, "No thank you"s, and even worse – "thank you, but no thank you". Sometimes, I'd get straight up ignored. But, Raul the fruit vendor fell for it, and that's all I needed. "I borrow 10 Rupees from Jaswal, and buy new dal puris from the Sweet Store with that money. Then, of the 20 Rupee I make from selling the dal puri, half goes to Jaswal" he sneered at the thought, but I urged him to finish, "and the other half to the Sweets store". But I was left confused: "So, how do you make any money?" "Well, that's the same question I asked myself, thank you very much". I leaned back on the non-existent wall. "So here's what I did. I know I can't change the money-lender from Jaswal, that pig-smelli-" "Why not?" "Well, what do you mean why not? If I switch, I lose everything! It's just – it's just a hassle, man, please understand that." OK, OK, for whatever reason, it was a hassle for this guy to just go to a better moneylender. "So, I get a loan from this guy, Jaswal for what – 500 Rupees" Now I was the one clapping: "Profit!" I claimed. But no: "No, no. You see, Jaswal is – he's against me. I saw the signs before, but I realized it too late" he satd through gritted teeth. "Son of a bi-!" he pounded the cart and some of the dal puris fell over on the side. Whoa. Guy needs a therapist. Or maybe this Jaswal guy was worse than I thought. He was: "It's 5 days, and I can't make the full payment. OK, he let me go. I don't have any land

he can take, so he knowshe has to watch me like a dog." Wow. Extreme – I like.
"Now 10 days. Then 20. Then 30. Now I have 50,000 Rupees due, and you know
that I can't pay that off evenif I do fifty jobs for the rest of my life." He was gonna
pound the cart again, but stopped short.

Figure 1: "Only the *dal puris* are mine, so don't tell them I buy all of
them, OK?" warned Raul, reluctantly posing for the guest picture. His
pushcart was stationed in front of the Pelakkad Deli and Sweets Shop
in Pallakad, Kerala

"Wait." he said, his eyes narrowing. "You! You! Gimme your godamn ID" he
said, grabbing me by the collar. Was I Jaswal? Or so he thought. I fished out my
ID from my wallet – no, that was my MetroCard. "Ok bhai, just take it down
a little, and let me find my ID, ok? I am not Jaswal." I considered making a run
for it, but hey – now the dividends are paying themselves in the form of this
good story. I finally found my ID, stashed somwwhere deep in my inner coat
pocket, under a couple of twisters, crumpled post-it notes (I assure you, none of
them had Maxwell's Equationsn them), and a ruby-white striped candy cane. He
let go of my collar. "Very sorry. This guy got in my head." he groaned, grinding
his head against the wall, as if that was gonna suddenly rain money from the
sky. Indeed it didn't. But it did start raining, so I guess part of Raul's wih came
true. Anyway, there I was, next to Palakkad Deli and Sweets, soaking in a rain,
probably about to get sick (I can indeed confirm that I got a mild cold the next

day), standing in front of a guy who had just grabbed my collar, asking me if I was his apparantely-crazed moneylender. Sure, I didn't get scammed or set ablaze, but this was somehow far worse. Well, thankfully I came to my wits and made a run for it. The little squat of a dal puri hit my back and I heard Raul's shouts in the rain, but I never turned back. I ran and ran in the far and distant rain until I finally came back to the hotel. Ah, home sweet home.

2 Raul's List

I might have run away from Raul and his pushcart, but millions of poor people like him can't do the same. See, this is the story of millions of Indians, Bengalis, and Pakistanis alike – all of whom are trapped in a cycle of loan after loan; day after day; year after year, much like Raul was. It is no doubt one of the most frustrating things and is just one of the many things that the poor man must reckon with, along with his children's education, his own nutrition, chlorinating his water every time he goes for a drink; taking the capsules and pills and vaccinations that he needs; saving up in the case that he will not survive the next economic shock his family faces – it's easy to see how quickly tiring the poor man's life can become. But now we find new light, a certain positivity when the poor man opens up businesses and clinics and schools. But to be entrepenuers in the first place, the poor man needs capital – the one of the two things he has a deficit of (the other being skill). So how does the poor man get the capital he needs, if no one trusts him to keep his word? This is the paradox of the poor man – and our job is to investigate it.

(I) The Reluctant Lender

(II) The Magic of Microcredit

3 The Reluctant Lender

The high level view only us so much.

Table 1: **A Hesitant Giver**

1 Why are banks so hesitant to lend to the poor?

2 What role do moneylenders play in giving loans to the poor?

3.1 Why are banks so hesitant to lend to the poor?

The facts are these: a lot of poor people (like Raul) have loans. But most of the mare from informal lenders, and not from formal sources like banks and cooperatives.

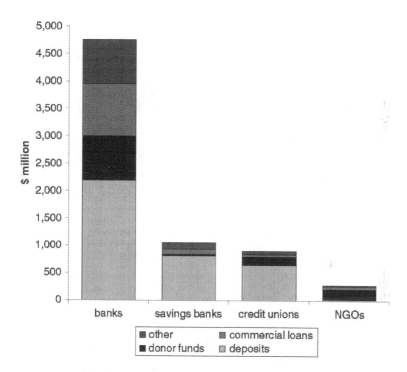

Figure 2: MFIs mostly get their funding from Banks, who have to lend 40% of their portfolio to the priority sector (In India, at least), which includes MFIs like SKS. This allows MFIs to jumpstart their growth, effectively contracting hundreds of contractors at an early phase. Furthermore, MFIs incentivize getting clients, so that lenders get increased comissions from more clients.

The poor often end up with loans from friends, relatives, shopkeepers, or local moneylenders. Their loans have very high interest rates and surprisingly low defaults. In Pakistan, the (average) effective annual interest rate is 78%, although this can vary widely (with a standard deviation of 38%) from a minimum of 18% to a maximum of 200%. This interest is usually paid back in an informal manner, at the wish of the moneylender and his borrower. There are typically no fixed

Refath Bari

deadlines for payments, and lenders typically have to spend time checking up on their borrowers to ensure loans are being used for the reason they were taken. It quickly becomes clear why interest rates are so high – it is because there are immense security costs in lending to the poor. As one proverb puts it, "A small debt makes a man your debtor, a large one your enemy".

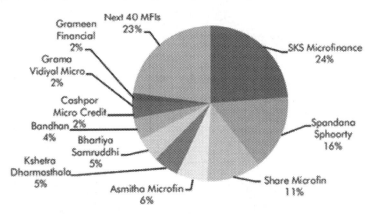

Figure 3: Microfinance is a big industry, especially in Asia (particularly India and Bangladesh). However, there are a few players who reign at the top – a few monopolies like SKS Microfinance and Spandana Sphoorty.

But the behaviour of lenders is equally justified: even though loans go rarely totally unpaid, even in the developing world, the lender must make sure the borrower keeps their word. He does so in a number of ways: checking up regularly on the borrower's business, perhaps if only to give suggestions on how to proceed; he may keep track of their location and their daily schedule to find them if needed. All of this takes time. And as one adage says, " Everyday is a bank account, and time is our currency. No one is rich, no one is poor, we've got 24 hours each." And with all that time devoted to any number of borrowers, the lender's time is all but stretched thin. And for this, he accounts by shooting up interest rates to accommodate for his time spent surveilling his borrowers.

3.2 What role do moneylenders play in giving loans to the poor?

But on second inspection, the poor man yet has more ways to trickery (and if you think this a bit too cynical, just consider that desperate times call for desperate measures -and for the poor man, essentially every day calls for desperate measures since he faces economic shocks on a day to day basis). First, there is the issue of willful default: what if the poor man claims that he no money on him, and yet still has some? How can the lender get his money back? It is for these types of worst-case scenarios that the lender must plan ahead for. And in doing so – and realizing that he cannot seize any asset of the poor man (i.e., if the poor man doesn't have land, or business assets, etc.) – the lender shoots up his interest rates once more. In fact, now may be the perfect time to discuss what we define as the multiplier effect. As the lender increases his interest rates for all the reasons we mentioned above (mostly security and monitoring expenses), the poor man becomes all the more likely to default or even run away with the money he borrowed. And because of this, the lender increases his interest rates once more, and so on and so forth. Therein lies the danger in high interest rates and lending to the poor – a combustible mixture that is often filled with i herent danger and risk. And it is because of this inherent risk of lending to the poor that their loans are filled with unimaginable interest rates (yet surprising y low defaults – in the case of Pakistan, the median annual default was only 2% There are countless horrifying stories and myths and legends of angry moneylender who never got their money back. In Afghanistan, for instance, money lenders pose as food vendors going from house to house, in reality – they were just conducti g their moneylending operations. There's also the tales of Eunuchs – the practic of showing an individual's body parts was considered bad luck in many parts of I dia and all the moneylender would have to do was threaten the breadwinner "a show ng" and he would be met with the money he had given to them. Moneylenders sometim s even go to the extremes – threatening physical assualt or otherwise damage to poor man's property, but this is quite rare. Instead, they resort to religious, ocial, and cultural devices such as appeal to an individual's religious beliefs, he always-reliable rule of peer pressure. But so much security and monitoring al o gives the moneylender the benefit of loyalty – he loans always to the same poo people, because its very hard to change moneylenders. First off, it would mean g ing through the expensive (time is money, once again) process of monitoring and s curity checks. But also, the new moneylender may not give the poor man the benefi of the doubt, and may indeed ask himself to what extent the poor man's credit tr stworthiness must be for him to abandon a hard-won relationship with a previous m neylender and seek a new one, despite the fact that changing relationships is expensive? Perhaps now is a fine time as any to acknowledge the fact that the poor man's loan sources are exactly those who he is closest to, because they are 1) the only ones willing to loan to the poor man and 2) the only ones who can effectively monitor the poor man. Think about it. Who better than your friend, your relative, your shopkeeper, or your local moneylender than to keep an eye on you? And you definitely won't run from them – that would mean abandoning your social network, which is the social equivalent of a death sentence for the poor man. Much the same way that the poor man does not migrate very far for jobs, just so that he can reside close to his social network – the poor man will not stray far from his informal loan sources, because it is unlikely that he will 1) be able to form these types of loan exchange networks in another community, and even if it is possible – it is a hassle and 2) be trusted by outside moneylenders, who may be suspicious of his past history as a borrower moving from place to place to escape interest payments. There is an up-side to having land now, however. For every additional hectare of land owned by the poor man, his average interest rate drops by 0.4%. Not revolutionary, but not bad either. In the case of willfull default, the moneylender has one of three possible routes: 1) he can seize any assets the poor man may own (seize collateral, if avaialable), 2) he can ask for a down payment on the loan, so that poor man is more invested to it, or 3) he can conduct a promoters contribution. Here's where it gets even more interesting: the more assets the poor man owns, the more collateral available for the moneylender to seize. So really, the ideal borrower would not be the poor man, but a rich one. In fact, it is the precise ideology behind the proverb "We lend only to the rich.", because in essence, the rich have that much more to lose. Falling a large height as an elephant hurts orders of magnitudes larger than falling a small height as an ant.

4 The Magic of Microcredit

The high level view only us so much.

Table 2: **A Definite Receiver**

1 How does Micro-finance work?

2 Is Microcredit magic?

4.1 How does Micro-finance work?

Gold is to the robber as microcredit is to the poor man: an oppurtunity. And it is an oppurtunity we cannot overlook. How do we begin? For that we approach none other than the poor man himself. One may begin with the simplest question possible – why don't the poor just use regular loans? For that, we look no further than Raul himself. Every day, Raul had to pay back a significant interest rate, thus being unable to considerably save up money. Instead, he had to take his daily earnings and give them back to his moneylender as interest and the Palakkad Sweets and Deli as repayment for the stock. Essentially, he was paying to be stuck in a poverty trap – a phenomenon that knows how to hide itself all too well. Now, with the question of Savings arises the question of semi-formal institutions such as savings groups, ROSCAs, and other such organizations that couple individuals together so that they encourage each other to keep saving, or paying back their loans as neccesary. Let us begin with the four basics of Micro-finance: (1) Micro-credit (the proliferation of small-scale loans to the poor) (2) Micro-savings (voluntary savings organizations such as self-help groups or ROSCAs) (3) Micro-insurance (the poor face many economic shocks, and as such it makes sense to provide them insurance) (4) Remittance Management (a minor aspect, no doubt, but important nonetheless because it enables the poor to make transfer payments via mobile phones).

Growth in MFIs

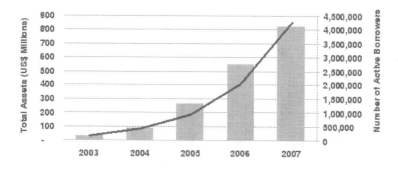

Figure 4: Microfinance Institutions such as SKS and Spandana Sphoorty have been growing fast in both rural and urban India, alike. Even in 2007, there were over 4.5 million borrowers engaging in microfinance institutions in India. From 2003 to 20012, microfinance became an international phenomenon implemented throughout the world, although most of the its borrowers are in Asia, primarily India and Bangladesh.

Microfinance aims to achieve five goals. (1) Eridicate Poverty through financial inclusion and providing the poor financial support (2) Protect the poor against economic shocks (3) Make sustainable businesses for the poor (4) Empower Women

Refath Bari

(of Grameen's 9 mllion borrowers, 97% are women). Now – here's where Micro-finance really comes in: the genius of microfinance is that it "turns" the poor man's best friend against him. Microfinance works by coupling poor villagers together so that they can all essentially keep each in self-check. Because what do we know about the poor man? One thing and one thing only: he values his social network above all (one of the reasons why he won't migrate very far, even if that means higher incomes). And so, by turning his own social network as a motivating factor to keep repaying his loans on a regular basis, we have ensured that he will never forget a payment ever again. And on this note, I should mark a mistake:

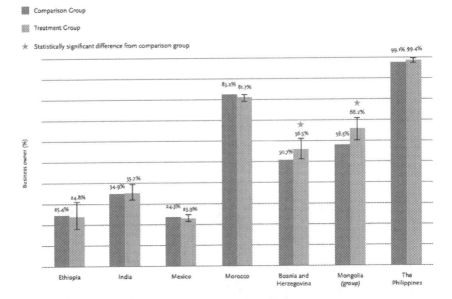

Figure 5: Microcredit has modest, but consistently positive effects, in-cluding increased business ownership across two of the seven coun-tries in which the study was conducted. Increased business ownership may just be the path out of poverty, because microfinance can enable small business owners to invest in rewarding assets, all whilst provid-ing them the experience of managing their finances, and without the danger of making them dependable on social service donations.

I have overwhelmingly used he, he, and he throughout this chapter, and indeed throughout the majority of this book – but the fact of the matter is that many of microcredit's biggest beneficiaries are women. In fact, of Grameen Bank's mil-lions of borrowers, 97% are women. Perhaps they have a higher repayment rate or greater trustworthiness, but at the end of the day, the story is the same: groups of local women gather and support each other to keep their word on loans and repay them all in due time.

Outcome	Bosnia and Herzegovina	Ethiopia	India	Mexico	Mongolia	Morocco
Business ownership	↑				↑	
Business revenue				↑		↑
Business inventory/ assets	↑	no data	↑	no data	↑	↑
Business investment/ costs			↑	↑	no data	↑
Business profit						↑
Household income						
Household spending/ consumption		↓		↓	↑	
Social well- being				↑		

Figure 6: Microfinance was hailed as a game-changer that would life hundreds of millions of the extremely poor onto the developmental ladder. For some time late 20th century, they were all the rage in the international development stage. While Micro-credit hasn't exactly lived up to its grand promise, it has still modestly improved the lives of the poor, and that is far more than we can say for other methods of poverty alleviation

As Economist Philip Mader says, "The innovation of microfinance is particularly notable for the fact that the resulting financial relation runs directly from the (very) poor to the (very) wealthy, globally – actors who have been only most tenuously financially connected in the past, with diverse layers of middlemen and organizations separating the owners of substantial capital from the pawnshops, moneylenders and credit associations of the poor. Thanks to microfinance, it is now possible for a Bill Gates to literally strike business deals with some of

Refath Bari

the poorest people on Earth and become entitled to asset streams generated by them, necessitating only the intermediation of an MFI."

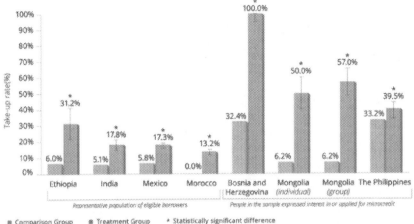

Figure 7: Demand for Microcredit has been modest, much like its effects. The danger in the industry of microfinance is that it is subject to herd behavior – this can play out to its advantages (as in the case that Grameen Loaners can use peer pressure to coax reluctant borrowers to pay back interest in a timely biweekly manner) or to its flaws (as in the case that if the majority of a village refused to pay back their loans, the whole village will follow afoot).

We need not stop there – the great thing about microfinance is that it has a failback mechanism. For the most reluctant of borrowers, or rather – least trustworthy of them, there always exists the reliable option of peer pressure. Indeed, there is no need it, as it turns out, for violent or crazy money-lenders (much like the one that gave Raul so much pain and headache, one Jasmal), when you have the simple option of peer pressure.

4.2 Is Microcredit Magic?

So much as a knock on one's door by the dreaded moneylender is enough to send the villagers a-running. Muhammad Yunus, the father of microcredit, is known as the "Banker to the Poor", because before him – the poor really had no stepping stones to the ladder of socio-economic development or mobility.

And the beauty of microcredit comes in the fact that it relieves both the borrower and the moneylender a great deal of stress. And stress, as we know by now is the poor man' killer. Microfinance works in part because of its strict rules: the borrowers must meet up once-or-so a week, each with their due amount of interest. The moneylender, who receives a portion of the interest repaid, simply counts up the dollars and checks if it is as much as expected – this is in stark contrast to the tradtional moneylender-borrower relationship, in which the moneylender must constantlty hover around the borrower, checking his whereabouts on a daily basis and constantly worrying about his money.

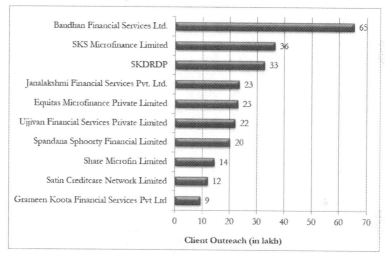

Top 10 MFIs with Client Outreach as of March 2015

Figure 8: Bandhan Financial Services LTD is by far the largest MFI in India, but it is one of the many operating in the country. Grameen Bank laid out the foundations for establishing Grameen-inspired MFIs throughout the world.

Now, with the microcredit way, there is an expectation set by the moneylender for the borrower – this expectation becomes common knowledge, and all parties adhere to it. The moneylender need not wait around or guess if his clients have the money. He knows the exact date and place that they will have it. If not, he can always use the tool of peer pressure to coax the borrower into repaying their interest. It gets better: the beauty of micr credit is that it allows microfinance institutions to walk that fine line between social good and commercial success. Many microfinance institutions have been overwhelmingly profitable, not just in Bangladesh, but around the world. In being so successful, these microfinance institutions are truly an example of a non-zero sum game.

Refath Bari

We need only look to their profits and influence to understand why: Grameen Bank had a profit of $28 million in 2017, $18 million in 2016, and only $300,000 in 2015.

Sir Fazle Hasan Abed's BRAC is the biggest NGO in the world, serving over 140 million poor people around the world. It also runs its own microfinance institutions via BRAC Bank, and is one of the five MFIs that have made that shares public (Grameen is also one of those five). And it's not only bangladesh – many countries have employed Grameen's methods in their own countries: In India, there's SKS and Spandana Sphoorty, founded by Vikram Akula and Padama Rejey, respectively.

Relative growth from 2012-2016

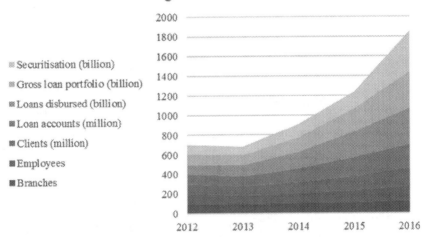

Figure 9: Muhammad Yunus and Grameen Bank's Joint Nobel Peace Prize in 2006 pushed microcredit to the frontier of economics, and ensured its worldwide recognition. It was during this period that Grameen Bank and hundreds of other MFIs like it were experiencing their greatest momentum, or just starting out.

These MFIs have three core aspects that make them enticeable to investor: strong profit margins (think above 15%), a commitment to eridicating poverty, and fast growth. One reason for MFIs' quick growth is that Indian Banks are required to give 40% of their loans to the priority sector, which includes MFIs like SKS, which turns out to be a quick way to raise money. All of these factors make microcredit an ideal means of fighting poverty.

Some will accuse me of being overdramatic; pompous; idealistic. I admit this. Microfinance is not a one-size fits all solution, and nor is it the holy grail. It-definitely works – households began wasting less money on nonessential and specialized adult goods such as sugar, alcohol, and tobacco. But the number of famliies that open businesses increased only from 5% to 7%. Not meaningless, but not groundshaking either.

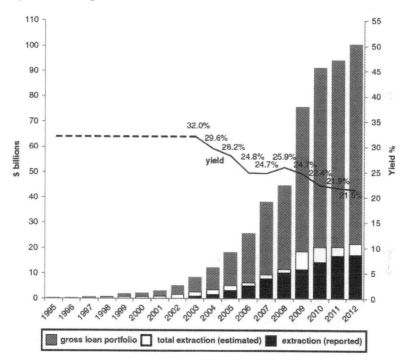

Figure 10: We see from the chart above that MFIs are by all means financially sustainable. There remain a few critics of MFIs who claim that although many MFIs have aspired to become subsidy independnet, very few have done so. And yet the evidence is clear: in 2006 alone, in a sample of 1300 MFIs, over 565 reported a postive return on assets (including infrastrucutre, staff, and provisions in case of loan default – willful or otherwise). As such, we find that hundreds of MFIs are financially sustainable – and this was in 2006. Due to steady growth and demand, MFIs are now raking in literal billions.

Nevertheless, microfinance is important because it afford the poor an oppurtunity to experience how it feels to save money. This is a precious experience that should not be taken for granted. As the poor become more accustomed to the experience of saving, they may begin to think more long-term than they used to and begin considering their actions by long-term consequences instead of short-term effects. At the end of the day, we come away with this: microfinance is an essential asset for the poor man, and it affords himan invaluable experience that will enable him to live a higher standard of life (if only by a little bit). Some MFIs have actually been scrutinized for being 'loan sharks' with absurdly high interest rates that defeat the whole point of microfinance, warn the creator of the idea, Muhammad Yunus.

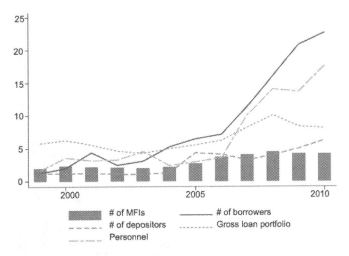

Figure 11: While the # of MFIs have only steadily increased (largely due to market competition), the # of borrowers has skyrocketed, largely due to highly-publicized campaigns and door-to-door marketing by MFIs. This is only possible due to the large number of staff these MFIs have been able to afford, which has also increased fairly quickly in the last decade alone.

Other MFIs have been investigated for potentially resorting to such extreme methods to retrieve interest that it resulted in a few farmer suicides. This caused local officials to make repaying loans back to the MFI Spandana illegal. In a matter of days, almost all borrowers stopped paying back their money. This resulted in a severe deficit for the MFI, and even after MFI went to officials to get the law quickly revoked, it had scarred the MFI. People only pay if they see others pay. People only buy into MFIs if they see their network does. That's the danger in MFI: their backup mechanism is the same as their sales generating mechanism: peer pressure. Peer pressure can cause people to pay their loans, but also make them refuse to pay, as some entire villages still do when Spandana offers them microcredit.

There are alternative models similar to Grameen Bank but that don't give money to the poor. Instead, they loan assets to the poor. Why don't we simply give the poor man free money? What's there to lose if we just donate to the poor? This is a common question, and one that isn't understood enough. Just giving money to the poor makes them dependable. Money is to the poor man as alcohol is to the drunk.

But let this in no way be mischaracterized as saying that the poor man is not creative. Indeed, if the poor are not smart, they will die. So all the poor entrep neurs I met over the course of my book are in every sense of the word, creative. This was long a folly of the Victorian Era, during which the poor were thought to have a limited capacity to plan for the future; as a matter of fact, as we've seen throughout this book, through Babu, Mo, Pommola, and Raul alike, every single one of the people we've met thus far offer an alternative perspective to the poor. Take Pomolla, for instance – she was a member of four Self-Help Groups, and even had a Savings Account opened at the local bank. What's more, she was expecting some returns on her own "mini-loans" (as she referred to them),a collection of four or five loans she'd made to various friends over the years that amounted to something like 200 Rupees, or so she claimed. What stun me was far more than the versatility of Pomolla – here she was, a mother tending to her children, a business-owner managing her clients, a money-lender overlooking her borrowers, and a saver protecting her assets. That right there is more than most people can handle, let alone our original conception of the poor as short-sighted, impateent people who have no sense of where they're going or where the wind is taking them. No, we must realize that the fact of the matter is that the poor are very much resourceful – in every sense of the word. They're taking advantage of every oppurtunity offered to them, and chasing every carrot on a stick. Indeed, such complicated savings instruments may very well be the symptoms of a broken financial system that doesn't cater to the poor, much like neglectful private and public education systems alike don't cater to the poor, ilterate children. And so, in this way, we find a common vein across all of the poor man's industries: Education, Health, and Finance. In all industries, exists a common neglector: an institution unwilling to cater to the poor. In Education, public and private institutions alike refuse to teach the bottom 20% of low-acheeving students, and the result is a sad waste of talent. In Health, public and private health care institutions alike refuse to provide the poor adequate health care, and the result is no less than a public health disaster. And now, we arrive to the subject of this chapter – Money. There is a deficit of financial institutions that agree to cater to the poor, and the symptoms of this deficit are poor people going out of their way to engage with existing, albeit poorly managed financial instruments such as Self-Help Groups and ROSCAs (although in many cases, these communal savings groups have helped the poor in saving up money, for three main reasons – they don't have fees, so one can easily make small deposits, and ROSCAs especially give each individual in a group a chance to access savings much faster than an individual could by themselves; lastly, they provide a means of financial advice for the poor). The moral of our story is this: the poor man is by no means short-sighted or lacking in creativity. We must throw away that conception if we are to help the poor. Instead, the poor man (or poor women, I should rather say, because most of the borrowers of MFIs, savers in ROSCAs or SHGs are poor women) actively engages in any financial institution that is willing to offer him a place to save his money. Even when the poor man is eligible to put his money in the bank – he does not do so. And why is that? Well, the oppurtunity cost is simply too great – banks involve fees for basically every action that one can conceive, and this makes it impractical for the poor man to open a savings account in the bank: there's a fee for opening an account, making withdrawals less than 1,2, etc.; you can now imagine why the poor man does not open bank accounts. Similarly, Banks don't want to manage the poor man's account, primarily because the oppurtunity cost is too great – it costs too much to monitor the account, and the savings account doesn't have much money anyway. As such, Banks leave the field of giving money to the poor to the moneylenders, who can now safely be assured that they are the only ones who the poor man can come to, to borrow money to make an investment. And yet in any given area in Udaipur or Palakkad, we find eight or nine moneylenders, not one or two. As such, there exists a competition that we may not expect. But, this competition doesn't matter because once the poor man makes a commitment to any one money lender, it will cost him more to change lenders, since he has to go through the monitoring and security checks all over again. Furthemore, the new lender that the poor man goes to for money will be suspicious: why switch lenders if it's so costly? Thus, the new lender will be faced with 'adverse selection'. And because the lender knows that you cannot switch, he can shoot up t e interest rates as much as wants – a symptom of monopolistic behavior on the lender's part (probably what happened to Raul). Instead, we can learn from the likes of BRAC, the largest NGO in the world by both borrowers and beneficiaries: it reaches over 140 million people on four continents. BRAC was the vision of Sir Fazle Hasan Abed, perhaps the most influential individual in the fight against poverty that you've never heard of (akin to James P. Grant). One of Abed's pivotal successes with BRAC was the idea of 'graduation' – he would loan assets such as cows to the poor. These income-pro ucing assets would afford the poor an oppurtunity to jumpstart their businesses, finance their investments, experience saving money. Furthermore, these assets would even provide a buffer between the poor and any unexpected financial shocks. Better yet, BRAC's graduation program has found significant success in Bangladesh, and is now being employed throughout the world: a comprehensive study published in Nature detailed a Randomized Control Trial consisting of a sample size of 10,000 poor people throughout six countries. In five of those countries, individuals who were part of BRAC's graduation program made more money, could afford more assets, had more to eat, and even had better mental health (probably the dividends of less stress; recall from Chapter 3 that the largest stressor for the poor man is money, unexpected shocks, and economic disaster; in this way, the poor man is in every way aware of his future – in direct opposition to the Victorian Era view that the poor are but short-sighted, impatient people). This was no fluke (an indeed, no Randomized Control Trial ever is, which is the whole point): in 2016 evaluation of BRAC's graduation program, Economists from the University of London assessed the impact of the program on 7000 extremely poor families in Bangladesh. It was a long-term study conducted over the course of a few years. The results were significant, if not worthy of celebration: families that participated in BRAC's graduation program had 37% more imcome than families that didn't, after four years. And the effects of BRAC's intervention was long-lasting, and was found to hold true even after seven years. From a financial perspective, however, BRAC's graduation program may be financially unsustainable, a prospect that Sir Fazle Hasan Abed considered. The gr duation program cost $500 per family, but the dividends were equally significant. However, in implementing the graduation program in other countries, Sir Abed says he will look for ways to decrease the implementation cost.

5 Moral of the Story VI

We've grappled with the old and new; the deficit and the alternative; the holy-grail and the modest solution. We've seen it all in this chapter, and now is the time to digest, recap, and understand what we've seen. First and foremost, we grappled with the Victorian-Era idea that the poor should be holed up in poorhouses that treat them like destitute beings that have no conception of past or future and have no ability to plan ahead for their lives. The idea that the poor are helpless, short-sighted, and handicapped is a common one, even today, amongst the populace.

But we cannot let this be. We've seen from the storie of the many poor people that I've talked with, brought food from, gave money to, and interviewed that the poor are – in every sense of the word – creative. Because if the poor man is not creative, he will die. And we know this because the poor face any number of shocks on any given day. I can give you an example right now. Today is May 30, 2020. Cyclone Amphana wrecked West Bengal and Kolkata, leaving thousandsof poor people without their properties or homes, and leaving disaster in its wake. It broke embankments, destroyed crops, wiped out thousands of homes and worst of all – it left 100 people dead. No more, no less. And now yo add on the layer of COVID19: even rural areas that had shelters couldn't (1) accomodate many people and (2) of those that it could accomodate, there was always the risk of the virus spreading amongst them. Two days ago, ago, an airplane from Lahore to Karachi crashed into a municipal village. 97 people were killed in the crash, a few buildings and homes burst into flames, and $400,000 damage was incurred, in terms of passenger baggage alone. And all in this in the wake of a global pandemic. Now, can you imagine the strife of the poor?

Table 3: Breaking the Falsehoods of Poverty

Fiction	Fact
Banks don't loan to the poor due to concern in regards to negative press coverage.	This is not true – as a matter of fact, social entrepreneurship makes for good business, and is actually a selling point for investors. Banks don't loan to the poor because the administrative costs of monitoring and securing loans from the poor outweighs the relatively meager interest returns from their inevitably-small loan. And it's a mutually exlcusive relationship, if you will – the poor are equally uninterested in opening a bank account, just because the costs of opening and withdrawing from said account will leave them with no savings anyway. Banks and the Poor have a mutually exclusive relationship that is probably best left alone.

Table 4: Breaking the Falsehoods of Poverty

Fiction	Fact
Microcredit is the holy grail we've been looking for to alleviate poverty.	We very much want it to be. That's in part the danger in believing in a holy-grail in the first place: true progress in the fight against poverty is made in small, incremental steps, via definitive randomized control trials, and effective policy. There is no silver bullet, and indeed there never has been or can be – because the fight against poverty is a war that's been thousands of years in the making, as long as human beings have been alive. But the great thing is that poverty is a measurable fact – there are thousands of developmental indicators we have to measure our progress. And we should never take progress for granted. And so, the reality is this: Muhammad Yunus' Microcredit is simply one of the many tools that we must wage in the fight against poverty. Sir Fazle Hasan Abed's BRAC offers us another possible solution: Graduation Programs (in the sense that the poor essentially 'graduate' out of poverty, and never look back). Both of these tools offer modest positive gains in the lives of the poor, increasing their business ownership, providing them financial stability, and above all – relieving their mental health. Neither of these tools claim to be a game-changer, and as a matter of fact – no one means will be a total game-changer, and we must come to accept that fact. We must realize that the whole is greater than the sum of any of its parts.

Refath Bari

Table 5: Breaking the Falsehoods of Poverty

Fiction	Fact
Microcredit has achieved fast growth due tor the immense demand for this new instrument of poverty alleviation. And for good reason too – it has been proven to have positive effects on the business ownership of the poor, as well as the expenditure of their savings and income. This quick money from banks allow MFIs to expand their reach via moneylenders, who are paid on the basis of how many clients they can attract. This fast growth has enabled MFIs to advance their initiative of eridicating poverty. In 2013, there were 213 million borrowers engaging with MFIs.	As explored above, MFIs such as SKS and Spandana Sphoorty have modest demand when they offer their services to all the poor people who are eligible. And indeed, their true source of demand comes from heavy publicization of the success stories of Microcredit. Furthermore, Banks in India are required to loan up to 40% of their portfolios to the financial sector, which includes Microenterprises (14% as of 2019), Small and Marginal Farmers (34%), and Agirculture (11%).

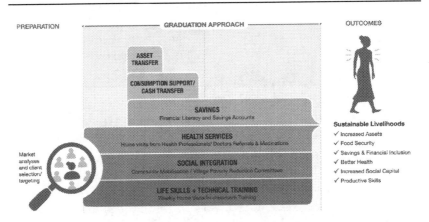

Figure 12: Here comes the advantage of BRAC, compensating for both of Microcredit's weaknesses: not only does it target the ultra-poor (those who live on 70 to 80 cents a day), but it incurs transformational changes in their lives. But this change does not happen in the course of a day, nor weekes, nor months of intervention. BRAC's interventions take anywhere from 18-36 months of intensive intervention, executed by field workers. And the effects of the interventions are just as long-lasting: they have been shown to last for a minimum of three years.

Table 6: Breaking the Falsehoods of Poverty

Fiction	Fact
Microcredit operates in a vacuum – as in it can operate without any supporting instruments.	By the nature of its idea, Microcredit does not and cannot operate in a vacuum. It is an institution – an idea – that fundamentally depends on the people. And as a matter of fact, Muhammad Yunus, the pioneer of Microcredit, and the man behind Grameen Bank, has expanded the services of Grameen into many other services for the poor, including Grameen Phone, Grameen Software Limited, Grameen CyberNet Limited, Gonoshasthaya Grameen Textile Mills Limited, Grameen Capital Management Limited, Grameen Knitwear Limited, and many others.

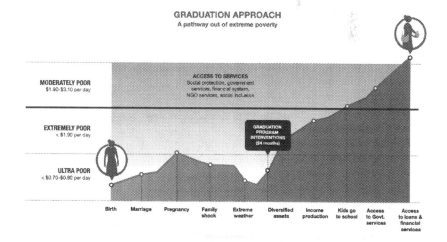

Figure 13: The pitfall of Microcredit comes with the fact that 1) it has modest benefits and 2) it cannot reach the ultra-poor, those who live on a daily income of even less than the United Nations' $1.90 extremely poor poverty line.

Refath Bari

Table 7: Breaking the Falsehoods of Poverty

Fiction	Fact
Sir Fazle Hasan Abed's BRAC and its graduation program has modest, and thus insignificant effects on the poor man's ability to own businesses, and other aspects of their life. As such, it is not worth the oppurtunity cost – just look at it: $500 per family, and for what? A 5% increase in business ownership? This is negligible, and should be scrapped.	Far from it; BRAC goes farther than any developmental intervention before it. It takes three often-independent developmental sectors and combines them into one unified approach: the Graduation Programme really takes it inspiration from three areas: financial freedom, social protection, and livelihood development. What the Graduation Programme does is far from just give the ultra-poor an asset: it sends field workers that intensively train the poor on skills that will be valuable for the local market. It does this on a weekly basis for anywhere from 18 to 36 months, coaching the poor to change their mindset and adapt new skills. BRAC workers train families to understand their financial portfolio, spend their money sensibly, and experience the value of savings. All this to set the poor family on a path to a sustainable life. The results should serve as inspiration for us all: the program changed people's livelihoods, their mental health, and their income, but most importantly – it changed their mindset; it gave the poor a reason to have hope. Many of the poor who took part in BRAC's program explained that they never imagined they could climb above the life that their parents, their parent's parents, and soon their own children would step into. The power of the graduation program truly is transformational and we should rightly recognize it for what it is.

Chapter 10

Dharavi

Refath Bari

55 Days in Dharavi

Dear Reader, we have arrived at the end of our journey. And now, it is your turn to take the reigns. Use all that you've learned to understand a fine case study on Poverty. The Case of Dharavi, let's call it. Dharavi is the third largest slum in the world, but that is by no means its distinguishing property. I ask you to join me in this final journey to understand the many facets of Dharavi, each of which is critical to the reformation of the slum. Granted, as last chapters go, this'll be an unconventional one. For one, there will be no Case Study (don't fear, of course, there's many stories to come yet), and no 'Moral of the Story'. Why? Because this story is still in the making. And you have the power to change it. Thank you for joining me on this wonderful journey, reader, and I ask you join me for one final ride. Let us commence.

Keywords: Dharavi, Bawana Colony, Janata Colony, Land Titling, Mixed Community Housing, Pucca Houses, Slum Redevelopment Scheme

1 A Caseless Introduction

There are 25 families on between the four and fifth alleyways of Dharavi. I know because I talked to every single one of them. But wait, you don't know what Dharavi is. It's tough to explain; really, you have to be there to understand the place, but let me try my best to give a faithful representation. At first glan e, Dharavi is no more than a slum. But take a second look. Go ahead. What do you see? Do you see the money? Hidden between the alleys? The broken pavements and the heavy mud? No? Let me show you. Dharavi is the third largest slum in the world by population. But it's much more than just a big slum: it's a rich one too. Look at the people; they've got barely any clothes, but they've certainly got education (or at least they understand the value of it, because most of the kids are in school). There's a school, public or private, nearly every nook and cranny.

But that's just school. OK. What about health? Well, being a slum, clearly there's not much of that (by definition). There's a universal sound in Dharavi, that rises above the constant hum of machinery, factories and recycling: it's the sound of coughs. Coughs, coughs, and coughs. Thick and small; loud and cranky; there's all sorts of coughs for all the different people. The polluted air even makes me go into a rage of coughing fits and I struggle to breathe, having to sigh every few seconds. Can I now return to the subject of people? Because really, that's what makes up this beautiful, beautiful place. I met all sorts of people. As I sto d amazed at all the different religions that compose Dharavi, I was slapped by the realization that was a microcosm of the US – it was America in a nutshell. The capitalism was there: just look at all the factories and all the rags-to-riches stories (hell, some of the millionaires in Dharavi were actually born there and became captains of industry). The people were there: Dharavi was dominated by no one religion – it was, in the finest sense of the word, a melting pot: Muslims, Hindus, Buddhists, Christians. You name it, it's there. What more do you need from a slum, for God's sake? I'll tell you what: Money. Dharavi is finely situated, by fate or luck we'll never know, smack-dab in the middle of India's "Wall Street" (the BKC, or Bandra Kurla Complex). Needless to say, that makes it really valuable. Think millions of Rupees. If you already are – congrats! -you're one of the hundreds of real estate developers eyeing one of the most diverse hubs of informal economy in India. Unfortunately, therein lies the prolem. lies the problem Real Estate developers hope to stick all of the thousands of Dharavi dwellers into high-rise buildings, clearing the rest of the space for malls, shops, and the like. But what they don't understand is that they are sacrificing the community of people for financial gain. But that's just a humanitarian standpoint. What really matters is the economic one: by crowding the poor into high-rise buildings, density will increase even more, making disease proliferation all the more likely. I need not say, then, dear reader what fate waits in store for the people of Dharavi. You know full well from the pages of this book what a critical role health alone plays in the economy: sick people mean lower labor productivity, means a slower informal economy. And we know that the informal economy is practically India's whole economy: for the last five years, it's been well over 90% of the economy.

2 Raul's List

I might have run away from Raul and his pushcart, but millions of poor people like him can't do the same.

3 At First Glance

How can a slum be worth millions? Dharavi is the answer. Its very existence is a contradiction. The home to over a million people from all over the world, Dharavi is rich in both ethnicity and value. A third of Dharavi is Muslim, 60% are Hindu, and the rest are Christians and other minorities. Walk on the street and you'll hear a symphony of language: from Tamil blending into Hindi flowing to Bengali pouring into English! Dharavi is a chunk of capitalism in an increasingly theocratic country. Following Prime Minister Modi's Citizenship Amendment Bill, which made Naturalization much harder for muslims, and internationally agreed to be a step forward for Mod's Hindu Nationalist agenda, Indian Muslim politicians such as Asaduddin Owaisi protested; Owaisi proclaimed: "We are heading toward totalitarianism, a fascist state; We are making India a theocratic country." Given these socio-economic conditions in the second largest country in the world, it's refreshing to see a tiny nugget of hope in Dharavi; Dharavi is defined as a slum, but it is first and foremost a land of hope: yes, the people are poor; yes the rivers are dirty; the street is noisy and the toilets are full. But setting does make a place; the people do; the people give life to Dharavi; the people make it come alive. Once at India's periphery, Dharavi grew into a colossal accumulation of workers all around India who created a massive informal economy in a land once thrown to the cows. Now, Dharavi is anything but ignored. Ask any real estate developer and their eyes light up when they hear 'Dharavi'. To the real estate developers, the politicians, and the bureaucracy, Dharavi is a goddamn gold mine, ready for a taking. On top of its billion dollar annual output, Dharavi is smack-dab in the middle of Mumbai, right next to Mumbai's Bandra-Kurla district (think Wall Street of India), making it even more valuable.

Dharavi is the richest and poorest slum in the world. With a population of a million people crushed in an area ⅔ rds of Central Park, Dharivi is one of the most densely populated areas in the world. And yet, despite disease, illness, injury, and poverty, the people somehow make it work. Dharavi's annual economic output is over a billion dollars. That means every resident produces goods worth a thousand dollars in economic output annually. But of course, this money is sucked up by business owners and politicians, leaving the actual residents of Dharavi with little to no money. With a prime spot right next to the business district and mass transit, Dharavi is hot on the market, potentially worth millions of Rupees. Many Real Estate Developers have an eye on the world's richest slum, with the hope of transforming it into a township of malls, offices, and luxury apartments. The Government of Maharashtra has declared itself a partner in the plan, calling it the "Opportunity of the Millenium ... [we seek a new Dharavi with a] world class cultural, knowledge, business and health centre" in the official 2007 Dhavari Redevelopment Plan. The Government expects at least 9000 crore just as premium for the redevelopment of Dharavi. But the redevelopment of Dharavi doesn't come easy. It's a plan that must take into consideration the struggles, the hopes, dreams, and the ambitions of each and every one of the slum's million residents. The ideal plan can leave no man behind, and the ideal plan exists. Every plan proposed thus far has had dangerous flaws compromising either the health and safety of the residents or the marketability of the slum. In this chapter, we examine Dhavari through its Geography, Ideologies, and the people, in a hope to establish what makes Dharavi truly special, and find the key to creating the ideal redevelopment plan for the richest slum in the world.

4 The Legal Foundation

Dharavi's location is a match made in heaven. At the heart of Mumbai in Maharashtra, Dharavi is surrounded by buzzling districts: Mahim and Bandra. is located just south of the BKC (Burga Kurla Centre), India's posh new business district, and a replacement to the old CBD (Central Business District).

Dharavi couldn't be in a better place. Originally home to fishers and farmers, it is now an increasingly industrialized informal sector of the Indian economy, contributing over 1 billion dollars in economic output every year. On top of that, Dharavi is in close vicinity to Mumbai's financial district, the Bandra Kurla business district (BKC). As such, Dharavi is the dream of every Indian real estate developer; the land of the poor is the dream of the rich, potentially worth millions of rupees. The Maharashtra government alone expects a premium for the redevelopment of Dharavi. However, current redevelopment plans for Dharavi threaten to sacrifice the communal bonds that exist in this informal economy. As such, redevelopment plans are still underway.

With a size of just 520 acres, Dharavi is just ⅔ rds the size of Central Park, smack-dab in the middle of Mumbai. BKC, just south of the airport, is much easier to access than the older CBD, and is essentially the Indian "Wall Street". As Dhavari rubs shoulders with the BKC, its land is highly coveted by Real Estate Developers. Dharavi is also highly accessible, surrounded by two of India's main railway lines, the Western and Central Railways. India's trains' doors are always open for ventilation purposes. As such, for the hundreds of Mumbaikers who travel to the BKC daily on the mass transit, passing by Dhavari means surviving a nasal assault, as the smell of the most densely populated slum in the world offenses the train. But to truly understand what has kept Dharavi so socially stagnant despite its outstanding economic viability, we must travel back to the 1980s, at the origin of India's Supreme Court.

5 The Fundamental Inequality

Mahatma Gandhi founded India in the hopes of establishing a socialist, secular, democratic republic. That great ambitious dream is now being choked by the ropes of the Indian Government and Supreme Court, whom by every new judgement, further insult the great Indian dream of a secular republic. Back in the 1980s, India's activist Supreme Court truly sought to represent its people. The problem with constitutions is that their interpretations can widely vary. The right to life and liberty can be interpreted as either a truly dignified life supplied with housing, health, and education or a brute, animal existence. The Supreme Court chose the former in 1980, advocating for the rights of all citizens and provoking the Indian Government when individuals were not receiving an adequate supply of basic necessities. But freedom doesn't die in a shot; it burns away slowly as a candle burns away the flame. Every judgement made by the Indian Supreme Court in the 1990s brought the country of 1.3 billion a step closer to authoritarian rule, with every judgement, undoing the pivotal work of Mahatma Gandhi. And thus, the Indian Supreme Court went from an institution worthy of the respect and admiration of 1.3 billion people to another rot of the Indian Bureaucracy, enabling the rich to commit crimes of unspeakable scale, and disabling the poor from fundamental human necessities like water pumps, garbage disposal, and affordable housing. Every now and then, the Supreme Court pulls up a case of an influential individual being punished in a guise to conceal the true farce of the Indian Supreme Court. And so, the greatest parlor of Justice in the Indian Government just serves as a shtick; an enabler for the rich, and a disservice for the poor.

History has taught us that Religion is the most powerful means of subduing a people. For the african-americans who were first shipped into America through the triangular trade, Christianity was the key to breaking their morale and ac-cepting their fate. 400 years and 500 km away, the Indian Government uses the same fundamental ideology. Castes are so obviously ingrained into the Indian Religious ideology that even I accepted them as fair divisions for the 1.3 billion inhabitants of India. But the fundamental reason for the existence of castes is the division of people into social classes; with thousands of castes spanning thou-sands of years, massive inequality is simply a given. In fact, inequality is the norm, a counterintuitive ideology for any inhabitant of the western world. But for the people of India, inequality is more than a given; it's a right. The rich deny the poor every basic human right conceivable – Water Pumps? Gone. Filtration Systems? Nonexistent. Garbage Disposal? Forget it. Hot Water? Now, that's a privilege. Remarkably, the poor justify the injustice themselves, and do the rich endorse it! And of course, being enablers of the rich, the Government does noth-ing to intervene. Government-endorsed injustice is not uncommon in the world; indeed, it's commonplace in countries like China, Hong Kong, and Myanmar. But the contradiction in India is in the coexistence of Democracy and Injustice. Democracy and Justice are conjoined twins. One without the other is like a fish out of water; it will just die. And thus is the cycle of Government based injustice – the Supreme Court enables the Rich, who deprive the poor, who accept their impoverishment as a given due to their caste. But the poor people of Dharavi are some of the hardest-working people I'd seen in my life. Many of them speak different languages, from Tamil to Marathi, and some come from all over India, Punjab, Hyderabad, etc. Why did they come here of all places? To answer that, we must understand the patterns of job migration.

6 Moving to the Cities

Why do jobs grow and concentrate on cities? Well, cities provide huge labor pools that rural areas just can't offer. Greater labor pools means a greater job market with potentially better hires; of course, all these workers are competing against each other, so salaries are completely up to the discretion of the employer. On top of that, none of the workers demand housing, health care, or other benefits. As such, jobs would naturally want to relocate to cities to take advantage of the cheap labor pool. But Migration is only part of the story. Take China, for instance, a communist regime with brutal migration laws; since 1958, China's hukou system shelled out parcels of residences to its people, either in the countryside or the city, and required express permission from the government for migration from the country to the city. And yet despite the regime's best efforts, over 130 million people in China have migrated from the rural country to the city without authorization. We distinguish here between two types of jobs: Exogenous and Endogenous. Exogenous being global, and Endogenous being local; For instance, an automobile plant may be exogenous, with customers spread nationally, or even internationally. On the other hand, an endogenous job may be a local restaurant, with customers distributed regionally, and is thus completely dependent on the locality. Unlike endogenous jobs, exogenous jobs aren't restricted to one area. In fact, they can move wherever policy pleases them, and as such, they're responsive to policy changes. As such, any policy guaranteeing business economical or operational advantages are bound to attract exogenous jobs to the given region. Furthermore, as a society prospers, so do jobs; and naturally, as technology increases, so do the number of local services endogenous jobs have to offer. It follows then that the growth of a population is proportional to the growth of endogenous jobs; in other words, as population grows, so does the demand for local services, and thus supply – AKA the number of endogenous jobs – also grows. As such, effective policy measures are all it takes to direct the movement of exogenous jobs.

7 Law of Adverse Possession

As with any country, India has written laws in its constitution and as passed by its legislation, but it also has unwritten laws that are "judge-made". The judicial system in India is as dependent on the strictly written law as it is on the interpretation of said law by the judges themselves. For instance, many legislatives measures have been struck down by the courts, because the judge deemed the laws unfit as per the Indian Constitution. Such laws are deemed "ultra vires" and struck down if they can be demonstrated to contradict the Indian Constitution. Of primal interest to Dharavi is the Law of Adverse Possession, one of the many idiosyncrasies of the Indian Housing System, which differentiates between possession and ownership. Owning a house isn't equivalent to possessing one. The Law of Adverse Possession states that given a property of Person A, if Person B possesses Person A's property with Person A's knowledge, but not express permission and Person B remains in Person A's property for at least 12 continous years, the Law of Adverse Possession states that Person A becomes the owner of Person B's possession. In the case of government property, the Law of Adverse Possession applies after 30 years. So how does this play in with Dharavi? Well, many of Dharavi's residents have been there for over 30 years, making the land legally theirs, and not the government's. It should also be noted that as in any other country, India's partitioning of land is per individuals who are each assigned a unit of land for a particular use, whether it be agricultural, construction, or for business. Before assignment, individuals must pay a fee to lease the land for any amount of duration, after which the owner of the land returns from the individual to the commons.

8 Mixed-Income Housing

There are several advantages to mixed-income housing for tenants. First is the tendency for greater interaction between different castes and classes of people, thus expanding the mental horizons of individuals who would previously be able only to interact with people of their own class. While there may not be a direct correlation between interactions and perception, it certainly doesn't hurt to expand one's set of interactions to a broader range of people. Secondly, mixed-income housing is economically beneficial for both sides of the coin: the rich, who most likely own, or subsidize major corporations or factories have access to a ready-made labor pool in the poor. On the other hand, the poor have access to jobs that they couldn't potentially find elsewhere. Furthermore, most endogenous/exogenous jobs require the service of the lower and middle classes, and the close geographical intimacy between three varying classes makes it much more economically efficient for businesses to operate and not seek out potential hires in other regions – thus reducing traveling costs and hiring costs significantly. And lastly, the isolation of minorities tends to make them even more isolated, and it becomes a positive feeding cycle as such minorities tend to get isolated not just physically, but also socially, operationally, and worst of all – economically, and mixed-income housing is the cure to that problem.

Dharavi's problem is not unique. At the crux of Dharavi is the problem of proper housing. People come to Dharavi not just for work, but also housing. Take Shakti Verma, a resident in Asalpha, Mumbai. Verma is a former business development executive who received his MBA from Amity Institute, Mumbai. Verma left his $100,000 Rupee a month paying job to create his own business. Verma claims that he would never have been able to afford a formal apartment in Mumbai with a fixed salary, and thus resorted to founding his own business. Verma's story is not uncommon; in fact, it's a story shared by Mumbaikers all over Maharashtra. Throughout Mumbai, you will find informal settlements officially denoted as slums by the Maharashtra Local Government; these slums are the people's response to inadequate government housing. Scattered throughout all of Mumbai, these slums are proclaimed by the government to be "Unfit for human habilitation. "; Slums are proclaimed by the Indian Government to be "residential areas where dwellings are in any respect unfit for human habitation by reasons of dilapidation, overcrowding, faulty designs of buildings, narrowness or faulty arrangement of streets, lack of ventilation, light or sanitation facilities or any combination of these factors which are detrimental to safety, health and morals. Thus, conceptually Slums are perceived as compact overcrowded residential areas (and not isolated or scattered dwellings) unfit for habitation due to lack of one or more of the basic infrastructure like drinking water, 3 sanitation, electricity, sewerage, streets etc" And yet, despite this bold proclamation, 52.7% of Mumbai is crushed into an area only 9% of Mumbai. But if slums are so detrimental to the safety and well-being of the population, why does one every two mumbiker live in them? The answer is simple: the lack of affordable housing options. In a nation where housing affordability is based solely on land availability, there won't be many options left for the poor. The scarcity of land in Mumbai, coupled with the fact that its land can't be expanded (since it's a coastal city bordered by the Arabian sea on three sides), makes housing a privilege, not a right, for the average mumbiker. But where did these sky-high apartment prices begin? Famous Indian Architect and Urban Planner PK Das believes the problem

Refath Bari

stemmed from a harmful governmental decision in 1991: "Upon independence, iIndia had pledged to be a socialist republic, which means the government had taken upon itself the exclusive responsibility of promoting social welfare projects including affordable housing or social housing. But come 1991, the year of liberalisation, the government dumps that responsibility and role and talks about facilitating the private sector. It began to depend on privatisation as a means of development .. leading to the state we are now in, where housing prices have hit the roof and slimmofication of cities has begun to threaten our quality of life. " The problem has gotten so bad that the national institute of urban affairs estimates that over 95% of households in Mumbai can't afford to buy a house in the formal sector. As Sahil Gandhi of the National Institute of Urban Affairs states in his paper Economics of affordable housing in indian cities: the case of mumbai, "This exercise reveals that a large proportion of households living in Mumbai are not in a financial position to repurchase their own homes. Clearly there is a distortion between the household's income and the price of the house they live in, there is distortion between the household's stock and its flow" Indeed, property prices have only grown in Mumbai, home of Dharavi, over the past decade, as demonstrated by Gandhi's paper. The response to the housing crisis was the proliferation of slums, which are in essence are analogous to affordable housing settlements in Mumbai. And yet, living in slums comes at a cost – it depresses families in the social ladder and puts their welfare at risk, due to the many diseases that can proliferate in a slum due to the lack of a sanitary environment. Families living in slums are only trying to make ends meet, like so many other mumbaikars; yet, they are often deemed dirty and called illegal settlers on their own land. Notable Urban Planner Shirish B. Patel defined the conditions apply in his piece in the Shirish B. Patel in his piece in the Economic and Political Weekly: "More recently, the chairman of Bombay First likened the squatters' occupation of land they do not own to stealing bread from a baker's shop. But neither pickpocketing nor stealing bread is a correct parallel. A more accurate analogy would be to say: "I am the captain of this ship. You are welcome to swab the decks and polish the brass and I will pay you. But there is nowhere you can live here. You have to spend the night over- board, swimming the shark-infested seas. If you are still there tomorrow morning, report at 8 for another day's work. Don't be late, because there are a dozen others eager to take your place at even lower wages." So while the rich get richer, the poor are not only not housed: they are set to competing with each other to get still poorer" had perfectly summed up the situation of the working class millennials of the cities with the analogy of a big ship, which has many workers, who perform every petty to intricate task on board, throughout the day, for which the captain pays them well, but does not allow them to spend the night on the ship. If they manage to survive the night in water, without getting eaten by the sharks, they must report to work the next morning. If not, there are plenty of fish in the sea." In essence, Mumbai's rich depend on the poor for all their utility services, and yet come night, when the poor demand housing, they're labeled encroachers in their own slums. And even if slum housing is more affordable, the poor end up overpaying for basic necessities such as clean water; on top of that, these people risk disease and infection every single day due to the immense number of diseases that harbor themselves in the unclean streets of a slum. The problem gets worse from here. Due to the lack of affordable housing, one may expect there to be a few homes left on the Mumbai market. Instead, there are over half a million vacant homes on the Mumbai market – the largest in India – left empty for investment purposes. Couple that with terrible governmental incentive to charge increasing rent prices, and you end up with landlords who couldn't care less if their entire apartment is godman abandoned. This is in part due to the Maharashtra Land Control Act of 1999, which is stated by the Maharashtra government it be "An Act to unify, consolidate and amend the law relating to the control of rent and repairs of certain premises and of eviction and for encouraging the construction of new houses by ensuring a fair return on the investment by landlords and to provide for the matters connected with the purposes aforesaid." Yet this act does anything but unify – it froze rents on many old Mumbai apartments at pre-1965 levels. As such, it has removed all incentive for landlords to lease out apartments and thus left thousands of vacant apartments which could be parceled out to the poor. The question of housing thus comes down to the Maharashtra government. But governmental public housing cannot possibly provide free or even affordable housing for all; the market simply cannot bear such demand. On the other hand, private housing isn't an option, either; over the past few decades, private developers have built relatively few housing opportunities such that if we were to project the amount of housing opportunities they could create, it would take them upwards of a century to meet the current demands for housing in Mumbai. The only viable option, then is self-building houses. As such, the Maharsastra government should focus on upgrading current informal settlements instead of obliterating them to make way for high-rise apartments which could potentially fund affordable housing.

9 Community Land Trusts

Real Estate Developers have been plagued with one question for the last millenia: How do you urbanize without displacing? In other words, how can one organize an existing region without displacing its current inhabitants? Many current urbanization plans choose to renovate areas by developing new properties (ie luxury apartments, malls, offices, etc.), while absolutely neglecting the current inhabitants, who would be forced to migrate to a cheaper region as current apartments are sold to wealthier individuals. The key to this dilemma lies in Community Land Trusts, which is simply a means of redevelopment that prioritizes the improvement of the current inhabitants' wellbeing rather than corporations' profit. To achieve this however, we look at Manhattan, specifically the Lower East Side, a region that shares many parallels with Dharavi: sandwiched between two prominent business districts, Wall Street and Midtown Manhattan, the Lower East Side is like a gem in the haystack for real estate developers. Furthermore, much like Dharavi, it's ethnically diverse, and never had a dominant religion or culture. So, in a proposal to reorganize the area without displacing the current inhabitants, the government proposed Community Land Trusts (CLTs), which consist of 3 key principles: First, the appreciation of land must profit no single private owner, but the entire group of inhabitants, which is why the land itself is owned by the entire group of residents; Secondly, there must exist a non-profit or a trust responsible for the land owned by the CLT. Lastly, if any property on the CLT is sold, the profit is shared between the CLT and the owner of said property. The property should be sold at lower than market rates, thus keeping prices in the property affordable. CLTs share 3 main objectives, including the affordable rehousing of residents without displacement (thus preserving mixed-income housing), provide affordable housing, and benefit the people, not the individual if the land appreciates in value. It should be noted that regardless of the redevelopment plan for Dharavi, there are a few common-sense rules that should be explicitly stated: 1) Residents should be able to remain in their residences until new housing is ready, 2) Redevelopment must begin with housing construction, and 3) the people of Dharavi must benefit from the redevelopment.

10 Land Titling

The story of Bawana is really a story of the rich stringing along the poor wherever they want. The morale of the story is that given the lack of adequate property rights, the rich can move the poor whenever, and wherever they like. Bawana is a recent tragedy that occured in New Delhi, India in 2011, and it teaches us a lesson regarding slums and informal settlements like Dharavi. At the time of Bawana, there was an unusual congregation of poor slum-dwellers around the center of Delhi. As Delhi was the capital of India, and increasingly grew to be a prominent business district, the land on which the poor slum-dwellers lived upon appreciated in value. But of course the rich – including real estate developers, investors, etc. – couldn't have that. And so despite the sturdy settlement established by the poor, developers began making plans for their removal. As such, the poor were shifted to an area on the outskirts of Delhi, where the value of the land was much lower. However, the residents still had to pay rents much higher than either Class A, Class B, or Class C citizens living in New Delhi, despite the fact that not only were they leaving on much cheaper land, but they had no security on their new land, either, due to their lack of property rights.

The story of Bawana is not isolated; the Janata Colony is much the same, if not a precursor. The movement of the poor in India is correlated to the appreciation of land at different times. Since the rich (ie real estate developers, promoters, advertisers, etc.) ensure that the poor lack any property rights whatsoever, they can string along the poor wherever they want. That's exactly the case with the Janata Colony. The Janata Colony was a colony of low-class Indians situated far from the central cities, near the outskirts of the state, near a nuclear reactor. Families were relocated to Janatha on small patches of land in the 1940s. And yet, despite the relocation; despite losing their homes, and receiving no compensation, the people made it work. In just a few years, temples, mosques, and even churches would begin sprouting in Janata. By the 1970s, the residents had built hundreds of homes, five mosques, six temples, and two churches all on their own. What's more, they built police stations and markets, and offices, and the population soared to 72,000 by 1980.

And then came the news. The BRAC (Bhabha Atomic Research Centre) considered Janatha a disgrace; an insult, as it was geographically close to the BRAC buildings. The enquiry officer stated that despite being obtained for resettlement of the poor, Janata Colony's land was recently brought by BARC for housing, a swimming pool, and other amenities. And so, the process of evicting 72000 people began, and with no property titles nor official documentation to protest with, the Janata Colony was razed to the ground, and once again, thousands of residents were displaced – moved into Cheetah Camp 1.5 miles away, where the land plot for each family was half the size that they received in Janata Colony. That was in 1981. Now, a few decades later, Cheetah Camp is the best it's ever been. Bustling with shops, markets, pharmacies, and stores, it's just the same as the Janata Colony was decades back. But it's just another lesson for those who know the full story. One day, five, ten years in the future, when another Indian corporate conglomerate decides the poor on earth are like graffiti on cement, they'll move these families again and again. This is the cycle of life for the slums of india. This is just another poverty trap. The continual movement of the poor means that even as a group, they never have a true place to call home. Poverty traps are as natural as they are man-made. In India, many poverty traps are the work of man, specifically men whose lives are devoted to ensuring the poor stay poor; men who will exhaust every possible avenue to deprive the poor of their basic human rights, from clean water supply to simple sanitation. These are the true criminals; these are the men who create artificial poverty-traps to burden the poor on top of their pre-existing misfortune, misery, and despair. By stringing the poor from place to place, not only do they expand the power of the rich, but guarantee that the poor will never have enough time to develop their own sustainable economy, thus creating an artificial poverty trap.

Dharavi is chiefly a capitalist economy. So naturally, if the poor work so hard, why don't they succeed? This is the question that has plagued third world countries in the east for the last century, and the key is the philosophy of the famous economist Hernando de Soto. Property rights are the answer to fixing this urgent crisis. Indeed, the solution lies in teaching the poor about finance, the importance of property rights, and the power of education. In Dharavi, work and home are combined, much like the cottage industry in 19th century America. As such, one should not just title his home, but everything – his business, his poppert, his credit, and all else, claims De Soto. By doing so, one ensures that he will not be the dog of the rich, and cannot be strung helplessly place to place, at the mercy of the upper class.

11 Free Housing

Who doesn't love free? Free healthcare, free primary education, but best of all – free housing. As with most things in life, what seems to be too good to be true usually is. The precursor to the novel concept of free housing was India's housing system in the 1990s, when anyone could take a bag of poles and stick them with a roof on the ground to call it a home. These developers would request permission from the Government of Maharashtra to develop a new settlement; once given permission, the developers would create settlements on the land, and sell the surplus to accomodate for the cost of construction. Thus, they would satisfy profits and development. But in the late 1990s, Balasaheb Thackeray, leader of the Sun Shiv government, founded the SRA (Slum Redevelopment Agency), and came up with a seemingly brilliant proposal to satisfy both ends of the deal – the residents and the developers: the ideal plan to provide residents free pucca housing and provide developers the profit they seek. The plan was to partition the given slum approximately half; half the land would be used for redevelopment purposes (ie high-rise apartments for current residents), whereas the other half would be used for malls, offices, and luxury residences. Thus, developers could regain the profit they sought from one side of the slum, while simultaneously providing current residents housing free of cost. Not only did the plan accomplish that, but it made the leap of assuming that the poor actually deserved basic human rights such as clean water and garbage disposal. Dharavi's redevelopment plans center on this exact plan. Yet the plan comes up dangerously short. The seemingly ingenious plan had serious flaws; no market research had been done. As a result, they overlooked the fact that there was no market available for such housing! In other words, there was not enough of a market available for so many middle and high-income apartments. As such, it wouldn't be possible to fund the free pucca houses. The moral of the story is that free housing is not a sustainable solution; yes, it may work in a few isolated cases, but for the problem of poverty as a whole, it cannot be scaled up or generalized, and therein lies the true problem with the ideal of free housing.

12 Densities

Density is a real problem in Dharavi. There's 277,000 people per hectare, a staggering statistic incomparable to any other province or locality. The closest country that even comes close is Hong Kong, which has a density of 144 people per hectare in its most crowded areas; Even so, Hong Kong has the advantage of underground transport, a key transportation innovation Mumbai has come short of. But with only a few hectares, Hong Kong isn't a worthy comparison for the world's largest slum, at over 244 hectares. A better comparison would be one of the world's most densely populated countries, Monaco, at a density of 200 people per hectare. But then again, being only a few hectares and having a population of 38,000, Monaco isn't much of a comparison to Dharavi in terms of either size or stature. And so, we can only conclude that Dharavi is one of the most densely populated countries in the world, if not the most densely populated. This dubious distinction would only be further impressed after the redevelopment of Dharavi. Under current plans to partition the land of Dharavi, 43% of the land would be retained for redevelopment and new housing for current residents, whereas the other 57% would be used to create new malls, hotels, and offices to accrue profit for real estate developers. Current residents would be crushed into smaller scale high-rise apartment buildings which – make no mistake – is quite attractive to the poor slum-dwellers and the developers for three reasons: 1) free housing, a bargain nobody would miss and certainly not the disadvantaged slum-dwellers of Dharavi. 2) free housing makes for a great voting shtick, as it quite appealing to the masses, 3) sure, residents wouldn't receive compensation for their old houses, but new apartments in high-rise buildings are much more effectual means of communicating status and wealth in a community, especially for middle-class citizens.

13 Redeveloping Dharavi

Over the past few sections, we've covered in depth all the separate components that must be taken into consideration in the redevelopment of one of the largest slums in all of Asia. In this section, we seek to summarize the above factors. First and foremost, we've come to understand the importance of permanence, especially when it comes to property. Thus, first and foremost, the people of Dharavi must ensure the land is their property, and not of the government or some otherwise foreign corporation. This can be done through the law of Adverse Possession, which applies quite fittingly, since Dharavi was designated as a government land, and many of its inhabitants have lived in it for over 30 years, which is the minimum amount of years required for the law of adverse possession to apply to government-owned land. Secondly, any redevelopment plan must share a few baseline characteristics, which include the following: 1) The goal of redevelopment must be to enrich the community, not the developers, 2) In the case of rehousing, residents must be permitted to remain in their houses and provided necessary amenities, including clean water supply and garbage disposal during construction. Just a few ideas for the redevelopment of Dharavi include the creation of a CLT (community land trust), which could be in the form of a non-profit (shareholders prohibited from receiving dividends), a trust, or some otherwise corporation in the benefits of the community, so that if the land of Dharavi appreciates further, the residents will be the beneficiaries, not the developers.

14 Stories from Dharavi

The first time I went, I ran to Dharavi at the strike of 3:00 PM. I expected there to be some kind of metal boundary between Dharavi and the rest of the world. In fact, all that separated Dharavi from the rest of the world were a bunch of narrow alleys and densely populated homes and businesses. I was stunned by Dharavi's prosperity. Given its reputation as the world's largest slum, I expected Dharavis living conditions to be much worse. My expectations weren't unfounded; having visited and stayed in Bengali slums for weeks at a time, I still recall the state of housing for Bengali slum-dwellers being a bunch of bamboo poles and tape. The border between Dharavi and other states is nearly seamless. The first day I came to Dharavi, I was wearing my normal average Joe clothes, with a regular t-shirt and jeans. But nobody would agree to an interview. In fact, when I approached many parents and children for their interviews, they almost opposed me, seeking not to speak with strangers such as myself. The next day, having learned my lesson, I reluctantly dressed up in my dress outfit; I wore a thousand dollar suit in a million dollar slum. Now, the slum-dwellers started before approaching me. I was able to pray Jammed in the mosque at 4:30 and explore the apartments around Dharavi.

We begin with the Mosque: I knew the mosque wasn't for everyone as soon as I entered. Despite being a slum, many of the muslims who arrived in the mosque for the Jammad seemed high-class. Many of the men wore marriage rings on their index fingers and had clipped nails. They could afford seemingly new, clean jeans and shirts, and the mosque itself was outfitted with strangely expensive equipment — most notably a clock that showed times at major cities around the world (an indication that the Imam expected foreigners to come to the Mosque, or simply a reflection of the rich diversity of Dharavi), a few wooden steps leading up to an inner room within the mosque. There were also books in arabic neatly stacked in four bookshelves to the right of the namaaz area. There was a microphone situated at the front for the Imam, and speakers surrounding the room. Not to mention the large carpet beneath us. Before the prayer room was a jainamaaz room, in which the people in the mosque could perform the traditional Muslim ritual prior their prayer. I had expected to be welcomed inside the religious institution of my birthplace, Bangladesh. Instead, I found myself twitching nervously as the hundreds of men around me stared at me and my dad, as both of us were praying in the mosque.

Still in the mosque, I found a peculiar story. Before the jammad began, I noticed there was a girl and boy standing behind my dad and I. We sat silent for awhile, waiting for some inquiry, until I finally turned around. "Hi, what's your name?" I asked, totally assured that the girl wouldn't know enough English to respond. "My name is Farakla Kald" in crystal clear English. Despite living in a slum, this girl had nearly perfect English, whereas I — having lived in the United

Refath Bari

States for a decade — still tripped over syllables and struggled to block my accent. I was stunned. "How old are you?" "11 years old", she responded. "So you must be in 9th grade" "No, I'm in 7th standard, Sir". I was taken aback by her pronoun usage. Sir? "So what is your school curriculum like? What subjects do you learn in school?" "Hindi, Tamil, English, Science, Math, Art, and Islam", she responded matter-of-factly. "What's your favorite subject?" "Science, sir. I like learning about leaves and photosynthesis and the like." "What do you want to be when you grow up?" "A doctor", she responded dutifully. "Do you like math?" "No,not really. I'm just learning about addition, subtraction, multiplication, and division." "You speak very good English. Did you learn it from school?" "Yes, sir. From my teachers." "Your teachers speak English?" I was pressured. "No, they only speak Hindi" Farakla said. "Wait, if your teachers don't know how to speak English, how can you learn it in the first place?" "From school" she repeated. "You said you won awards, in what, English?" "No, I've won gold medals in Art and Drawing, Sir" "Wow, what do you like to paint?" "I can draw anything, Sir. You give me anything, and I can paint it." "So you can paint me?" My dad perked. "No, sir that's a little too complicated, because it has shadows and other things that are hard to paint. I mean simpler things ""What's the last thing you painted, Dharavi?" "No, sir. Our teacher took us outside and we had to paint scenery."

Dharavi is a slum, first and foremost. So what do you see when you think "Dharavi"? Because if you google it, you'd never realize there are people who actually live there. Every single image of Dharavi on Google is a drone shot from above. All you can see are the roofs of the shantytown below. This is why poverty continues to exist; not one of the pictures above are of a local in Dharavi, or its community; instead, the only thing that meets the eye are roofs and roofs till the end. This is the dehumanizing element of poverty that objectifies a class of people into a group of "humans" who don't deserve the same rights as regular citizens. What's more, political nonsense and ignorant bureaucracies have squandered the hope of the people of Dharavi for a better Dharavi. Years of political disputes have wasted the vested trust of the Dharavi people, and effectively stifled all opportunity for Dharavi to transform from the once-shantytown it was to the still-shantytown it is. If you search up "Dharavi" on Google, you'd never realize the strength of its people. All you'll see are aerial images from the sky – as if no one actually had the resolve to go and physically meet the faces of poverty that live in Dharavi. Dharavi lives in Mumbai, but if you ask any of the residents who pass Dharavi every day on their commute to work, the first thing they say is the smell. Dharavi is just one of the places Mumbai's trains pass between destinations; the train doors are always open for ventilation; as such, when commuters pass Dharavi, they instinctually recognize the smell – the distinct, sick smell of poverty. Even the many foreigners that seek to explore Dharavi do so through the filter of a tour, which by definition is not only selective in what it can show, but can only show so much. Dharavi is lucky, in a way: whereas most slums are situated on the outskirts of their countries, a reference to their physical and social neglect, Dharavi is situated right in the center of New Delhi, next to the BKC (Bandra-Kurla Complex), India's socio-industrial complex. The result is a fascinating blend of people who work day through night in the hopes of providing a better life for their children or their families abroad. Dharavi is almost a franchise, in that it attracts people, who seek to learn new trades or skills to make enough of a living to support their families. But it wasn't always like this.

There are thousands of pictures of Dharavi around the internet, but all of them are aerial images. That's a telling sign that people are not willing to meet the faces of poverty as human to human, but as a human to slum-dweller, establishing a socio-economic barrier between themselves and the people of Dharavi, making the slum-dwellers inferior. Dharavi 80 years ago is not Dharavi today. Back then, soon after the Green Revolution spurred immense agricultural growth in Punjab, Dhavari was an area anyone with a roof could claim a home. But now, Dahravi could be a millionaire's land. Indeed, it has given birth to a few millionaires, in the midst of all its poverty. The stark inequality of rich and poor is reflected by Dahravi's location itself. Located in the midst of the bustling capital of New Delhi, Dharavi is a stark reminder of the economic inequality that exists in India between the rich and poor. In fact, it's a physical, topological projection of the massive inequality between the rich and poor of India's slums.

The Death: There are so many ways to take a life, and all ways come alive in the slum. It almost seems like every person has a thousand forces acting against them – disease, debt, poverty, risk of injury, and so many more. Indeed, there's two things certain in Dharavi: Death and Misery. It's a bleak picture down here, mostly due to the buzzing industrial complex coupled with a complete disregard for labor regulation. Forget minimum wage, parental leave, health benefits, vacation days, or labor unions. Dhavari's got none of it. Arm cut off by the fleecing machine? Too bad; a family just lost its breadwinner. Legs broken in a car accident? Now you're defective, and might as well be fired from your job. It's easy to become desensitized to the death that naturally comes with living in a slum. Slums have been well-documented for their dirty living conditions – few, if any water pumps; people openly defecating; and no sanitation whatsoever. Of course, with these living conditions comes the high prevalence of disease and illness. So what happens when a worker falls ill? This was my first thought when I came to Dharavi. The answer was in the buildings. Dharavi is special in that it actually attracts individuals seeking to learn a new trade, instead of being stuck in the same job for the rest of their life. Take the story of Mukhal. Mukhal grew up in Punjab, a region northeast of India, and the home of the Green Revolution, India's version of the agricultural revolution.But every revolution comes with pitfalls, and Punjab's was no exception. By the mid 2010s, Punjab farmers were suffering from low household incomes, and were increasingly burdened with debt. Mukhal's father's father's father was a Punjab farmer, one of the first to profit off the Green Revolution in the 1970s. As such, Mukhal naturally took up his family's profession and continued his father's legacy, becoming a Punjab farmer. But becoming a Punjab farmer in 2010 was very different from becoming one in 2000. One was a life of glory, financial security, and promise; another a life riddled with debt, insecurity, and depression. Soon, Mukhal realized the scale of his debt, over 300,000 Rupees. Regardless of how hard he worked, night-to-day, his debt only grew worse. So he began selling his precious farmland. But it did nothing to alleviate his debt. In fact, it made matters worse, and Mukhal began complaining to his family regarding their overwhelming debt. Mukhal decided to gamble; not by going to a Casino, but going to Dharavi – a place rumored to be the land of the determined, and home of the hopeful; a tiny nugget of capitalism smack-dab in the center of Mumbai. A decade later, Mukhal tells me his gamble paid off; he now lives comfortably with his wife and two sons in their high-rise apartment.

When I first met Lakshaba, I thought she must have been joking. But her eyes were depressed into her face, her face wrinkled with decades of pain and suffering, and her lips showed no sign of comedy. And so I realized; it was all true. Her husband of 40 years, Karbith worked at a garment factory for nearly 20 years, until one wrong day, his arm caught up in the spindle machine. He returned home from the hospital after a month, with a stub where his arm used to be. The painkillers he took left him in a daze, and he got addicted to the point he wouldn't show home for days. And thus, Lakshaba had no choice but to take up a job, and care for her three children at the same time. Her life was stretched thin, and her mind stressed constantly. When her husband returned every few months, she would think he had finally recovered; the reality was much darker. He had wasted the family's savings and needed increasingly more money for the drugs he was addicted to. He would recover only to fall prey to the same cycle of addiction once again. And so she spent her days working constantly to the point of near exhaustion, trying to make up for the money the Karbith lost. The day of judgement came on the 21st of May, 1983. Lakshaba threatened to divorce

Karbith, but Karbith didn't care anyway – he just didn't care anymore; his only concern was that he would lose his only source of money to buy drugs – his wife. And so, Lakshaba had no choice but to divorce Karbith and care for her children until they were self-sustaining. Now, at 85, she sits still in her brown wooden rocking chair, and stares at me intently as I ask "What do you regret most?" "All the things I couldn't have: an education, a family, and most of all, a happy life. When I think of my life, all the memories I remember are tragedies: the machine that broke my husband's arm; the time he told me he wasted all our life savings on drugs; and the day I divorced him. Is it bad? Is it bad that all my memories are so sad?" She knew my response, and so I sat back, holding back the tears that would inevitably come.

The Misery: Describe poverty in two words. Many would say smell and sacrifice. The smell is evident, but the sacrifice comes as a surprise to many. Where is the sacrifice in poverty? What can you sacrifice when you have nothing? I learned the answer on my trip to Dharavi in December 2019. Begging is an absolute staple in every slum. People beg up high, and down low; they advertise their past service, their current hunger, and their future disabilities all for a extra few coins at the end of the day. Being a child of Bangladesh, I thought I'd seen the extent beggars would go to for a dime in the bucket. But in the 33 miles I walked in Dharavi, I saw not one beggar. I was about to pack it up and call it a day, but then I spotted him. I met my exception on the 34th mile: a child with a stub for an arm. I could almost smell there was something peculiar; something odd about the way he held up the stub, as if asking for something. And then he finally came up to me, and shook his little tin plate, the sound of little metal coins clinking against little metal plates. What could I do? I was so broken as to what to do, that I couldn't say anything for a while. I asked the boy where his parents were. 34 minutes later, I found myself in front of two old, haggardly parents struggling to explain how their son ended up with a stub where his arm was. They finally ended up saying he was born this way. My suspicion arose from my knowledge and experience that most poor families would sacrifice their children' body parts to make money. As I suspected, upon closer examination, and asking around the slum, I could only come to the conclusion that the parents were responsible for cutting off their son's arm. I knew it all along, but the vindication nevertheless shocked me. That a parent would sacrifice their child's health and wellbeing for money raises serious ethical and financial questions. At what point does a mother agree to cutting off her son's arm? What choices does she consider as alternatives? Is there a breaking point? How is the decision even made? Is it made with careful deliberation, with consideration of all advantages and pitfalls? Or is it made in a haste? And then there's the logistical aspect. At what age does a parent decide that he must cut his child's arms off so he can make money? Why doesn't the parent just get a job or force the child into child labor instead of cutting off his arms? Does the parent take the child's future into consideration? That he won't be able to work at most jobs because jobs for the poor are labor-intensive jobs that require back-breaking work and cognitive and physical functioning? These are the heavy questions that these parents torment themselves with. But when I asked them, their only response was "What could we do?" But the misery doesn't end there.

We've already explored self-induced poverty traps, such as that of education, and missing women, but what about drugs? Extreme poverty occurs overwhelmingly in regions where much of the population is addicted to drugs such as opioids or heroin. As USNews' Steven Reinberg reports, most Opioid overdoses occur in poverty-stricken neighborhoods in the US. The Center for Disease Dynamics, Economics and Policy finds that over 63 million Indians are driven to poverty every year due to spending on drugs. Researchers C.C. Garg and A.K. Karan agree that "expenditure on drugs is "one of the major causes of impoverishment in India." The medical system is neglectful, but we must examine it intricately. It begins with the addict himself, who goes to the pharmacist, if he's rich enough. Otherwise, most slum-dwellers have independent suppliers who provide drugs for cheaper. As most pharmacies in India are unregulated, providing the drug itself is up to the chemists' (pharmacist) discretion. The problem with this system is exposed through Kalbir. Kalbir is an educated, and thus moderately-wealthy worker in Dharavi, who frequents the Chemist shop often. Working a labor intensive job, he ended up cutting off part of his finger, for which the local hospital prescribed painkillers – heroin. At first, Kalbir simply showed up with his prescription and the money, and the chemist gave him the heroin. The first few times, the drug eased his pain. But gradually, Kalbir realized he couldn't live without the drug. It wasn't an addiction per se, just an instinct, a compulsive feeling that pulsed and pained his body whenever he wasn't on the drug. Thus began the cycle. It started with a visit, maybe two every day. His visits grew, from two to three, until eventually, he would see the chemist five or six times a day. And thus began the addiction. Soon, the chemist stopped asking for a prescription; Kalbir became entrapped in an inescapable cycle of high and low. Finally, a few years later, he began getting tired. His savings were reduced to almost zero, his family was devastated, and his morale was nonexistent. Kalbir's wife finally got him to abstain. He told me his recovery process feels like torture. At first, he used to count every single minute or hour he was without smack. Minutes became hours became days became months. Now, Kalbir is 9 months sober (hasn't used heroin for 9 months), but the compulsion remains. Every time he goes to the chemist, his urge pulses him, but he remains firm. "If there was less people, maybe I go get some", he jokes. "I don't even need prescription, he [the chemist] knows me." Kalbir's story is a common one for many drug addicts – the pain, the relief, the addiction, and the recovery. But his story also exposes the flaws of the Indian medical system; most slum-dwellers in Dharavi work labor-intensive, back-breaking jobs day-to-day. Couple that with India's lack of any worker regulation whatsoever, and lack of any hygiene or sanitation and the result is a dangerous combustion of disease, illness, and pain. All it takes is one bad day; one unlucky stroke of the hand for injury to overcome all of life – and it's all the more likely in the midst of these unregulated and unsanitary conditions. Thus begins a positive feedback cycle: slum-dwellers living in unsanitary conditions working labor-intensive jobs almost constantly are bound to end up with either disease or accident. In the case of an accident, they'll most likely get prescribed painkillers, which – in many cases – will result in addiction, which will have a plethora of devastating side effects to the slum-dweller's income, savings, and household. If the worker recovers, he goes straight back to the same job that landed him in that dangerous cycle of pain and addiction. This positive feedback cycle is what constitutes a poverty trap.

The Politics: Kashmir was alone when I first met him on the corner of the market. He was decked in regular clothes; he came in his normal duti, teared against every fabric of his leg. We walked along the bustling market. "So how'd you lose your house?" I asked. He answered with silence, but slowly began to warm up. The actual house went five years ago, he said, but the journey started fifteen years back. In 2004, Karmith had returned to Dharavi after many years, hoping to learn a new trade or skill, as do many other rural migrants. Karmith knew that with his new trade and skills, he would be able to better financially support his family and give him hopes to lessen the burden of his debt. But by the time he started to settle in his house in Punjab, in his old home, he realized his own brother was occupying his house for many days, and sometimes weeks at a time. Karmith had neglected the house for over 15 years, back in 1989, when he provided his newlywed smaller brother with the house to provide his brother comfortable living quarters. And thus, with his own permission, and his own neglect, Karmith had ended up giving his house to his brother Darmit for over 15 years. Now, with the brothers contesting for the piece of property, it was up to the discretion of the Indian Supreme Court to decide which brother received the house. With Karmith contending that he was the original owner, and Darmit explaining that he had been possessing Karmith's house for 15 years continuously – with Karthmith's initial permission – both brothers had strong cases to win. Darmit was declared victorious by the Indian Supreme Court, a stunning clarification of Indian Housing Policies. And thus ended up Karmith, homeless and a sad slum-dweller with no household. And thus, in search of a new trade in the hopes of creating significant household income, he was just one of the many rural migrants to come to Dharavi – that lost land of dreams, of hope, and of ambition – in the hopes of establishing a significant household savings, of which he would send back a certain portion back to his family in Punjab every month.

Work: Back in the '70s, anyone with two sticks and a hand could call Dharavi home. By the 1970s, Dhavari's massive population earned it the dubious nickname of "The Biggest Slum in Asia". WIth over a million inhabitants working night and day, Dharavi is a place of passionate work, and passion leads to hope.

"When did your son die?" is probably not the best question to start off with, but nevertheless, the mumbiker didn't seem to mind. "2006" was his only response, but it was all I needed. I realized that Prodeep's house was nearly void of any furniture, clothing, or any other common personal belongings. All that remained on the wall was a gold-like frame surrounding what I presumed to be Rochit's son. Slum-dwellers are in a unique position; they're pressed financially to the point where some of them believe it to be neccessary to deprive their children of their childhood and force them into child labor. This is by no means a condemnation. In fact, many of these parents believe child labor is justified, comparing the lives of their children to their own childhood. What they fail to take into account is the reason they're forced to put their children in child labor is poverty, that beast that takes and takes and takes. And so, faced with no option but to work back-breaking jobs night and day, these children sacrifice their health at a remarkably young age to support their families, risking disease, illness, injury, and worst of all – death. That was the risk that Prodeep took when he demanded Rahan to work 8 hours a day at the local garment factory, in the hopes that Rahan's income would supplement his own. But with his eye blinded by the shine of money, Rahan had committed a fatal mistake: he asked the garment factory owner whether Rahan could work 4 hours overtime to make more money. The owner accepted Prodeep's request, and now Rahan worked 9 AM to 9 PM; no holidays, no breaks; no insurance; just work, work, work, and work. But like anything, you only know what you have once it's gone. Prodeep thatha didn't realize the scale of his fatal mistake until January 5th, 2006. It was a few days after New Years, and the family rejoiced over a resolution to a debt-free life by the end of the year. Their resolution cut short on January 5th; Rahan's arm cut short in the spindle of the textile machine in the garment factory. He returned home with a bleeding stump where his arm used to be. The local hospital found an infection in the stump, and informed Prodeep and his wife what to expect: "we can keep him on life support for the next few months, which will cost you a total of 50000 Rupees upfront, as you have no insurance. Without life support, he won't last very long. Other than that, we don't see much of an alternative " But of course, Rahan's family, despite their household savings, had no such money. In one way, Prodeep was relieved, as he had no choice and all his responsibility in the matter was absolved. But in every other way, he was already dead inside. Prodeep's wife assured him that a life on life support is not a life worth living anyway, and that Rahan would go to a better place after Earth. It was no comfort to Prodeep. Now, a decade and a half later, Prodeep sits in the same room his son nearly bled to death in, 13 years ago. He sits and he sits and he sits. And he looks at the picture at the wall, and thinks of what could have been.

Hope: Let me assure you. If you're depressed by now, you have every right to be. Poverty at ground zero is as strikingly horrific today as it was a hundred years ago. But there is some semblance of good hope in mothers like Savitrabai. Slum-dwellers like Savitrabai are a truly unique class of people. Despite being entrenched in poverty, there exists a sense of almost "shared poverty", a shared obstacle that must be overcome as a community, not just individually. But of course, the people are the bread and butter of a slum. So what about single mothers like Savitribai, who live in Dharavi? What do you see when you see a single mother?

Born in a family of five, Savitrabai was always the competitive type. Having grown up in an educated family, she always understood the value of education. Then she made the wrong turn. "I was on it for years. It took everything from me – my family, my income, my savings. I was nothing after I came out; nobody." Smack did it. As goes many stories like this, Savitribai was once injured in a leather production factory. She was just one unit in a massive assembly line, and her job was to fold the soft leather into a rectangle, and place it on a mat, on which descended a large pressing machine every 20 seconds; this machine would depress the surface of the leather, and flatten it to the point where it looked like a flat piece of texture. March 15th was the day it all went to hell. Pressured by the speed of the assembly line and stressed by troubles at home, Savitrabai kept her hands under the pressing machine for just a second too long. What happened next is the story of a thousand screams, a desperate bid for health, and a scary encounter with death: the machine pressed the skin and bone of Svitrabai's hand, with the sound of breaking bone killing her ears. Savitribai limped to the local

Refath Bari

hospital, where they gave her a cast and prescribed painkillers. You can guess the end by now. What followed after was a story of pain, addiction, recourse, and recovery, and back to addiction. The ability to end a cycle is an extraordinary power, and that's exactly what enabled Savitrabai to break out of her own, self-imposed barriers, motivating herself through her children and schooling. But by the time she broke the cycle, the cycle had broken her. Her income was nonexistent; her savings – saved over all those years – was squandered on drug after drug, and reduced to essentially zero. And her children were neglected on a frightful scale: they had malnutrition, they were deprived of clean water and food on a daily basis, and worst of all, they were denied an education by their own drunken mother. Now, a decade later, Savitrabai admits that she still must suppress thoughts of the drug that convulse her body every time she passes the pharmacy. But then, she reminds herself of her children, and all fades away. Now, her children are in a school near Dharavi, learning basic arithmetic and literacy skills. As a single mother, she works during the day when her children are in school at a textile mill, and that income is spread over the family, and part of it goes to the rent of 800 rupees a month for their apartment, which they share with two other families. That is a story of hope; the story of a mother who overpowered all odds to break her addiction before it could break her. This is the story of Dharavi, the land of the determined; the home of the hopeful.

Here we are, standing at the very edge, at the very end: There are moments in my life when I explicitly knew I was experiencing a defining moment. The 5th of January, 2020 was one of them. I was walking on the fairgrounds of Dharavi, recording and speaking with the villagers, the pharmacists, the business owners, and shopkeepers. I was learning more about the people that made Dharavi an infusion of hope, drive, and sheer will. What I saw next I will never forget. Amid the hustle and bustle of the largest slum in Asia, I found one girl in red. She was surrounded by little blue books on all sides, and a blue pencil with no eraser in her hand; the literal personification of a needle in the haystack: all around her were notebooks, pencils, and erasers. I had only seen such images online, and I never believed them. For all I knew, they were staged, because how can the poor understand the value of education if they never had it before? I only recently understood the value of education, after understanding its true rarity. And so, I was simply walking along the narrow alleyway when my journalists' eye suddenly spotted a black girl in ragged pink clothes writing on a scrappy, small marble notebook outlined with the ignasia of "Dharavi Preliminary Primary Education School". The notebook was slightly bent around the edges and was the child's English grammar notebook. Upon asking her for her name, she replied 'Puja'. I was astonished she even understood my query, which was in English. I spotted her father, body half naked peeking one eye out from behind the door. I sat down on the steps leading up to Puja's cramped home. "Can you read that sentence?" I asked her, pointing to the second sentence in her English Grammar notebook. "If you are sick, drinking two glasses of water will fix your sore throat.". Next to the sentence, Puja had circled True. "Can you tell me what that sentence means?" I inquired. Smiling, she shook her head in response. The answer to that small question itself represented a failing in the educational system of Dharavi. For an education system to exist is not enough; it must promote the fruits of learning; it must actively engage all students in discussion and ensure that no child is left behind. I changed the subject to mathematics. "1+1" I wrote on Farjana's paper. Notably absent from her pencils were erasers, and her pencils themselves were the size of stubs. I was literally knocked off my perch when she neatly wrote 2 with her black-brown striped pencil. "OK, ..." I noted, raising my expectations. "1+2" I wrote, hoping that the first correct answer wasn't a happy accident. And indeed, it wasn't! "3". She wrote neatly next to the equal sign. "1+3". She wrote 4. "1+4". She wrote 5. "OK, let's change one of the addends' '. 2+5. She wrote 7. I was already elated with joy; that a 4 year old girl living in a slum under quite possibly inhumane conditions could have already learned addition. I upped the ante. "Let's go for multiplication". Puja smiled at me, unafraid and elated. I was amazed at the child's enthusiasm and passion for learning at such a young age in such disparate conditions. "OK, let's go 2 times 4". She wrote 6. "OK." I stoped. I realized we had reached a pausing moment. And so I stopped. "This is different. This is multiplication, not the same as addition." Her father suddenly jumped in the conversation "You said times, that's why she doesn't understand. She will understand if you say 2 multiply 4". And so, I proceeded with the next example "4 multiply 3". Again, Fajana inscribed 7 on the paper, and so I realized the problem wasn't in the diction nor the notation. She simply didn't know multiplication. And so, I scribbled little dots on the paper, explaining "4 multiply 3 is 3 groups of 4 dots. So, how many dots in total?" "12" she said, staring at the paper intently, practically jumping for the next example. "OK, so try 3*6" Fajana began drawing the dots on paper as her mind started connecting the dots themselves. It was amazing how rapidly she picked up the usage of abstract symbols like dots to understand the operation of multiplication. She ended up with 9. "OK, so tell me how you got 9." She showed the 3 dots added to the 6 dots was a total of 9 dots. "Ah, but remember, this is multiplication. So, we are thinking about groups", I said, drawing the correct solution. Fajana stared at my solution, taking some time to internalize it. "OK, so let's do 4 multiply 4" I said. Again, Fajana drew the

Refath Bari

dots and again repeated her mistake of misinterpreting the multiplication sign as addition. Soon after, she got 8, as expected. But thankfully, I understood her point of confusion, and drew the correct solution again. Now came the magic. This time, I raised the stakes, "OK, let's do 3 multiply 7." Puja drew 7 groups of 3 dots and wrote 21 with confidence. I was simply floored, but quick to recoup my expectations, believing the answer to be a happy accident, since I had grown used to the phrase "What seems to good to be true usually is." But It wasn't! Sure enough, the magic was real. And so, I tried bigger numbers "3*8" I wrote. Again, she drew 8 groups of 3 dots and ended up with 24. "OK, then. Let's try this" I said, raising the stakes considerably: "6*8". 3 minutes and 8 groups of 6 dots later, Puja confidently wrote a huge 48 on the paper, smiling as she did so, knowing she was right before I even said anything. I couldn't talk anymore. I knew what I saw, but my eyes couldn't believe it. To this day, I still don't.

The Journey

Refath Bari

55 Days in Dharavi

The following is the album for *55 Days in Dharavi*

Keywords: Dharavi, Kerala, Mumbai, Chennai, Palakkad, New Delhi, India, Bangladesh, Chittagong, Pune, Maharashtra

1 The Places

You've heard the people. You've read the places. Now it's time to see what you've read for so long. Follow me on my journey through India, from Kerala to Mumbai to Pune to New Delhi. You'll find here some of the people who've inspired me, supported me, and shared me in my ambition to create a better world without poverty or hunger. Perhaps now is a fitting time as any to find the story behind *55 Days in Dharavi*: The hands struck 12 and the 55th and final day had come. The boy knew it was time to go. He wished all 34 families he had studied farewell. The lives of poor in the face of a pandemic was an essential story in the pages of history, he promised to an especially skeptical family. He glanced it at his watch. 12:20 PM. The flight was only 4 hours to go. The boy rapidly paced through the cracked pavements of Dharavi, in desperate search for an exit. And there he found a curious sight: the girl made no sound, but the sight said enough. Her 7-year old hand skillfully graced the pages of a blue pad, as books surrounded her on all sides. This was the sight he had sought the last 55 days. Her pencil tip was old and gray from overuse, and she had no eraser. "Here," said the boy, throwing her one of his. As he moved closer to the girl, black eyes stared from the back door. This girl was the boy's ticket to the poor, but his real ticket sat crushed in his black coat. He unfolded it and glanced at the departure time: "3:45". His watch said it was too late. The hands struck 4. The boy was not returning to America.

Refath Bari

Figure 1: I shudder when I see this picture now – never has the ideal of "Standing on the Shoulders of Giants" been more evident. Here I am, in front of two of the greatest giants in Poverty Alleviation: Nobel Prize Laureate Muhammad Yunus and Developmental Economist Jeffrey Sachs. I had the rare and utmost privilege of expressing my greatest dreams to the two giants: a dream of eradicating poverty.

Figure 2: Dr. Yunus was in every respect my mentor and personal guru. He would often give me life advice when I strolled into his office in Chittagong with mom and dad. Here, however, he seems to be in a particularly playful mood (we were playing hide and seek, and I'd just lost)

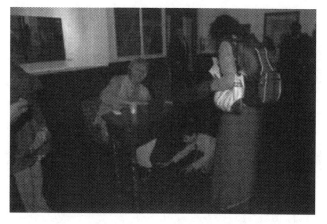

Figure 3: See the little blue boy under the table? That's the author, saluting his Guruji in the traditional Bangladeshi greeting. This was at one of Dr. Yunus' book signing ceremonies, where he would often parcel out advice to rich and poor alike.

Figure 4: My first meeting with Dr. Yunus in his Chittagong Office was quite eventful. When I first entered Grameen Bank's main headquarters in Dhaka, Bangladesh, I was shocked to be greeted by hundreds of women parceled into small groups, with each group having a lead advisor of some sort. Now I know that I was watching a revolution in the making: the Grameen Revolution.

Refath Bari

Figure 5: This is a particularly vexing picture: this a train station bridge so that rich (or at least middle class) can literally walk above the people of Dharavi, thus circumventing the smell of the infamous slum. Two train stations border Dharavi, making it all the more accessible: the Mahim Train Station from the East and the Sion Train Station from the West. Both stations lead to the BKC (Bandra Kurla Complex), India's financial hub. Here I stand on the Mahim Skywalk, constructed to provide commuters 'relief' as they travel through Dharavi.

Figure 6: This is a Sikh temple, called Gurdwara, where the people of Dharavi go and pray. The Gurdwaras often give free food, as one of the most important tenets of Sikhism is to provide food to those in need. This has become an especially important role to play, especially during the Coronavirus Pandemic, when the Sikhs (25 million Sikhs in the world) cater to the needs of a city in crisis.

Figure 7: In a matter of just ten weeks, 30 Sikhs have served over 145,000 meals. The devotion and clockwork precision of their efforts is staggering: they wake up at 3:30 AM, arrive at the Gurdwara at 4 AM, and assemble vast amounts of basmati rice, dal, and beans to give to anyone in need (Sikh or otherwise).

Figure 8: Mr. Ranbir, retired construction worker and evergreen optimist, hails from Punjab, India. "I love everybody", he says in broken English. "They say, 'we no like Muslims'. But no, I love everyone. Muslims, Hindu, Christian, everybody, everybody.", he assures me. Maybe Mr. Ranbir is the optimist the world's been looking for.

Refath Bari

Figure 9: The author is currently conducting research on the Geometry of Space-Time with Dr. Kabat, former Columbia University Professor and MIT PhD in Physics. The author also sat in Dr. Kabat's Physics class in 2011 as a 9 year old.

Figure 10: Here's a look at one of the many narrow alleyways that compose Dharavi. Just to give you a sense, most of these alleyways can just barely fit a person in-between them (that's how dense the living standards are), and it certainly doesn't help that the blue tin roofs of the shanties literally block sunlight for 24 hours a day. That means these people don't see light for much of their lives in Dharavi. That's a scary pretense to agree to.

Figure 11: I'm in my dad's NYU graduation (in 2015) with Dr. Catherine Milne and Dr. Pamela Fraser-Abder. Over the years, we've gotten to know each other especially well and I am incredibly grateful to have the privilege of standing on the shoulders of these giants. This book is a culmination of my five years relationsip with Dr. Cath.

Refath Bari

Figure 12: There's something I can't show you out-of-frame that's surprising the two women behind me. Indeed, for these people of Dharavi who work nonstop day and night for money to support a better life, little can surprise them – they deal with economic shocks on the scale of extreme monsoons, floods, natural disasters, automobile accidents, hunger, and now – COVID19.

Figure 13: As you hold in your hands this book, I hope to return to the children of Dharavi to give them this book. I hope this book will inspire them to ruthlessly pursue education and may their natural inquisitiveness lead them to a better future than their parents could afford.

Figure 14: This is Puja. This story has exactly four working parts: the girl, the father, me, and the problem. But you will see that the whole is far greater than the sum of its parts: as Puja's father looked intensely at the stranger teaching his daughter, my notion that the children of slum-dwellers were illiterate was shot to hell, as I watched Puja discover in a few minutes a math concept that most third graders understand in a few months.

Figure 15: I found sunlight even in Dharavi, but this was no happy accident: it was a consequence of the consistent, constant labor of the poor. As they work nonstop from 8 AM day to 8 PM night, they work towards a better life not just for themselves, but also for their children.

Figure 16: I spoke with Spike Lee of my hope to transform *55 Days in Dharavi* into a film of the same. Promoting a more equitable, sustainable, and realistic view of poverty is an essential goal to achieving the UN's Sustainble Developmental Goal of eliminating Hunger and Poverty, and mass media communication forms such as film is the exact means of accomplishing that.

Figure 17: I may have irritated some of the people of Dharavi, who always seem to be in a rush! It is truly a bustling center of industrialism – perhaps just not fully developed – filled with a people that harbor a dream of a better, healthier life.

Figure 18: It's always a great experience celebrating the triumphs of effective interventions with my mom, dad, little brother, and *thatha, thathu.*

Refath Bari

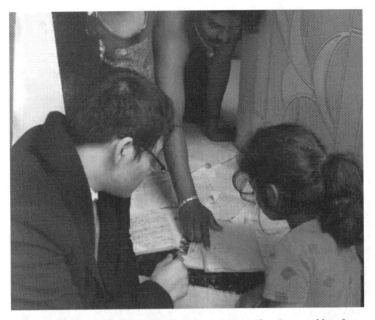

Figure 19: As I write this, my eyes tear as I remember Puja and her father. Her father ultimately joined in on our discussion of how to multiply numbers using a manipulative/dot representation. She was only four (Kindergarten), but she learned in two minutes what an American (PISA 2018 #25) or Singaporean Child (PISA 2018 #2) learns in two months – in the third grade. I met Puja 7,774 miles away two months ago. And I never really left. Crushed in my pocket, sat my ticket to the US, but here in front of me, was my ticket to the poor: Puja. I spent months preparing for my visit to Dharavi, Mumbai, studying learning theories, economic models, and poverty traps. But nothing could prepare me for this: when I found Puja, in her lightless home, in an alley somewhere between a couple hundred nooks and crannies, I expected the typical disaster story – a child that lost her love for math because of a school system that neglected the bottom 50% of students who were poor or challenged. But what I found slapped my notion to hell: here was a four year old showing Vygotsky's ZPD (Zone of Proximal Development) in action: age was no barrier for her. What she learned at four, most learn at eight. Poverty was no barrier for her. There I found her, in Dharavi. It has no sunlight; not much clean water; electricity probably hasn't reached that corner of the globe yet. And yet there is light. It comes from Puja. Puja is a living testament to the power of education: the fact that Education can bridge all barriers. She is proof that education is the great equalizer.

Figure 20: One of the wonders of Dharavi I had the joy of experiencing were the Dosas. The amazing thing was that they were actually selling quite a few Dosas, and would wrap them in tea leaves or newspaper upon giving them to me (they were all soaked in oil). I also got a few Shingaras, which they wrapped up real quick.

Figure 21: I actually sat in Dr. Michio Kaku's Astrophysics class when I was 8. We are back in contact, discussing possible means of implementation of a curriculum that popularizes science among children in Dharavi.

Refath Bari

Figure 22: Dr. A. Q. M. Badruddoza Chowdhury was the President of Bangladesh until 2002. At the time, we were discussing various means of proliferating educational programs and subsidies for the illiterate and poor of Bangladesh's many slums. I am currently in conversation with him to discuss possible implementations of a medical team to treat slum-dwellers vulnerable to COVID19.

Figure 23: Dr. Yunus always entertained our visits, even after winning the Nobel Peace Prize. Here is the mark of a man down to earth: as we mutually celebrate an international recognition that the man deserved for many years to come. To this day, he remains Bangladesh's only Nobel Laureate.

Refath Bari

Figure 24: Let me be honest: this picture has no relevance whatsoever to this book. However, I grew up in Bangladesh reading the poems of Al-Mahmud, who is the poet laureate of Bangladesh. As such, I couldn't resist putting this picture of us together.

Figure 25: Dr. Kaku is no foreigner to popularizing science for the masses – in fact, he's been doing it for decades, through his Radio, Television, and Film series. As such, it was only natural that we recruit him in the campaign to raise awareness of the true effects of education for the poor – a task which the doctor was eager to embark on.

Figure 26: I joined Dr. Brian Greene of Columbia University — one of the last remaining String Theorists (an endangered population, no doubt) – to popularize science not only in the United States, but also throughout Asia, including India and Bangladesh, through his popular science outreach program, the World Science Festival.

Refath Bari

Figure 27: Mathematics has long remained a disputed component of India's National Curriculum. How should it be approached? Through a purely skills-based perspective that teaches students a disparate set of algorithms that should be memorized for execution? Or through a much more difficult – and not necessarily more fruitful, in terms of student achievement – methodical goal of explaining the underlying motivation behind every mathematical idea?

Figure 28: Dr. Kabat, my research advisor, keenly watches as I explain the generalization of the Galilean Transformations to a four-dimensional vector space of Space and Time. And who but the genius peeks out from behind? The picture was taken in 2013.

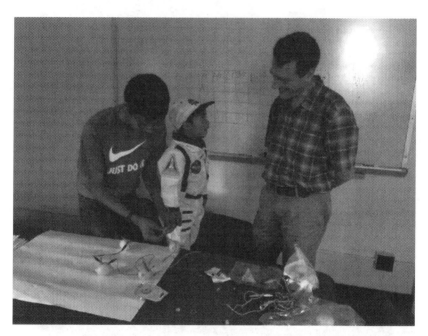

Figure 29: Hands-on Experiments are the most fruitful means of achieving student engagement in the classroom, according to Jerome Bruner; this can be achieved via manipulatives, demonstrations, or even experiments as is the case here. This is a crucial pedagogical technique that should be encouraged in all classrooms in the developing world, which is exactly what I and my little brother explored with our advisor. The picture was taken in 2015.

Refath Bari

Figure 30: Dr. Kabat & I share the morning on a day when the light clearly didn't favor our direction. And who but my dad to watch us over our shoulders?

Figure 31: Following the success of an informal intervention (checked via Randomized Control Trials) in various districts of Maharashtra, the team all reconvened for a joyous celebration.

Figure 32: My own *nanu* created a school for the poor and illiterate in Bangladesh, which currently has a student enrollment of over a thousand children. The school has recently received a grant from the Bangladesh Government for its' student body's proficiency in Math and Science.

Refath Bari

Figure 33: As a Muslim myself, it was quite the wonderful experience celebrating a traditional Indian holiday in the homes of one of the families we studied. They graciously hosted us for a few days before we wishing us farewell on our intervention.

Figure 34: I outline the plan for the interview we will execute throughout the various states of India, including Kerala, Tamil Nadu, Uttar Pradesh, Punjab and Rajasthan, and Mumbai.

Figure 35: Perhaps the most effective means of popularizing educational reform and social subsidies for the poor is via mass media outlets such as Hollywood. Here we stand with the Oscar-winning actress Melissa McCarthy.

Refath Bari

Figure 36: As a five year old child, I had the rare privilege to act in a film directed by MMR Gulzar and I was cast as the child of Diti and Azizul Hakim. Here we are on the final day of shooting, with the full cast.

Figure 37: I describe my hopes for a more equitable education for the poor that ensures not just the quantity of elementary schools, but also the quality – a fundamental factor that is nevertheless often overlooked when it comes to international talks on the United Nation's Sustainable Development Goals.

Figure 38: I discuss the practicality of implementing a specific intervention and its corresponding Randomized Control Trial with my little brother, who himself has received recognition from the President of the United States, Barack Obama

Figure 39: The team celebrates a successful randomized control trial in the Ashok Hotel in New Delhi, India. We found a happy accident waiting for us there: hundreds of children who sought to create a better future for their own lives – in essence, a celebration of the minds of prodigies (of which my brother is one!)

Figure 40: Fan Art of Puja and Refath Bari drawn by Eshi, a Bangladeshi Artist.

Figure 41: Fan Art of Puja and Refath Bari drawn by Eshi, a Bangladeshi Artist.

Bibliography

Refath Bari
55 Days in Dharavi

The following are the citations for *55 Days in Dharavi*

1. Nath, Samir Ranjan, and Kathy Sylva. "Children's access to pre-school education in Bangladesh." International journal of early years education 15.3 (2007): 275-295.

2. Banerjee, Abhijit V., Abhijit Banerjee, and Esther Duflo. Poor economics: A radical rethinking of the way to fight global poverty. Public Affairs, 2011.

3. Banerjee, Abhijit, and Esther Duflo. "More than 1 billion people are hungry in the world." Foreign Policy 186 (2011): 66-72.

4. Hallegatte, Stephane, et al. "Managing What Cannot be Avoided: Risk can be reduced by improving resilience." (2016): 135-173.

5. AlSayyad, Nezar. "Editor's Note." Traditional Dwellings and Settlements Review, vol. 26, no. 2, 2015, pp. 6–6. JSTOR.

6. ANJARIA, JONATHAN SHAPIRO, and ULKA ANJARIA. "Slumdog Millionaire and Epistemologies of the City." Economic and Political Weekly, vol. 45, no. 24, 2010, pp. 41–46. JSTOR.

7. ASER 2019 - ASER Centre. http://www.asercentre.org//p/359.html. Accessed 19 Feb, 2020.

8. BOOYENS, Irma, and Christian M. ROGERSON. "Re-Creating Slum Tourism: Perspectives from South Africa." Urbani Izziv, vol. 30, 2019, pp. 52–63. JSTOR.

9. Brook, Daniel. "Slumming It: The Gospel of Wealth Comes for Dharavi." The Baffler, no. 25, 2014, pp. 136–45. JSTOR.

10. Cutting, William A. M., and Gopa Kothari. "Children In Third World Slums." British Medical Journal (Clinical Research Edition), vol. 296, no. 6638, 1988, pp. 1683–84. JSTOR.

11. DANDAVATE, UDAY. "Icons of Mumbai." Economic and Political Weekly, vol. 45, no. 47, 2010, pp. 29–31. JSTOR.

12. DEMPSEY, NICOLA. "Revisiting the Compact City?" Built Environment (1978-), vol. 36, no. 1, 2010, pp. 4–8. JSTOR.

13. Duflo, Esther, et al. "Peer Effects, Teacher Incentives, and the Impact of Tracking: Evidence from a Randomized Evaluation in Kenya." American Economic Review, vol. 101, no. 5, Aug. 2011, pp. 1739–74. www.aeaweb.org, doi:10.1257/aer.101.5.1739.

14. Engineer, Asghar Ali. "Bombay Shames India." Economic and Political Weekly, vol. 28, no. 3/4, 1993, pp. 81–85. JSTOR.

15. "High-Rise Eviction." Economic and Political Weekly, vol. 42, no. 25, 2007, pp. 2364–2364. JSTOR.

16. Kalan, Jonathan. "Think Again: Megacities." Foreign Policy, no. 206, 2014, pp. 69–73. JSTOR.

17. Patel, Shirish B. "Housing Policies for Mumbai." Economic and Political Weekly, vol. 40, no. 33, 2005, pp. 3669–76. JSTOR.

18. "Unstated Premises of Maharashtra's Housing Policy." Economic and Political Weekly, vol. 42, no. 33, 2007, pp. 3359–64. JSTOR.

19. "Urban Layouts, Densities and the Quality of Urban Life." Economic and Political Weekly, vol. 42, no. 26, 2007, pp. 2725–36. JSTOR.

20. Sanyal, Kalyan, and Rajesh Bhattacharyya. "Beyond the Factory: Globalisation, Informalisation of Production and the New Locations of Labour." Economic and Political Weekly, vol. 44, no. 22, 2009, pp. 35–44. JSTOR.

21. SATTERTHWAITE, DAVID. "Upgrading Slums: With and For Slum-Dwellers." Economic and Political Weekly, vol. 45, no. 10, 2010, pp. 12–16. JSTOR.

22. Sen, Amartya. More Than 100 Million Women Are Missing. Dec. 1990. www.nybooks.com, https://www.nybooks.com/articles/1990/12/20/more-than-100-million-women-are-missing/.

23. SENGUPTA, MITU. "A Million Dollar Exit from the Anarchic Slum-World: 'Slumdog Millionaire's' Hollow Idioms of Social Justice." Third World uarterly, vol. 31, no. 4, 2010, pp. 599–616. JSTOR.

24. Taubenböck, H., and N. J. Kraff. "The Physical Face of Slums: A Structural Comparison of Slums in Mumbai, India, Based on Remotely Sensed Data." Journal of Housing and the Built Environment, vol. 29, no. 1, 2014, pp. 15–38. JSTOR.

25. Wadhams, Chris. "Housing and Local Economic Development – An Agenda for Low Income Urban Neighbourhoods?" Community Development Journal, vol. 28, no. 4, 1993, pp. 321–33. JSTOR.

26. Zimmer, Ron. "A New Twist in the Educational Tracking Debate." Economics of Education Review, vol. 22, no. 3, June 2003, pp. 307–15. ScienceDirect, doi:10.1016/S0272-7757(02)00055-9.

27. Durand-Lasserve, Alain, and Lauren Royston, eds. "Holding their ground: Secure land tenure for the urban poor in developing countries." (2002).

28. Ravallion, Martin, and Gaurav Datt. "Why has economic growth been more pro-poor in some states of India than others?." Journal of development economics 68.2 (2002): 381-400.

29. Ravallion, Martin, and Gaurav Datt. "Why have some Indian states done better than others at reducing rural poverty?." (1999).

30. Cornwall, Jeffrey R. "The entrepreneur as a building block for community." Journal of Developmental Entrepreneurship 3.2 (1998): 141.

31. Barendsen, Lynn, and Howard Gardner. "Is the social entrepreneur a new type of leader?." Leader to leader 2004.34 (2004): 43.

32. Seelos, Christian, and Johanna Mair. "Social entrepreneurship: Creating new business models to serve the poor." Business horizons 48.3 (2005): 241-246.

33. Breman, Jan. "Footloose labour: working in India's informal economy." (1996).

287

Refath Bari

34. Asadullah, M. Niaz, and Nazmul Chaudhury. "To madrasahs or not to madrasahs: The question and correlates of enrolment in Islamic schools in Bangladesh." International Journal of Educational Development 49 (2016): 55-69.

35. Asadullah, Mohammad Niaz, Nazmul Chaudhury, and Amit Dar. "Student achievement conditioned upon school selection: Religious and secular secondary school quality in Bangladesh." Economics of Education Review 26.6 (2007): 648-659.

36. Arends-Kuenning, Mary, and Sajeda Amin. "School incentive programs and children's activities: The case of Bangladesh." Comparative Education Review 48.3 (2004): 295-317.

37. Khanam, Rasheda. "Child labour and school attendance: evidence from Bangladesh." International Journal of Social Economics (2008).

38. Asadullah, M. Niaz. "Returns to private and public education in Bangladesh and Pakistan: A comparative analysis." Journal of Asian economics 20.1 (2009): 77-86.

39. Asadullah, M. Niaz. "The effect of class size on student achievement: Evidence from Bangladesh." Applied Economics Letters 12.4 (2005): 217-221.

40. Cameron, Stuart. "Whether and where to enrol? Choosing a primary school in the slums of urban Dhaka, Bangladesh." International Journal of Educational Development 31.4 (2011): 357-366.

41. Asadullah, Mohammad Niaz. "Returns to education in Bangladesh." Education Economics 14.4 (2006): 453-468.

42. Nath, Samir Ranjan, and Kathy Sylva. "Children's access to pre-school education in Bangladesh." International journal of early years education 15.3 (2007): 275-295.

43. Ciapponi, Agustín, and World Health Organization. "Systematic review of the link between tobacco and poverty." (2014).

44. Banerjee, Abhijit, and Esther Duflo. "More than 1 billion people are hungry in the world." Foreign Policy 186 (2011): 66-72.

45. Garrette, Bernard, and Aneel Karnani. "Challenges in marketing socially useful goods to the poor." California Management Review 52.4 (2010): 29-47.

46. Peretti-Watel, Patrick, et al. "Cigarettes and social differentiation in France: is tobacco use increasingly concentrated among the poor?." Addiction 104.10 (2009): 1718-1728.

47. Hackbarth, Diana P., Barbara Silvestri, and William Cosper. "Tobacco and alcohol billboards in 50 Chicago neighborhoods: market segmentation to sell dangerous products to the poor." Journal of public health policy 16.2 (1995): 213-230.

48. Hallegatte, Stephane, et al. "Managing What Cannot be Avoided: Risk can be reduced by improving resilience." (2016): 135-173.

49. Hundeland, Per Sigurd, Martin Carlsen, and Ingvald Erfjord. "Qualities of mathematical discourses in kindergartens." ZDM (2020): 1-12.

50. Sachs, Jeffrey D. The end of poverty: Economic possibilities for our time. Penguin, 2006.

Author Biography

Refath Bari

55 Days in Dharavi

Biography for Refath Bari, 55 Days in Dharavi

Refath Bari is a student at Brooklyn Tech, a Specialized High School. He is currently conducting research on Special Relativity with Columbia Scientist Dr.

Refath Bari

Daniel Kabat and has received a perfect SAT Math Score. He is Captain of the Math Team and has represented Brooklyn Tech at various Math Competitions including WWTBAM, AMC 10, Purple Comet, NYML, IML, Mandelbrot, USAMTS, MATHS, DMI, and the Breakthrough Junior Challenge. He is the winner of the NYC Hackathon, and his app won recognition from Jumaane Williams, the NYC Public Advocate, for "Best Use of NYC Open Data". It is now being considered for mass release in Staten Island by Senator Andrew J Lanza. He is the two-time winner of the Brooklyn Tech Hackathon in 2019 & 2020 and first-time winner of the 2020 Brooklyn Borough Hackathon. He won the Subject Field Expertise Prize for his award-winning app, Rescuer in 2019. His team placed 2nd place in Columbia's Annual Math Tournament and he is a high scorer at many of the above mentioned contests. As per his NYC IML score, he currently ranks 11th place in New York City.

Printed in the United States
By Bookmasters